Xian Sacraments: Sacramentum =
Mystery

1. Baptism
2. Confirmation
3. Holy Eucharist =
4. Marriage
5. Holy Orders - Deacons, Priest & Bishops
6. Penance for Sins
7. Anointing of the Sick

forgotten
POWER

WILLIAM L. DE ARTEAGA

forgotten
POWER

THE SIGNIFICANCE OF THE LORD'S SUPPER IN REVIVAL

GRAND RAPIDS, MICHIGAN 49530 USA

ZONDERVAN™

Forgotten Power
Copyright © 2002 by William L. De Arteaga

Requests for information should be addressed to:

Zondervan, *Grand Rapids, Michigan 49530*

Library of Congress Cataloging-in-Publication Data

De Arteaga, William L.
     Forgotten power : the significance of the Lord's Supper in revival / William L.
De Arteaga.
        p. cm.
     Includes bibliographical references and index.
     ISBN 0–310–24567–2
     1. Lord's Supper — History.   2. Revivals — History.   I. Title.
BV825.3 .D4 2002
234'.163 — dc2

2002000829

Interior design by Beth Shagene

Printed in the United States of America

---

02 03 04 05 06 07 08 /❖ DC/ 10 9 8 7 6 5 4 3 2 1

CONTENTS

PART 4:
Biblical Patterns and Contemporary Opportunities

IMPORTANT DATES TO REMEMBER

The following listing of dates in chronological order is intended to help you see the historical sequence of events discussed in the course of this book.

IMPORTANT DATES TO REMEMBER

1517	Martin Luther initiates the Reformation
1529	Martin Luther and Ulrich Zwingli meet at Marburg Castle
1560	John Calvin requests the use of tokens for distribution in his church in Geneva
1621	King James I forces Parliament to pass the "five articles of Perth"
1634	King Charles I bans revival meetings and mandates that communion be offered only at parish churches
1642–1646	English Civil War
1649	Oliver Cromwell assumes control of England and Puritan period begins
1660–1685	Restoration period in England
1662	Puritan Synod passes the Half-Way Covenant, allowing grown, unregenerate children who accept orthodox doctrines to baptize their children
1672	Solomon Stoddard's full conversion experience
1679–1680	Solomon Stoddard opens communion to all congregation members, upheld by majority vote of the synod and recommended to other churches
1688	Protestant King William of Orange assumes the crown and Scottish Presbyterians are released from persecution
1713	Jonathan Edwards reconsiders the fenced sacrament of Puritan tradition
1724	John Wesley begins his clerical career
1726	Jonathan Edwards becomes assistant minister to Solomon Stoddard
1729	Solomon Stoddard dies; William Law publishes *A Serious Call to the Devout Life*
1730	John Wesley, Charles Wesley and William Morgan begin attending holy communion weekly and visiting the sick and imprisoned
1732	William Grimshaw ordained into the Anglican clergy; John Clayton joins John Wesley in the Holy Club
1734–1735	Jonathan Edwards holds series of sermons on "justification by faith alone"
1736	John and Charles Wesley arrive in Georgia

1737–1743	First Great Awakening
1738	John Wesley returns to England and founds Fetter Lane, has his famous Aldersgate experience
1739	Samuel Blair leads revivals in Pennsylvanian congregations; George Whitefield conducts revivals in Bristol
1739–1741	John Wesley preaches at revival meetings in Bristol
1740	John and Charles Wesley withdraw from Fetter Lane
1741	George Whitefield holds revival in Northampton
1742	Sacramental cycles held at the village of Cambuslang, Scotland; William Grimshaw begins preaching at St. Michael's at Haworth
1745	John and Charles Wesley publish *Hymns on the Lord's Supper*
1748	George Whitefield travels Scotland
1749	Jonathan Edwards announces he will demand evidence of conversion experiences from those seeking communion
1755	John Wesley holds the first Methodist covenant service
1770	George Whitefield dies
1771	Francis Asbury arrives in the American colonies
1781	John Murray moves to Massachusetts; John Wesley ministers in Manchester
1784	John Wesley begins ordaining Methodist ministers in the United States; Methodism and Anglicanism are separated
1790–1796	James McGready begins preaching in North Carolina, then Kentucky
1797–1805	Second Great Awakening
1799	Revivals begin at the Red River church in Kentucky; William Penn Candler develops the altar call
1801	Barton Stone offers public sacrament at Cane Ridge, Kentucky
1805	Baptists begin holding camp meetings and stressing immediate baptism to seal conversion
1806	Presbyterians sought to invalidate the licenses of many revivalists in Cumberland
1825	Charles Finney holds his first revival meeting
1827	Critics of Charles Finney mount a pamphlet war against him
1830	Charles Finney begins using the anxious bench
1850–1914	Victorian period in England brings back total abstinence and Reformed communions

INTRODUCTION

A MINI-SACRAMENTAL REVIVAL

The special revival began on a bright fall Sunday morning in 1986 when Fr. Gray Temple, rector of St. Patrick's Episcopal Church in Atlanta, presented one of his usual brilliant sermons. Fr. Temple had been well educated as a theological liberal, but he became a charismatic and began preaching evangelically after experiencing a hairraising vision from the Lord on the reality of the demonic kingdom. That was something not found in liberal theology![1]

The sermon that morning was on Jesus' command to love one another. In a moment of inspiration, Fr. Tom Belt, the assistant pastor, stood up and suggested a specific response, namely, that the congregation take time then and there to visit and affirm one another. Although some Pentecostal churches do this, this is *simply not done* in Episcopal churches. The rector reaffirmed Fr. Belt's suggestion and urged that during the communion distribution every member of the congregation follow the Spirit's lead and pray for and love one another *as they received communion at the altar rail.*

What followed was a most glorious communion service. As the elements were distributed, people hugged and laid hands on each other in prayer. Clusters of three or four persons formed to minister to one another. Words of prophecy and exhortation were given, and reconciliations took place. The largely charismatic congregation had experience in the gifts of the Spirit, so neither the "word gifts" nor the laying on of hands for prayer was strange to them. What was unusual was the power, gracefulness, and beauty in which the gifts flowed that Sunday at the communion rail. Most people left deeply touched by the Spirit of God and sensed that something special had just happened. The same format was followed the next Sunday — with equally glorious spiritual fruit.

However, some complaints trickled in. Mistakes had been made. A woman complained that someone had laid hands on her suggestively. Someone else felt that many were praying too loudly at the altar. Others in the congregation missed their periods of "recollection" with the Eucharist (i.e., a time of silent meditation and prayer with Jesus — the usual practice of devout liturgical Christians).

To correct these errors, Fr. Gray restricted the communion prayers to the "experienced" intercessors of the church. This meant only those in the local chapter of the Order of St. Luke (OSL), a fellowship dedicated to the ministry of healing, could function as altar intercessors. The OSL intercessors continued praying with the communicants at the altar and in fact did an excellent job. Physical healings took place, and one marriage was miraculously healed and saved from divorce through the spontaneous (and silent) prayer of one of the intercessors. Nevertheless, several lay leaders at St. Patrick's discerned that in spite of the continued successes by the OSL intercessors, the Spirit was grieved by the exclusion of the general congregation from the communion ministry.

A few weeks later one of the OSL intercessors made a serious mistake by praying over and laying hands on a phobic woman as she received the consecrated bread. The lady in question had been repeatedly molested as a child and just recently been brutally raped. She dreaded *any* touch. The intercessors were then banished to the side of the altar, where persons wanting intercessory prayer would go and receive prayer — a practice now common in charismatic-liturgical churches. Everything was in proper order again, but the special time of revival slipped away.

At the time I had spent a decade among several churches and groups within the charismatic renewal movement and had done substantial research on church history. Yet I recognized something unique had happened at St. Patrick's that should have continued. In a later telephone conversation with Fr. Belt after he had moved on to another parish, he also expressed regret that these special communions were shut down. He believes the mistake was a theological one, in assuming that communion was an *individual* sacrament rather than its biblical meaning of a *communal* meal. In fact, theologians have long understood the corporate nature of the Eucharist but have had few clues as to *how* a communion service can become corporate.[2]

WORKING DEFINITIONS

We need to pause here for some key definitions. *Revival* is a much used and abused word. Often it means little more than a scheduled evangelistic meeting with an out-of-town preacher — often announced on the church marquee: "Revival: This Friday and Saturday Night!"[3] In this book revival means an occasion when the Holy Spirit descends upon and invigorates a Christian community for a period of time. The congregation knows something special is happening. Unbelievers are converted, and those who have already accepted the gospel are renewed in their devotion. There are noticeable changes in behavior of the reviving congregation, such as an increased desire to evangelize and a rapid increase in the fruit of the Spirit. Sometimes there are unusual physical manifestations, though this does not always happen.

Traditionally, when revival hits a congregation, the renewed presence of the Spirit produces fresh conversions among persons who are inexplicably drawn to the revived church or touched by evangelistic outreach of the congregation. When revival comes to a congregation such as St. Patrick's, where the people are already born again and

Spirit-filled, what intensifies immediately are the fruit and gifts of the Spirit. This is sometimes termed a *refreshing* rather than revival.[4]

The *sacraments* have been defined in different ways throughout the ages. Tragically, some of these definitions have been the cause of church division. The Anglican-Episcopal tradition, which has attempted to be a middle ground (*via media*) between Reformed theology and traditional Catholicism, defines sacraments as "outward and visible signs of inward and spiritual grace, given by Christ as sure and certain means by which we receive that grace."[5] To this traditional understanding I would add that sacraments are covenant signs that *express God's faithfulness and character as covenant maker*. They are among the "means of grace," which include prayer and worship and which welcome us into and sustain us within the kingdom.

Most scholars in the area of sacramental history distinguish between the two main Christian sacraments — baptism and the Lord's Supper (the "dominical sacraments"), which were clearly mandated by our Lord — and other sacramental forms that have come and gone among Christians of various ages (e.g., the medieval rite of anointing kings). This is not to disparage these lesser forms, as they may be excellent ways to reaffirm the many-faceted covenant relationship that God has established with humankind and especially his church. For example, Roman Catholicism declares that marriage, properly blessed by a priest, is a full sacrament. The Reformers found this assertion untenable and pointed out how the early Christians recognized marriage only as a civil necessity. In fact, it was not until the Roman Empire fell into ruin and civil magistrates became rare that priests began to bless marriages. Conversely, foot-washing, which many Protestant denominations take as an "ordinance" and perform regularly, was not accepted by the Roman Catholic or Eastern Orthodox churches as a full sacrament in spite of its firm biblical warrant (John 13:4–15).

It is not the purpose of this work to argue for or against an official or expanded list of sacraments. Our chief concern will be with the Lord's Supper, which is recognized by practically all Christians as a major sacrament (or *ordinance*). However, we will suggest that some of the polemical issues about the correct number of sacraments could be avoided by affirming that the Holy Spirit has from time to time inspired certain ritualized acts to express faith-filled and grace-giving covenants. Thus, marriage may not have been directly instituted by Christ, but certainly the various Christian ceremonies of affirming the marriage union have become a grace-giving event that reflects the parallel covenant relationships between husband and wife, and Christ and his church (Eph. 5:21–32).

COMBINING WORD, SACRAMENT, AND PRESENCE

The central task of the present work is to show that sacramental worship enhances, sustains, and strengthens revivals. The covenant presence of God's graces during sacramental worship reinforces the Holy Spirit's special presence and work during the revival period. Sacramental worship also gives the reviving community a more complete vision of God's character as faithfully and consistently present.

The aborted revival at St. Patrick's demonstrates this theme. Powerful revival can occur when three elements take place simultaneously. First and most important, the evangelical gospel is proclaimed, and people are given an opportunity to respond to it. Second, such preaching is combined with worship that includes God's covenant signs (sacraments), especially the Lord's Supper. Third, the *manifest presence and gifts of the Holy Spirit are accepted* in spite of the fact that such a presence is disruptive to religious traditions and routine order.

The biblical evidence for claiming that such three-dimensional revivals are the main biblical pattern for revival is examined in chapter 13, where both the Old and New Testament evidence for such types of revival is considered. The fact that St. Patrick's revival was quickly quenched for "good" reasons, in terms of the traditions of worship and decorum, signifies another recurring theme. Revivals of this highly effective type are delicately balanced and draw much opposition from within the church — much of it well meaning. Sustaining these multidimensional revivals requires leadership especially sensitive to direction from the Holy Spirit and solidly grounded in Scripture.

Word-Sacramental-presence

Ironically, such multidimensional revivals have not often occurred within highly liturgical denominations such as Roman Catholicism or Eastern Orthodoxy.[6] Rather the Word-sacramental-presence combination has most often occurred in the Protestant branch of Christendom. Martin Luther and John Calvin, the Reformation giants, laid the foundations for this type of revival by advocating a spirituality that balanced the effective preaching of the evangelical Word with devout sacramental worship (ch. 4). Their critique of Catholicism was that exaggerated sacramental theology and pseudo-sacramental acts, such as praying with votive candles, had weakened the proclamation of the Word. It was the firebrand Reformer Ulrich Zwingli who devalued the importance of the Lord's Supper by denying both the "real presence" of our Lord in the sacrament and its grace-giving act. Unfortunately, after the eighteenth century his sacramental theology became ascendant among evangelical Christians.

The Protestant revivals examined in this volume, all of which were multidimensional, depended on the classical Reformed view of the sacraments — that is, that the sacraments are truly means of grace and that the Lord's Supper gives the believer a special presence of Jesus. They also occurred before the middle of the nineteenth century and therefore are missing an element that many evangelicals assume to be essential to true revival, the altar call. Part of this story deals with the thorny issue of becoming Christian in the classical Reformed pattern before it was assumed that incorporation into the body of Christ was as simple as a walk to the front of the revivalist's tent.

Two Church Traditions

Part 1 will lay the groundwork for the assertion that multidimensional revivals are the most effective and fruitful of revivals. This is demonstrated by examining the best cases of churches that are missing one or more of its elements. To this end I share with the reader my youth as a Roman Catholic. I was brought up in a pious Catholic family living in a devout Irish-American Catholic neighborhood of New York City. The spirituality of that community was sincere, pious, and sacramentally centered. In spite of a totally Catholic education, which included an undergraduate degree at (Jesuit) Fordham University, my faith faded and then died as I confronted the secular world of the 1960s. In fact, few Catholics I grew up with maintained a true Christian faith as practicing Catholics. A majority settled into nominal Catholicism, with sporadic church attendance and sufficient public morality to maintain their professional status or self-esteem. The failure of traditional sacramental Catholicism to protect its followers from the ravishes of secularism and the modern world is the central focus of chapter 1.

After a period of atheism I was touched by the Lord and called back into active faith. Through attending mostly evangelical or Pentecostal meetings and attending a charismatic Church of God, I entered the world of evangelical-charismatic Christianity (ch. 2). In this tradition, which is consciously nonliturgical and minimally sacramental, there are few nominal Christians. Every layperson has a sense of mission and church ministry. Bible study is continuous and effective from childhood to "senior citizen" status. However, it is not uncommon for many within this tradition to have a flawed moral sense. I quickly found, for instance, that business people who loudly proclaimed they were "born-again" evangelicals often had the worst reputation for honesty and service among their colleagues.

This gap between faith and morality, called antinomianism, has plagued Protestant Christianity from the earliest days of the Reformation. It is a sub-Christian behavior that is the opposite to Catholic nominalism. The Catholic nominal person believes weakly but often lives an outwardly moral life — the result of the intense moral teaching (sometimes legalism) of traditional Catholicism. By contrast, the evangelical or Pentecostal believer often has a weaker moral sense but believes in church doctrines strongly, passionately arguing such marginal issues as the exact manner of Christ's second coming.[7] Thus early in my renewed Christian walk I came to understand that both main streams of Western Christianity — the liturgical/sacramental Catholic and the nonliturgical evangelical (and Pentecostal/charismatic) — were operating at a "wounded" or incomplete mode.

SACRAMENTAL REVIVALS IN HISTORY

Fortunately at this time I began looking at the history of church revivals. To my utter astonishment I discovered a little-known facet of church history. Protestant evangelical revivals of the seventeenth and eighteenth centuries were *deeply sacramental*. The combination of sacramental worship and evangelical preaching resulted in revivals among Puritan Congregationalists and Scottish Presbyterians that give us the first historical examples of multidimensional revivals (chs. 3–7). The Presbyterian Scots experienced 150 years of sporadic revivals culminating in the great communion service at Cambuslang in 1742, where about 30,000 came to worship together and thousands communed (chs. 5–6). Ironically, after the greatest success at the Scottish town of Cambuslang, opposition mobilized against the revivals. Ultimately these revivals were discredited as "enthusiasm" and out of order.

Sixty years later Presbyterian ministers on the Kentucky frontier carried out the same tradition of preaching and sacramental worship and triggered the Second Great Awakening (ch. 7). That awakening transformed America from a nominally Christian and Deist nation into a more truly Christian one. Unfortunately, that revival has often been pictured as little more than frontier roughness because of its uncontrolled manifestations such as the "jerks" (uncontrolled bodily movements). As in Scotland, fear of the excesses ended the revival among the Presbyterian churches.

My historical investigations led to an examination of yet another sacramentally centered revival that began during the peak years of the Scottish Presbyterian revivals. The Wesley brothers' accidental revival, which birthed Methodism, must be ranked as the most successful revival of the church age. It lasted almost a hundred years and transformed for the better the moral and spiritual climate of both the United Kingdom and the United States.

The Wesleys expanded the multidimensional revival by including social concern for the poor and careful discipleship. The sometimes unusual manifestations of the presence of the Holy Spirit, such as desperate cries for mercy or "the fallings," were understood as a *normal* part of revival and were neither encouraged nor suppressed.

The Wesley brothers also created a corpus of glorious hymns, including some of the best communion hymns of Christendom.

The Methodist revival birthed whole communities of born-again, sacrificial, and holy Christians who were comfortable with the manifest presence of the Spirit. The Wesley brothers consciously battled the temptations toward antinomianism on the one hand and religious formalism on the other, to form a balanced, vital evangelicalism rarely seen in Christendom (chs. 8–12). The Methodist revival began to decline only after the brothers had died and the various Wesleyan groups began to lose the original balance of Word, sacrament, and presence.

PRESENT POSSIBILITIES AND ETERNAL REALITIES

Our last section will show how revival swept an Episcopal church in central Florida to produce a modern manifestation of multidimensional revival. Then we will see how another Florida church, Christ the Redeemer Church near Jacksonville, has pioneered the way to balance Word, sacrament, and Spirit in a totally contemporary setting. Finally, in chapter 16 we will reach our conclusions by returning to the Wesleyan revival as a model for the present-day church.

It is important to note what this book is *not* about. It has nothing to do with "liturgical reform." Liturgy is associated with sacrament and may be thought of as the poetic expression of sacrament. Yet after much investigation I am not convinced that one form of liturgy, such as the austere Reformed pattern of the Lord's Supper, is either less or more effective as a means of grace than the most elaborate, high-church forms of sacramental ministry. What does seem to make a difference is the faith and understanding of the Christian community that something significant can or will happen during sacramental worship.

The practical aim of the book is to demonstrate to Christians in the nonliturgical churches that sacramental worship is not contrary to vital evangelical faith or revival. In fact, the strengthening of the evangelical proclamation with sacramental worship is the Bible's best plan for revival. A concurrent aim is to show the sacramental branch of Christendom that liturgical worship without evangelical proclamation and the gifts of the Spirit is futile in standing up to the pressures of the contemporary world.

NOTES

1. Taped interview with Fr. Gray Temple (c. 1983) in author's collection. For the liberal view of the demonic, see Henry Ansgar Kelly, *The Devil, Demonology and Witchcraft: The Development of Christian Belief in Evil Spirits* (Garden City, N.Y.: Doubleday, 1974). A brilliant, biblically based response is found in James Kallas's work, *The Satanward View: A Study in Pauline Theology* (Philadelphia: Westminster, 1966).

2. See, for example, the Eucharistic theology of the great French Catholic theologian Henri de Lubac, summarized in Paul McPartlan's *The Eucharist Makes the Church: Henri de Lubac and John Zizioulas in Dialogue* (Edinburgh: T. & T. Clark, 1993), esp. ch. 1.

3. A vigorous critique of this cheapened meaning of revival is found in Iain H. Murray's brilliant work entitled *Revival and Revivalism: The Making and Marring of American Evangelicalism, 1750–1858* (Edinburgh: Banner of Truth Trust, 1994).

4. Significantly, the leadership of the Toronto Airport Christian Fellowship often uses the term *refreshing* to describe what is happening in their meetings.

5. *The Book of Common Prayer* (1979), 857.

6. For a history of revivals prior to the Reformation, see the classic work by Fr. Ronald Knox, *Enthusiasm: A Chapter in the History of Religion* (New York: Oxford Univ. Press, 1950).

7. A balanced introduction to eschatology, the doctrine of the last days, and one that respects the different views of Christians across the centuries, is found in the *Christian History* issue dedicated to the topic: "The End: A History of the Second Coming" (vol. 18, #61). Although not an academic journal, *Christian History* is a marvelous place to find balanced historical perspective on many issues. The editors of *Christian History* have ready access to the finest evangelical (and now charismatic) scholars, and the individual issues contain guides to further readings. I will cite them further in the course of this work.

PART 1

THE
TWENTIETH-CENTURY
PATTERN OF CHRISTIAN
SPIRITUALITY

Sacramental Spirituality without Revival: Traditional Catholicism

A Chest Full of Sundries

I looked on with both sadness and pride and helped when I could. I was eleven years old, and my sister, nineteen, was packing a travel chest full of sundries such as toothpaste, bar soap, and writing paper. This was part of the requirements to enter the novitiate and become a Sister of Charity, a Catholic nun. At the time (1954) entering postulants were expected to bring this kit of basic supplies (waved in case of family poverty). The sundries kit was a residue from the Middle Ages, when women brought a partial dowry to the convent as a sign that the family was not avoiding the cost of marrying her off. My aunt had provided dozens of tubes of toothpaste, an awful-tasting brand that has long since been discontinued. My sister, Gloria, bought most of the other supplies with the money she earned from the part-time job she held while attending school. As I looked on, I secretly hoped that when the tubes were all squeezed out, the mother superior would somehow send her back home. Gloria had served as a "co-mother" to me, and I knew that although we would visit, I would miss her terribly.

Gloria entered the novitiate with thirty-nine other young women at Mount Saint Vincent College (New York), where over 150 others were being formed into Catholic nuns. The basic program lasted three or four years, depending on the educational level of the postulant. The Sisters of Charity had been founded in the nineteenth century by Mother Elizabeth Seaton (now declared a saint), and they were dedicated to teaching and nursing. My sister's admitted aversion to blood precluded the nursing vocation.[1]

My sadness was mixed with pride at having a sister who would be part of the spiritual elite of the church. We had repeatedly heard from the sisters and brothers in our parochial school that the vocation to the religious life was the highest (and most difficult) calling of life. I had thoughts that I too might someday follow into the religious life and become a teaching brother or priest.

This happened less than fifty years ago. Yet it seems as if it took place on a different planet. We Catholics assumed that the church would go on unchanged from antiquity, its doctrines and theology stable and established since the Middle Ages by the great theologians of that era. The Roman Catholic Church had survived the Reformation, whereas the Protestant world was hopelessly divided by denominations and factions within denominations. In our view of the Protestant world, we saw little but weak belief among the more liberal denominations and rampant emotionalism among the fundamentalists. The Pentecostals were written off as cultic and beyond the pale of consideration. All this disorder in the Protestant world was caused, we believed, by not having the pope and the stability of Catholic doctrine to lead them.

If anyone had predicted the present state of the Catholic Church at the beginning of the twentieth-first century, we would have assumed the revelation to be an absurd, demonic lie. Novitiates empty? Church attendance down to less than 30 percent of baptized Catholics? Theological factions among the bishops and priests? Theological liberalism and faithlessness in the seminaries? Catholic colleges and universities where the doctrines of the church were more often ignored and ridiculed than taught? Nonsense! That could never be!

And yet it is true. It happened in our lifetime.

SACRAMENTAL SPIRITUALITY AND CATHOLIC CHILDHOOD IN THE 1950S

My family lived through this transition from traditional piety to the current pluralistic form of Catholicism. In the 1920s my parents' families had been next-door neighbors in Rio Piedras, Puerto Rico. Both families practiced the nominal Catholicism so common to middle class Hispanics of that era. My father was orphaned when he was twelve and sent off to a Catholic (Christian Brothers) boarding school in Plattsburgh, New York. There the brothers fostered in him a devout Catholicism that he never abandoned. He met my mother again in 1929 in New York City, where her family had immigrated after the death of her father. My mother and father married in 1931 and established their home in Manhattan, in a neighborhood that was predominantly Irish Catholic.

On a rainy Sunday morning, during their first year of marriage, my father set out for mass, but my mother refused to accompany him. He commented as he left, "If you don't go to church the devil will take your soul!" My mother stayed home but literally quaked from fright while my father was at mass. She never missed Sunday mass after that.

Gloria, their second child, was the only girl. She was born critically ill and not expected to survive. Mother, by now more devout, prayed desperately, "Lord, if you allow her to live, I will give her completely to you." She lived, and God accepted the vow. When Gloria was in the second grade, she approached mother and asked meekly, "Can you give me two hundred dollars when I'm eighteen?" My mother asked why, and she answered, "I need the money to become a nun." She had just heard that novices need to take into the convent several years' supply of sundries — about two hundred dollars' worth.

We all went to the parochial school adjacent to our church, the Church of the Incarnation. Already in the 1950s there was a tremendous moral and behavioral gap with the local public schools.

Catholic schools were safe, disciplined sanctuaries of moral education and learning. In contrast, New York public schools were
suffering from the natural by-product of secular humanism: pur-
poselessness, crime, and vandalism.

Sisters of Charity and Christian Brothers staffed Incarnation
School. Boys and girls were separated in the fifth grade, with the
Christian Brothers training the boys and nuns continuing with the
girls. In later years I ran across accounts of neurotic nuns or brothers
who severely beat or abused the school children. Some of those stories were undoubtedly true, though I found that the nuns and brothers at Incarnation were kind; admittedly, some did have a heavy hand
(or ruler). All were dedicated to doing God's will, as they understood
their calling, and to our spiritual and educational welfare.

My first-grade teacher, Sister Mourine, was particularly saintly.
She was very Irish and perpetually cheerful. She took obvious pleas-
ure in reading us Bible stories and saints' stories and in teaching us
how to pray (I was ahead of the class, since my sister had already
taught me most of the prayers). Sister Mourine managed a class of
sixty students with good cheer, love, and discipline. In later years,
when the American public came to revere Mother Teresa, I would
say, "I knew someone like that."

I vividly recall my second-grade reader, a book of saints' lives.
There were picture stories of St. Francis and the birds, St. Martin
cutting his cloak to share with a beggar, and St. George slaying the
dragon. I was fascinated by the colored illustration of the blessed
knight shoving a lance through a dragon's midsection (sort of a croc-
odile with stump wings). A beautiful maiden stood to the side. I asked
Gloria about the dragon, and she improvised that "at that time" there
were dragons, thus preserving for me trust in the Catholic Church
and everything it taught.

In the second grade we were prepared for Holy Communion, a
major stage in life for Catholic children. First we were given instruction on confessing our sins and were processed through our first
sacramental confession, the oral confession of our sins to a priest.
Then we carefully rehearsed for our first communion. Our parents
bought special communion suits for boys and white dresses for the

girls. We were instructed to "talk to Jesus." I was shocked at the moment of my first communion to find it was not like a telephone conversation; I spoke mentally, but I did not hear a voice respond.

In school we were taken through the confessional cubes once a month. But in our family we went to confession practically *every* week. From my present perspective, I see that the Protestant critique of confession has some validity. It does make the Christian believe that the atonement is "doled out" a week at a time through the priest's powers. Moreover, we could never really rest in our salvation, as any "mortal sin," such as disobeying the rule not to eat meat on Friday, put us in danger of hell. Nevertheless, the practice of weekly examination of conscience and the continuous discussions of what was serious or minor sin cultivated a high awareness of the moral law. It is not at all strange that Roman Catholics, not evangelical Protestants, led the first and strongest opposition to legal abortions in America.

The sacrament of confirmation came in the sixth grade. It was supposed to impart the gifts of the Holy Spirit. The Baltimore Catechism, the official doctrinal teaching text for Catholics at the time, explained:

> Which are the gifts of the Holy Ghost?
> A. The gifts of the Holy Ghost are Wisdom, Understanding, Counsel, Fortitude, Knowledge, Piety and Fear of the Lord.[2]

Unfortunately, this theology of confirmation was dependent on the Old Testament definition of the gifts of the Spirit (see Isa. 11:2). This was an incomplete understanding that developed early in church history, before St. Paul's writings had been unequivocally accepted as part of the Bible (fourth century). Thus the sacrament of confirmation did not take into account the gifts listed in 1 Corinthians 12, such as speaking in tongues or prophecy. In fact, we had no knowledge of such gifts. In the 1950s only a few scholars in the Catholic Church had a positive appreciation of Pentecostalism and its recovery of all of the gifts of the Spirit.[3] Had anyone broken out in tongues or prophetic utterances at the bishop's laying on of hands on our heads, they would have been considered insane or insolent. Unlike my first communion, I was not disappointed with confirmation since *I expected no spiritual experience*. As a pious Catholic boy, I simply trusted the sacramental rite as important in spite of any evidence or change in my spiritual life.

The Catholic brothers and sisters taught us the doctrines, theology, and moral understandings that had been the teachings of the Church since the Middle Ages and codified by the Council of Trent (1545–1563). The doctrine of the sacraments was repeatedly and carefully taught. Each sacrament gave a particular grace (called "sacramental grace") appropriate to it, as well as a "sanctifying grace" to help the person to achieve holiness. For instance, in the sacrament of matrimony the person received the specific sacramental grace, which helped in the duties and stresses of marriage, and a sanctifying grace, which helped one grow in personal holiness.

This sacramental theology, especially the understanding of Holy Communion, was based on the theology of St. Thomas Aquinas. Here entered the famous doctrine of *transubstantiation*, taught as the high point of Catholic truth. Because of its philosophical subtlety and difficulty, it was taught only to eighth graders, many of whom would soon go to public school and thus receive little or no further Catholic instruction. The doctrine of transubstantiation assured that every believing Catholic had an appreciation of the "real presence" of Jesus at communion.

Knowing the Bible was not considered central in Catholic instruction, though it was not ignored. Large sections of the Old and New Testaments were read at every mass, a liturgical custom that dates back to the Jewish synagogue. This was a most sensible tradition before the advent of the printing press. Unfortunately, the transition to private and family Bible-centered devotions was not made in this era, as this was too "Protestant." For example, our family had a Bible, but I cannot remember my father ever reading it for devotions or during family prayer time. The center of our family prayers was in the recitation of the rosary, especially for the conversion of atheistic Russia. Still, our private prayer life was good, with much prayer time spent in church (open all times in this era). My sister modeled this, for she often dropped into church for five minutes after a shopping trip.

For some in our parish the combination of sacramental life and prayer resulted in fully mature Christian lives. A few in the parish lived lives of evident holiness. I particularly remember a lady with the unusual name Brunilda. She chose not to become a nun, which was her intense desire, because she had to care for her widowed and handicapped mother. She sacrificed both the prestige of being a nun and the security such community life would give in old age. Brunilda, like a few in the parish (including my sister), attended mass daily and drew great strength from daily communion.

CATHOLIC PREP SCHOOL

The excellent Catholic prep school I attended was associated with Manhattan College. The Christian Brothers on staff demonstrated the same self-sacrifice and concern for the welfare of the students that I had come to expect as normal.[4] Yet serious problems arose. As we matured, we learned scientific skills and critical thought processes based on the interaction of reason, experience, and evidence. Our faith, however, was based on sacramental piety, tradition, and authority and was entirely lacking in experiential evidence.

For example, we still (mostly) believed that the saints had the power to do miracles, including healings and exorcism, yet none of us had ever seen a miraculous healing. The sacrament of extreme unction was not considered a healing rite but rather a special send off into the heavenly world; no one expected healing from it. We had heard about exorcisms, but these were so rare that in spite of living amidst a pious and well-staffed Catholic community, we knew of no priest who had done an exorcism.

Was there a difference between rumor and rare event? Was the power to heal illness with prayer something akin to St. George's slaying the dragon? The noted English monk-theologian Dom Aelred Graham, writing in 1970 and reminiscing about a similar Catholic boyhood, addressed the issue succinctly:

> Today, over half a century afterward, I still think that the priests and nuns who introduced me to the Christian sacraments could not have done it better; they truly represented a "mothering"

Church. . . . [But] it may be that the Church has yet to present her message according to age and the stages of mental development. She does, or did, well with children; not so well with adolescents and grown-ups, especially those who are thoughtful and reflective.[5]

In my senior year at prep school I ran into Joe, a friend who was two years ahead of me and well into his college studies at a local Catholic college. We had a conversation about the Catholic faith. Joe now saw Christianity as a myth, useful for keeping moral order but having no intrinsic relation to truth.

"No, no, that's wrong!" I insisted, but he merely smiled knowingly. He assured me that intelligent and educated Catholics thought as he did and that I was still at an "immature stage." "You'll see, you'll see . . ." and he waved me off. His word struck me as tragic (and I hoped not prophetic).

WITNESS TO THE FALL OF CATHOLIC ORTHODOXY

When I entered Fordham University in September of 1961, it was vying with Notre Dame for preeminence among American Catholic universities. It was an exciting time to be a Catholic; John F. Kennedy had just been elected president, marking the full acceptance of Catholics into the political mainstream. Church theologians probed toward a transition from its medieval consensus theology to more modern forms of theology. What we as entering freshmen did not anticipate was that the new forms of theology presented to us were often little more than philosophical faithlessness. Rather than entering a new "promised land" of modern reflection on ancient creeds and biblical truths, we walked into a mine field where the traditional modes of theology were blown apart, and nothing positive or credible would replace them.

This was both sad and ironic, for the Jesuit order of priests, who taught at Fordham, had long been the orthodox "shock troops" of the Catholic Church. The "Society of Jesus" (Jesuits) had been founded by St. Ignatius of Loyola (1431–1556) as an order of highly educated priests and Catholic apologists to win back Europe from Protestantism. In Poland, France, and other sections of Europe they were largely suc-

cessful. The Jesuits remained scrupulously orthodox from their founding until the decades after World War II. Then, unknown to the public, the Jesuit seminaries had become heavily influenced by liberal
theology and biblical "demythologizing" — the doctrine that miracles
are "scientifically impossible." Thus, for instance, the miraculous stories of the Bible are no more reliable than the legend of St. George
and the dragon.[6]

When we began our studies, we discovered that the theology and
philosophy departments were divided among contending factions. A
few traditionalists hung on to the theology of St. Thomas Aquinas as
if the modern world had not happened. In my junior year I had one
such professor for moral theology. Our only textbook was a set of St.
Thomas's *Summa Theologica*, and he taught the course like our
grammar school catechism class. He instructed us on "correct doctrine," and we were supposed to accept it without question. He was
an easy grader, so most of us got an A or B+, a rare thing in that era.
But the course was both insulting to us as young men seeking truth
and an injustice to orthodox Catholic theology and doctrine. It
seemed to us as if orthodoxy could only sustain itself by unreasoning
authoritarianism.

At the other extreme was a group of younger radicals who had
accepted theological liberalism. The specific form of liberal theology then in fashion was the "death of God" theology, which popularized radical demythologizing and glorified the so-called insights
of the nineteenth-century anti-Christian philosopher Friedrich
Nietzsche. Nietzsche was the son of a devout Lutheran minister and
was raised in a Europe decimated by Protestant cessationist theology.

Cessationist theology affirmed that miraculous events such as
healing and prophecy ceased after the apostolic period. This sapped
the faith expectancy of any further miracles in the current age and
left mainline Protestant Christianity a religion lacking in belief of
the miraculous. Ultimately the authority of Scripture and the divinity of Christ could not be sustained with such a theology. As a consequence, the sense of God's presence and touch in everyday life was
lost.[7] Nietzsche saw that few of his generation really believed in the
Bible and Christian doctrines. Instead the majority, especially in the

educated classes, paid lip service to Christianity as socially useful myths, but no more; in reality, therefore, God was dead.

This "Death of God" movement in the 1960s, as it was called, claimed Christianity had to create a theology that was nonsupernatural and ethically relativistic and that avoided "God talk." The movement was given wide coverage in the press, including a cover story in *Time* magazine.[8] Presenting this theology to us as a "mature" spirituality destroyed for many of us any lingering faith in the validity of the miraculous elements of the Bible or of the church's great saints. In a class in my junior year a young lay theology instructor ridiculed the resurrection by quipping that Jesus' body "rotted like stinking fish." That blasphemy was greeted with giggles of nervous approval, including mine. We were "free" from the dogma of the catechism and of the "old foggy" traditionalists, such as that of my moral theology professor.

A few professors attempted a "middle ground," probing toward new theological understandings while attempting to affirm orthodoxy and avoid the apostate fashions. Under one of these professors, the saintly Fr. Gleason, we were introduced into some of the best writings of modern Catholicism.[9] Unfortunately, the moderates were focused on the liturgical reform movement and spent much of their energy in that direction. They assumed that changing the Latin mass to a popular language would unleash a surge of devotion. In fact, much of the focus of the Second Vatican Council (1962–1965) was on that very issue. Ultimately the liturgical reforms and revisions, including the use of the vernacular for the mass, did nothing to increase lay devotion. In fact, many now believe it merely brought confusion. Perhaps more important, it diverted the attention of the moderate faction from the impending real problem, the rise of radical theologies.[10]

In retrospect, the biggest fault of the orthodox moderates was not forcefully confronting the emerging radical theologies. They were victims of the politeness and goodwill of their generation. It would have been biblically appropriate for some faculty member to have carried out "prophetic dramas" like an Old Testament prophet, perhaps barging into the class of my radical professor, throwing a rotting fish on his desk, and declaring: "Thus will *you* be, but the Lord arose!"[11]

There were not enough professors within the orthodox center to hold against the temptations of radicalism and apostasy, which always come dressed in the costume of "progressive theology." Nor were we sufficiently informed about the church's splendid heritage of spirituality and discernment. For instance, I learned from a history professor, not a theology professor, of the Bollandists. This was a group of seventeenth-century Catholic scholars who critically evaluated the church's legacy of saints' records. They separated the accounts into myths (such as St. George and his dragon) on the one hand, and reliable witness of the church's continuing miraculous power on the other.[12] My history professor talked about the Bollandists as a passing bit of information. Had this knowledge been actively presented to us as a theological issue and as a basis for the practice of discernment, we may have maintained a fundamental trust in the reality of the miraculous, including the biblical record.

At Fordham, our Catholic faith eroded day by day. By my senior year I still resisted Joe's prophecy and was not an atheist, though many of my friends were. I still held on to a glimmer of hope that the supernatural world was real and that Jesus was the Son of God. Yet I was in fact a functional deist — believing that there was a God, but he was far away. I continued to go to mass, though with little of my childhood devotion.

My final descent into atheism came two years after I graduated, while I was serving in Vietnam. Gloria sent me one of those Good News New Testaments written in modern English. I came across the passage where Jesus cursed the fig tree (Mark 11:14), and it occurred to me (a sort of demonic illumination) that Nietzsche was right — Christianity was a religion of resentment! I slammed the Bible down and began a forlorn six-year quest to live as a heroic atheist, the Nietzschean ideal. The radicals at Fordham had taught me well!

Most of us in the class of 1966 believed the radical wing was the wave of the future. Our hero was Fr. Herbert Rogers, the in-house radical Jesuit, and our designated villain was Cardinal Occtaviani of the Roman Curia, who attempted to hold back the progress of

Vatican II. In a tragic sense we were right. America, and American Catholicism in particular, were at the edge of a moral and cultural abyss ushered in by the Vietnam War. The older institutions and ways of thinking were disdained under the banner of revolutionary change. The Catholic universities suffered as much as the other institutions of higher learning in America, coming into an era that some have labeled the new "dark ages" of leftist politics, political correctness, and sham scholarship.[13]

In the 1970s and 1980s Fordham University became a center of a newer form of radicalism, liberation theology. This theology chose Marx instead of Nietzsche as its prophet and believed that Christian Marxism would end the poverty of the Third World. Had not the fall of European Marxism intervened, this tragic theology may well have captured all of Latin America the way it did Nicaragua.[14] While liberation theology declined, several other radical theologies arose, including theologies of the radical women's movement. Within this faction exists some of the most bizarre manifestations of contemporary theology, a few of which are reworked forms of paganism and witchcraft.[15]

This description of what happened at Fordham University is not an extreme example but is in fact typical of what happened to most Catholic colleges and universities.[16] Recently, the head of the religious studies department of a Detroit area Catholic college, a radical feminist, publicly declared that Joseph probably raped Mary and that Jesus was illegitimate. She challenged the administrative authorities to discipline her for her stand: "If they try to get rid of me, they know I'll sue them." No action was taken against her.[17] In fairness to Fordham's current status, there has been a resurgence of orthodoxy at the university under the direction of Avery Cardinal Dulles, considered by many as the most important living American Catholic theologian.

What happened to the Catholic colleges and universities also happened to the institutions of higher learning of the other mainline Christian denominations. My wife recently visited her former college in Maryland, a Methodist institution. When she attended, there was compulsory chapel, Methodist spirituality was taught, and a moral and Christian atmosphere was pervasive. It is now as totally secular as any state college.

This has been the common fate of Christian institutions of higher learning in the United States. They have succumbed to the forces of secularization and the temptations of federal grants, which have forced them to downgrade religious worship and instruction. Theology departments have become departments of religious studies, where Eastern religions or Native American religions are treated as equal to Christianity. For Protestant colleges and universities the pattern has generally been a descent from traditional denominational belief, to nondoctrinal liberal theology, to pure secularism, and currently into an adamant anti-Christianity.[18]

NOMINALISM AS NORMATIVE

Recent studies show that of those who call themselves Catholic, only a little over 25 percent attend weekly mass, a tremendous decline from that of the 1950s.[19] But even before the American Catholic Church entered the destructive and radical 1970s, its salient characteristic was the large numbers of *nominal* Catholics produced. Many adults slipped out of practicing their faith and attended church only on social occasions and holidays, though they still called themselves Catholic. The elaborate and traditional sacramental system, such as attending mass, receiving communion weekly, and making confession, most often did not lead to a mature, holy Christian life. In the Irish community of my childhood, alcoholism was too often a common outcome of this incomplete spirituality.

Nominalism as the fruit of Catholicism increased after the 1960s as the ethnic element of American Catholicism became less important. The old Irish and Italian neighborhoods dissipated into the suburbs, and the social pressure to be a Catholic *because* you were Irish, Italian, or Polish disappeared. In tragic irony, the political triumph of American Catholicism in electing the first Catholic president, John F. Kennedy, was also symbolic of its failure. Although his mother, Rose Kennedy, was a pious woman, her sons succumbed to the secularization of their elite schooling and lived only the most superficial and nominal of public Catholic lives (and as we now know, private lives of licentiousness).

The ascendancy of nominalism was particularly tragic because American Catholicism was perhaps the best and freest manifestation of the Catholic tradition. Unlike European or Latin American Catholicism, the Catholic Church in the United States was neither subsidized nor fettered by the state. Every penny of church support and maintenance was freely given. Nor was the American Catholic Church class bound. Unlike many areas of Latin America, it was not divided between a Spanish or middle-class clergy on the one hand, and a quasi-pagan, indigenous peasantry on the other. In fact, to carry things even further back, recent sociological analysis of European Christianity has shown that the fabled "age of faith" (the Middle Ages) was in fact an age of great nominalism. Everyone in Europe was baptized as Catholic, and a few took the faith seriously, but a majority were in fact nominal, nonpracticing Catholics.[20]

DECLINE IN SACRAMENTAL SPIRITUALITY

Decades of contention and theological radicalism have done much to undermine the sacramental piety of the majority of American Catholics. Belief in traditional doctrines, such as the "real presence" of Jesus in the Eucharist, has given way to symbolic and memorial theologies alien to classical Catholicism. A recent poll indicated that as few as 30 percent of Catholics in their forties or younger believe in the real presence at the Eucharist; this is another indication that nominalism has increased and overwhelmed the core doctrines of the church.[21]

This sacramental malaise is so common that Catholic educators now accept it as normal. Typical is the lament by Amy Welborn, a theology teacher at a Catholic high school. In a recent article in *First Things* she points out that of her seniors, who have received four years of religions instruction, less than a quarter go to mass on Sunday regularly. The most common question she has to answer in her professional life is "Why go to mass?" Welborn believes that the problem of this drastic declension in sacramental piety has two sources: the weakened sacramental theology now common, and the confusion produced by three decades of so-called liturgical reforms, which have attempted to make the mass "relevant" and "exciting." In fact, these have trivialized the typical parish mass.

When Welborn took her students to the local monastery, they reacted completely differently to the mass. They experienced awe and a sense of true worship. The local monks were not traditionalist; rather, they merely took the mass seriously as *worship*. One of her eighth graders expressed it succinctly: "In [our parish] church on Sunday, it's like it's all about us or something. This [monastery mass] was about God."[22]

Those parishes influenced or staffed by radical priests and nuns have the greatest problems in maintaining a vivid sacramental piety. Radical theology often discounts, in focus if not in theory, the seriousness with which earlier generations affirmed the real presence in the Eucharist and its transforming grace. For the political radicals sacramental piety is suspiciously too personal and certainly has little potential for political correctness.

This is reflected in a recent bestseller by a Catholic laywoman, Martha Manning's *Chasing Grace: Reflections of a Catholic Girl, Grown Up*.[23] Martha grew up in an Irish Catholic household. Her father had spent several years in seminary, and she and her sisters went to Catholic parochial and high school. Tragically, as Martha admits in the preface, she would "like to believe" the basic doctrines of the church but doesn't now.[24] Instead, her present Catholic life is what can best be called "active nominalism." Manning likes the social act of going to church and has adopted Catholic varieties of feminism and liberation theology to give meaning and purpose to her life. The sacraments are seen as *markers* of life's transitions, but there is no hint of any real grace received or life transformed.

Once again, nominalism has become the norm within the American Catholic Church. The fruit of this is that Catholics have left and continue to leave their church in astonishing numbers. The Vineyard denomination, a charismatic grouping of churches that has a typically low appreciation of the sacraments, has one-third of its members coming from Catholicism.[25]

THE CATHOLIC CHURCH TODAY: A WOUNDED GIANT

Today the Roman Catholic Church in America staggers from the wounds of the past thirty years. The great numbers of devoted young men and women entering the religious life as priests, nuns, and brothers have collapsed.[26] My sister's order, the Sister of Charity, is a typical and tragic example of American Catholicism. The numbers of novitiates entering yearly fell from about forty per year in the mid-1950s to *zero* in the 1990s. Mr. Walter Mathews, Director of the National Charismatic Catholic Office, has kept specific tabs on his fellow graduates from Regis High School, the Jesuit high school of the New York area. Out of 143 graduating seniors of his class (he graduated ten years after I did from Manhattan Prep), only *twelve* are serious Christians, and of these not all have remained Roman Catholic.[27]

Catholics in America are divided into rival factions, united by a common liturgy and history. In some of the larger cities separate parishes serve one faction or another. More commonly, Catholics have learned to live with various factions within a single parish.[28]

There is a small traditionalist faction that believes that Vatican II, with all the changes it brought, was a great mistake. They believe that a return to holiness can be achieved by simply turning back the clock, as in returning to a Latin mass and making St. Thomas's theology absolute again. There are, in fact, small Catholic congregations scattered throughout America that attempt to carry out this program, usually with limited success.

On the other extreme, the theological radicals have become a major element in American Catholicism. Many of the present-day clergy leaders and educators formed their spirituality within the anti-Vietnam movement and have a distinct antifree-market, left-wing ideology and political agenda. This faction is highly influenced by the demythologizing interpretation of Scripture, liberation theology, and "victim" theologies (such as radical feminism).

The moderate reforms of the 1960s generally drifted into one of two camps. They became radicalized with the anti-Vietnam War movement and liberation theology, or they retrenched and reaffirmed the basics of Christian orthodoxy. This neo-orthodoxy has been much encouraged by the present pope. It has gained increasing influence in recent years with the establishment of the several journals, including *First Things*, edited by Richard John Neuhaus, who calls his movement "dynamic orthodoxy."[29]

Allied with the neo-orthodox faction are the charismatic Catholics. The Catholic charismatic movement arose in 1967 and spread rapidly in the 1970s. This movement attempted to integrate the Pentecostal understanding of the gifts of the Spirit into traditional Catholicism. After the 1980s the movement lost steam and was shunted off to the margins of Catholic life, becoming merely one faction among many.

All of this is only approximate. In an individualist society such as America, it is not uncommon to have charismatic liberal Catholics, or theological conservative Catholics who are politically radical. Many parishioners try to live out their religious life without choosing theological sides, accepting various theological mixes, even if they don't make rigorous logical sense. They go to mass and try to raise their families in the midst of the temptations and stresses of an increasingly pagan America.[30]

As bleak as this picture is of American Catholicism, the situation of the Catholic Church in other countries, particularly in Europe, is much worse. In France today, less than 3 percent of those adults under twenty-five are practicing Catholics. The beautiful churches and cathedrals of that country are more museums than places of active worship. France has a special anti-Catholic and anti-Christian component in its history, dating from the Enlightenment and French Revolution, so the low attendance figures are somewhat understandable. Significantly, a similar collapse has occurred in formerly pious Catholic Quebec, but within *thirty years*, not three centuries. I do not bring this up with any sense of glee. Rather, it is important at this point to dismiss the idea that what went wrong with American Catholicism was that it was not traditional enough. In Quebec we have a demonstration of the contrary. The most traditionalist and sacramentally proper form of Catholicism in the Americas did even worse in standing up to the stresses of modernity than the American Catholic Church.[31]

THE SUNDRIES CHEST RECONSIDERED

Why did the pious, sacramentally based Catholicism of the 1950s do so poorly in resisting the forces of secularization and paganization that swept America? Many factors need to be considered, both secular and spiritual. The disconnect of many Catholics from their ethnic identity exposed the nominalism of many in the church. Irish Americans in an Irish neighborhood in the 1940s or 1950s experienced social pressures to be active Catholics and to send their children to Catholic schools. When their children grew up and moved to the suburbs, however, there was no reason to maintain Catholic practice unless there was a serious adult commitment. In this sense, the decline of ethnic Catholicism may be considered a grace from God that exposed the nominal status of many of its members.

The leadership of the church, both clergy and lay leaders, were thrown into confusion and contending factions with the decline of traditional Catholic theology after Vatican II. As doctrinal certainty and self-confidence ebbed away, newer radical theologies further eroded the fundamental biblical beliefs embedded within traditional creeds and theology.

The same forces of secularization assaulted American Protestantism as well. Yet specific sections of Protestantism, such as the conservative evangelical, Pentecostal, and newer charismatic denominations, flourished rather than declined in the post-1950 America.[32] These denominations do not center their spirituality on the sacraments. They have maintained their doctrinal integrity because their clergy and laity have a deeper knowledge and understanding of the Bible than their Catholic counterparts and are thus less dependent on theological fashions.

More fundamentally, these biblically based denominations have a vivid understanding that the core message of Christianity is salvation by faith in Jesus Christ alone. Catholic theology asserted this in its foundational documents, but it did not transmit this understanding of the gospel in the field where lay Catholics lived, worked, studied, played, and prayed. In fact, the doctrine of salvation by grace was overwhelmed by the traditions, activities, and sacramental actions of Catholic life.[33]

Another major factor has been in the lack of lay empowerment, especially *spiritual empowerment through the gifts of the Spirit*. Lack of the active spiritual gifts meant a seriously weakened witness of the gospel. Everything that the traditional Catholic experienced in his or her prayer life could be explained away as a psychological state. Who had been healed by prayer? Who had experienced a radical change in his or her spiritual life because of fulfilled prophecy or deliverance from evil spirits?

In the last section of the book we will get a glimpse of what happens when a liturgical church (Episcopalian) combines traditional sacramental piety and orthodox theology with an evangelical understanding of the gospel *and* the Pentecostal gifts. But now let us move to examine a form of Christianity that has little sacramental expression but does proclaim the evangelical gospel and practice the gifts of the Spirit.

NOTES

1. The Sisters of Charity were visually distinct from other Catholic nuns in that they wore a black bonnet, the common nineteenth-century headdress, rather than the veil and white cardboard combination of most orders of nuns. A glimpse of their strict training and disciplined life can be seen in the movie *A Nun's Story*, in which Audrey Hepburn stars as a Belgian missionary nun. The novitiate and rule of life pictured in the movie was stricter than that of Sisters of Charity, but the general pattern was the same.

2. Question 177 from the original Baltimore Catechism. The text of the catechism is available online at: www.catholic.net/RCC/Catechism /2/Welcome.html.

3. Among the few was Ronald Knox; see his classic work, *Enthusiasm: A Chapter in the History of Religion* (New York: Oxford Univ. Press, 1950), a study of Pentecostalism before the present century. Thankfully it is back in print.

4. To modern readers this account of Catholic life in the 1950s may seem nostalgic. The problem is that in many ways the moral and civic climate of America *was* much better then than now. For a confirming view see Kevin M. Ranaghan's memoir of parish life in the Bronx in the 1950s, "Growing Up Catholic," *New Heaven/New Earth* (March 1989), 2, 10.

5. Dom Aelred Graham, *The End of Religion* (New York: Harcourt Brace Jovanovich, 1971), 27.

6. Malachi Martin, *The Jesuits: The Society of Jesus and the Betrayal of the Roman Catholic Church* (New York: Linden, 1987). Fr. Martin is an ex-Jesuit who is highly informed about the history of his order, but his work suffers from exaggeration and tendency to melodrama.

7. On the theology of cessationism, see my *Quenching the Spirit* (Lake Mary: Creation House, 1992, 1996), and Jon Ruthven, *On the Cessation of the Charismata* (Sheffield: Sheffield Academic Press, 1993).

8. The key books of this destructive theological fashion were John A. T. Robinson, *Honest to God* (Philadelphia: Westminster, 1963); Thomas J. J. Altizer, *The Gospel of Christian Atheism* (Philadelphia: Westminster, 1966); and Harvey Cox, *The Secular City* (New York: Macmillan, 1965). This short-lived theological fashion should go into history by its acronym, "DOG" theology. Certainly its advocates were "barking up the wrong tree." Most significantly, Harvey Cox recently admitted that he was in error and (almost) repented. See his most recent work, which traces the history of Pentecostalism and predicts it will be the predominant Christian movement of the coming century: *Fire from Heaven: The Rise of Pentecostal Spirituality and the Reshaping of Religion in the Twenty-First Century* (Boulder, Colo.: Perseus, 1996).

9. Among other things Fr. Gleason introduced me to the work of Dietrich von Hilderband, whose book, *True Morality and Its Counterfeits* (New York: McKay, 1955), stands as a Catholic classic. This work alerted me to the problem of Christian pharisaism, which eventually flowed into my book *Quenching the Spirit.*

10. On the futility and ultimate failure of the liturgical reform movement, see Joseph Cardinal Ratzinger, *Milestones: Memoirs 1927–1977*, trans. Erasmo Leiva-Merikakis (San Francisco: Ignatius, 1998), 146–49.

11. On the importance of being "prophetic" as against the pseudo-virtue of being "nice" in the context of Catholic doctrine, see the work by the eminent Methodist theologian, Stanley Hauerwas, *In Good Company: The Church as Polis* (Notre Dame: Univ. of Notre Dame Press, 1995), ch. 6, "The Importance of Being Catholic."

12. Their splendid work was continued and updated in the 1930s by Fr. Herbert Thruston. See Joseph Crehan, *Father Thruston: A Memoir with a Bibliography of His Writings* (London: Sheed & Ward, 1952). I found out about Fr. Thruston, the great Jesuit scholar of spiritual phenomena, two decades after I graduated from Fordham.

13. The literature of the academic collapse is vast and growing. Allan Bloom made the clarion call in his book *The Closing of the American Mind* (New York: Simon & Schuster, 1987). More recent important works include Dinesh D'souza, *Illiberal Education: The Politics of Race and Sex on Campus* (New York: Random House, 1991). On the decline of the Catholic universities, see the review article by Mark Noll, "Football, Neo-Thomism and the Silver Age of Catholic Higher Education," *Books and Culture* (Sept./Oct 1995), 31–33. For a brilliant critique of present-day Catholic universities, see Ronald Herzman, "Catholic Educations," *First Things* (October 2000), 39–45.

14. On the rapid rise of liberation theology throughout the Catholic world, see Ratzinger, *Milestones*, 136–39.

15. Susan Wise Bauer, "Conversations: Re-Imaging Women," *Christianity Today* (May 24, 1999), 66.

16. See Ralph Martin, *The Catholic Church at the End of an Age* (San Francisco: Ignatius, 1994), 26–29.

17. Cited in ibid., 29.

18. James Tunstead Burtchaell, *The Dying of the Light: The Disengagement of Colleges and Universities from Their Christian Churches* (Grand Rapids: Eerdmans, 1998). This book contains almost 900 thoroughly researched pages. An excellent review and summary can be found in *First Things* (October 1998), 43–50.

19. Martin, *Catholic Church*, 36.

20. Rodney Stark, "Secularization: The Myth of Religious Decline," *Fides et Historia* 30 (Summer/Fall 1999): 1–19.

21. Cited in Brian W. Harrison, "The Crisis in Eucharist Faith," *The Christian Activist* (vol. 8), p. 3, from the online edition at www.christusrex.org/www1/CDHN/crisis.html.

22. Amy Welborn, "Why Go to Mass?" *First Things* (August/September 1998), 24. Welborn echoes the sentiments found in Ratzinger, *Milestones*, 146–49.

23. Martha Manning, *Chasing Grace: Reflections of a Catholic Girl, Grown up* (San Francisco: Harper, 1996).

24. Ibid., xiv.

25. See Martin, *Catholic Church*, 38; esp. Dean R. Hoge et al., *Converts, Dropouts, Returnees: A Study of Religious Change among Catholics* (New York: Pilgrim, 1981).

26. Martin, *Catholic Church*, 37. For a detailed study of the decline of the women's religious orders, see Ann Carey, *Sisters in Crisis: The Tragic*

Unraveling of Women's Religious Communities (Huntington, Ind.: Our Sunday Visitor, 1997).

27. Telephone conversation with Mr. Walter Mathews, July 17, 1997.

28. On the present divisions of the Catholic Church, see Bob Zyskowski, "Opposites Distract: Is Polarization Pulling the Church Apart?" *U.S. Catholic* (March 1998). Available online: www.uscatholic.org.

29. *First Things* is indeed a magnificent journal and representative of the best orthodox thinking of American Catholicism. One can read the entire corpus of *First Things* by going to www.firstthings.com/menus.

30. Zyskowski, "Opposites Distract."

31. See Preston Jones, "Quebec after Catholicism," *First Things* (June /July 1999), 12–14.

32. Roger Finke and Rodney Stark, *The Churching of America, 1776–1990: Winners and Losers in Our Religious Economy* (Piscataway, N.J.: Rutgers Univ. Press, 1992).

33. This is extensively documented in Martin, *Catholic Church*, part 2, chapter 2, "Faith and the Breaking of Pride."

Revival without Sacramental Spirituality: The Evangelical-Charismatic Experience

Invited into the Kingdom

My flight from Catholicism and attempt to live the "God is dead" philosophy as a "heroic Nietszchean," responsible for creating my own values, proved destructive. With my integrity and morals ebbing, lying to cover up faults or gain advantage became the norm. Unhappy and filled with self-pity, I failed both as playwright and play-boy, but at my lowest ebb God called me into the kingdom with a recurring dream.

In this dream I am wandering lost and alone in a tumbleweed-filled desert on a cold, clear night and stagger upon a tent. It has a charcoal fire in it and a table spread with bread and a chalice. I understand that I am dreaming and that this warm and inviting tent represents the church.[1] The dream repeats for several nights, and every time I stand in front of the tent and rail, "You are a mirage! I must be brave and live in the desert!"

God did not give up, and as the dream came again and again, one day I stood in front of the tent, considered my life situation carefully, and said, "I choose to enter." I partook of the Lord's Supper, and a feeling of joy and peace came over me. Thereupon I woke up to a new relationship with the Lord and a reborn prayer life.

Providentially, I soon joined a local Catholic charismatic prayer group. There I received initial discipling and advice. It was 1975, and the leadership encouraged attendees to go to interdenominational meetings and special services at non-Catholic churches. In this way I encountered various evangelical-charismatic churches and para-churches.[2] I was enchanted by these groups, especially by their strong faith and knowledge of the Bible. For a season I believed them not only much superior to the Catholic Church of my youth, but practically flawless.

FGBMFI

My first experience with a group of worshiping non-Catholics was a large gathering of the Full Gospel Business Men's Fellowship International (FGBMFI). In the 1970s this men's group had an anointing to evangelize many who were "turned off" to normal church attendance. They met in hotels, featured nonclergy speakers, and brought in business people by the thousands.[3] I cannot recall the speaker in that first breakfast meeting, but I recall vividly what happened when the director of the local chapter came to the podium. With a broad smile, he began what had become a ritual: "How many Baptists do we have with us today? Raise your hands." About a quarter of those attending responded.

"How many Catholics do we have?" About the same number raised their hands.

"How many of God's frozen chosen [chuckle] . . . you Presbyterians." A lesser number raised their hands.

He went on to ask about several other denominations. Here was ecumenism without the trappings or pretense of ecumenical dialogue. We worshiped together, listened to a talk on practical spirituality, and after the official meeting prayed for each other and swapped "war stories" of healings, deliverances, and other personal spiritual events. These FGBMFI men, as well as others in the charismatic renewal movement, chanced accountable prayer and prophetic utterances and risked failure and correction.

For people such as these, the philosophical argument that "God is dead," the theological position that miraculous powers ceased after the apostles, or the notion that biblical miracles were some sort of significant "myth" was total nonsense. They lamented, prayed, and joked about the sad state of official mainline theology, that their seminaries were "cemeteries," and so on. They possessed an absolute confidence in the Bible as truth, including the descriptions of healings and other miracles.

Like the Promise Keepers of the 1990s or the Methodists of the 1750s (see chs. 8–12), the FGBMFI was consciously nonsectarian and adamantly supported the local church. Although much worship took place at their meetings in the form of praise songs and prayer, they encouraged their members to be loyal participants of their own churches for Sunday services. In spite of their intentions on this matter, many men made the FGBMFI the center of their spiritual lives — a comment on the dead spirituality of their home congregations. The FGBMFI liturgy of praise songs, preaching or witness, and ministry time was exciting and worth valuable Saturday mornings.

Sadly, like every nondenominational charismatic service I attended in the following decades, the celebration of the Lord's Supper was conspicuously absent. This was ostensibly because of a lack of consensus both on the theology of the Lord's Supper and on its form of celebration. The more fundamental reason was that so few of the evangelical-charismatics understood the Lord's Supper as spiritually essential, let alone an important part of worship or revival.

Equally unfortunate but to be expected, immaturity and exaggeration were apparent from the very beginning of the charismatic revival. The movement generated modern versions of "St. George and the dragon" stories. Harold Hill, one of the most popular writers of the movement, claimed in *How to Live Like a King's Kid* that a NASA computer scientist ran an astrological regression on a powerful computer. The scientist amazingly discovered the "missing hours" when the sun stood still in the sky by Joshua's command (Josh. 10:12–14) and when God moved the sun back ten degrees after Hezekiah's illness (2 Kings 20:8–11).[4] When pressed for details and sources, Hill's story dissolved into rumor. This type of myth-making allowed the charismatic critics, both evangelical and secular, to dismiss the whole movement as hype.

MOUNT PARAN CHURCH OF GOD

At the same time, however, I encountered some of the best spirituality of the charismatic renewal. My Catholic prayer-group leader suggested we go as a group to hear the preaching of Dr. Paul Walker at Mount Paran Church of God, a church at the northwest edge of Atlanta. Pastor Walker delivered sermons that were exciting, passionate, and tremendously uplifting. He was also powerfully anointed, and the whole church radiated the presence of God as he preached. Walker's command of Scripture was (and is) utterly amazing. Like many Pentecostal "preacher's kids" he had memorized much of the Bible from childhood. At various points in the sermon he would cite a string of Bible verses to buttress a point.

When Dr. Walker took over the Mount Paran Church in 1960, it was just another small Church of God congregation.[5] His natural gift of preaching increased its membership immediately. Located in the midst of a rapidly growing and increasingly sophisticated city, the young pastor continued his education. He earned a master's degree in theological studies from Emory University and then a Ph.D. in counseling from Georgia State University.

Walker understood that the traditional Pentecostal preaching of "hellfire and brimstone" would no longer work. Rather, he developed a preaching agenda that began "with basic needs, and trie[d] to show people how those needs can be met through the Word of God."[6] He also moved the congregation away from the legalism of the Pentecostal Holiness code to a less culturally bound but biblically based way of life.

The major spiritual breakthrough came in the early 1970s when the antiwar movement bred a large "hippie" community throughout America. The 13th Street area of Atlanta was the focal point for thousands of these unwashed, counterculture youths. Dr. Walker understood their spiritual despair and confusion and walked the 13th Street area, personally inviting them to church and praying for their needs.

Many came. Some Mount Paran members objected to the presence of the unwashed youth. Walker affirmed that *all* would be welcome. He suggested that those who objected allow the Holy Spirit to correct the newcomers' dress and hygiene. That in fact happened, and many were "snatched from the fire."[7] Some ultimately became established church leaders.

God blessed Dr. Walker's faithful evangelism with an explosion of church membership. When I first visited the church in late 1975, it was the center of the charismatic renewal in Atlanta.[8] Its Sunday night services attracted groups of Christians from many mainline denominations. I sat in the "Catholic section" in the upper balcony with others of my prayer group.

The central spiritual event at Mount Paran, as in most evangelical and charismatic churches, was the *altar call*. After a sermon the public was invited to respond by coming forward to kneel for receptive prayer. This method of response developed in the middle of the nineteenth century and was initially given only for salvation (to initially receive Jesus as Savior).[9] But by the 1960s many charismatic churches were using it to minister emotional healing, family reconciliation, and especially physical healing. At Mount Paran, Pastor Walker would invite the elders to cominister at the altar with anointing oil. A steady flow of witnesses validated healings and deliverance from alcohol and drug abuse.

Interestingly, other than baptism, anointing with oil was the only traditional sacramental form that was taken seriously at Mount Paran. Anointing and laying on of hands in prayer were understood to be an effective combination for healing. Baptism was respected because it is plainly taught in Scripture and because there were personal stories circulating by those who had received visions or other spiritual experiences at the moment of baptism. This served to reinforce the importance of the sacrament given in Scripture, though there was no *theology* of sacramental grace. By contrast, the Lord's Supper was distributed quarterly out of scriptural *obedience*. If evaluated honestly, communion was viewed as less spiritually effective than either the altar call or the anointing and laying on of hands for healing. Many other charismatic and Pentecostal churches mirror this sacramental situation.

My mother visited me during this period. Ever the Catholic, she was, however, open enough to enjoy the services at Mount Paran. One Sunday evening when they distributed communion, she whispered to me, "This is not real communion, is it?" I could not argue with her. The underlying evangelical theology left the congregation without any *expectancy* that something spiritually significant would happen at the "ordinance."[10]

THE FLY IN THE ANOINTING: ANTINOMIANISM

While I marveled at the spiritual effectiveness and efficiency of the evangelical-charismatic churches and parachurches, I also noted a distressing factor. A number of biblically well-studied, often long-term members had low levels of integrity and moral development. They "God-talked" all the time but *lived* as if they had been converted only recently and knew little of the moral demands of the gospel. Later I came to understand this as a temptation that is as old as the founding of Paul's churches. The apostle had to defend himself against the misunderstanding that the forgiveness of sins through faith in Jesus absolved a person from the moral law: "Why not say — as we are being slanderously reported as saying and as some claim that we say — 'Let us do evil that good may result'? Their condemnation is deserved" (Rom. 3:8).[11]

The antinomian temptation recurs whenever the doctrine of salvation by grace is strongly emphasized and not counterbalanced with the doctrine of discipleship and sanctification. It is not surprising that the great Reformer Martin Luther had to deal with an outbreak of antinomianism among his own immediate followers.[12] During the period of the English Civil War and Commonwealth (1640–1660) several radical antinomian groups arose. They drifted into immorality and became an embarrassment to their Puritan allies.[13] An extreme form of antinomianism was practiced by Rasputin, the infamous monk who influenced the court of Czar Nicholas in the years preceding and during World War I. Rasputin believed that in order to truly repent, one had to sin vigorously. His life thus became a cycle of orgies and penances.[14] We will note later that the Wesley brothers battled a less depraved form of antinomianism early in their evangelical careers (see ch. 8).

Among contemporary American evangelicals the centrality of the salvation experience and the dramatic impact of a person's initial altar call, combined with the doctrine of "eternal assurance," can tempt such persons to carelessness on personal morality and growth in holiness.[15] I came to discover that evangelical businessmen, including many who loudly proclaim their faith, often have reputations for dishonesty and unreliability. On one occasion I talked with a former member of Mount Paran, a woman who had been converted from a pagan lifestyle but was now backslidden. She worked in real estate and recently experienced several commercial "dirty tricks" by evangelical Christians. She blurted out bitterly, "I'll never trust another born-again Christian as long as I live." This conversation shook me, and I investigated the problem among my Christian friends from several churches and groups. They also reported that the problem was unfortunately not rare. Dr. Walker alluded to the problem on various occasions and attempted to counter it both from the pulpit and with adult education programs.[16]

My wife and I had a demonstration of just how completely this antinomianism has soiled American Christianity when we went to the movie *Murphy's Romance*. In it Sally Field plays a young divorcee struggling to support her child by boarding horses. Her ex-husband comes back, and just as before, cheats, lies, and continues to live licentiously. He does, however, want to reunite with his ex-wife and child. To convince her that he has changed, he declares that he is a "born-again Christian" and has "made an altar call." The audience in the theater snickered and laughed in derision, signifying their experience with such characters. Carolyn and I peered at each other in the flickering light, deeply ashamed. The screenwriter of this movie had captured a major fault of American evangelicalism.

Significantly, this antinomianism was not restricted to laypersons but had insidiously spread into the leadership of several major evangelical-charismatic ministries. Scripture proclaims that "God cannot be mocked" and that judgment comes first to the church (Gal. 6:7, 1 Peter 4:17). The years 1985 through 1994 were the years of public judgment on the church. The antinomianism and shallow theology of the period infected many in the national leadership of the renewal. The scandals of the TV evangelists — Jimmy Swaggart, Jim Bakker, and others — placed all of Christendom in a bad light. These evangelists had moral failures that were not brought to account and corrected by a pastor but continued until exposed by the secular press. Evangelical critics who disliked the renewal were joined by charismatics who believed some charismatic theology to be heretical. A flood of anticharismatic books hit the market.[17] It was a period of much confusion for those who called themselves charismatic, and it seemed that the special, expansive work of the Spirit had come to an end.

A NEW WAVE OF THE SPIRIT

But the Holy Spirit had not withdrawn from the American scene. Rather, the Spirit was raising up new leadership and was flowing through different groups. A newer move of the Spirit developed under the leadership of a former rock musician, John Wimber. He was raised in a family that never mentioned God, and after conversion he derived his ideas about what church should be by reading Scripture. From his Vineyard Church in Anaheim, California, and from his teaching post at Fuller Theological Seminary, Wimber developed a string of influential churches that accepted the charismatic gifts yet distanced themselves from the antinomianism of the earlier renewal.

Wimber called his movement a "third wave," in that it came after the Pentecostal and charismatic revivals. It attracted many evangelical churches who wanted the gifts and the power of the Spirit but did not like to be called "charismatic." These Vineyard churches also aimed at evangelizing the younger generation and created a new brand of church music that would appeal to youth. Strong revival broke out in several of the Vineyard churches as early as the 1980s, with many of the participants experiencing the phenomenon of being "slain" and falling to the floor, sometimes staying there for hours under God's healing and anointing power.[18]

Simultaneously, another revival stream came from the independent itinerant ministry of South African evangelist Rodney Howard-Browne.[19] In 1991 his services also began manifesting revival phenomena, especially "holy laughter," by which a person would begin to laugh uncontrollably for no apparent reason. Often deep emotional and spiritual healing took place after these bouts of laughter. In 1993 Howard-Browne had a short preaching engagement at Carpenters Home Church in Lakeland, Florida, which blossomed into a major revival that attracted thousands, including many pastors from across the nation. Again, holy laughter and being slain in the Spirit were the predominant manifestations.

In 1993 Howard-Browne held a revival at Kenneth Hagin's Rhema campus in Tulsa, Oklahoma. There a Vineyard pastor, Randy Clark, received the laying on of hands from Howard-Browne four times. When he returned to his home church, revival spontaneously broke out there too. Pastor John Arnott of the Toronto Airport Vineyard Fellowship heard of Clark's experience and invited him to speak in Toronto for a few nights in January 1994. Strong revival broke out, which has continued six nights a week until this day. The laughter, healings, and being slain in the Spirit took place continuously, but a new controversial manifestation, prophetic roaring, appeared at Toronto.[20] This manifestation has caused considerable controversy and ultimately separated this church from the Vineyard fellowship of churches.

The Toronto location has been the most influential of the current revival cities.[21] Pastors, clergy, and lay leaders from all over the world have flocked to Toronto to experience the "Toronto Blessing." Pastor Arnott and his team have been especially influential in the United Kingdom, where in the Anglican Church over five hundred churches have undergone revival and expansion.

My book *Quenching the Spirit* appeared in 1992, before the current revival broke out. In it I described the perennial problem of Christian pharisaism. That is, every revival is opposed by church people (Christian "pharisees") who cannot discern the presence of God in a revival because of its unexpected manifestations and "messiness." Pastor Arnott, Bud Williams, and many other leaders of the revival have used the central arguments of *Quenching the Spirit* to effectively defend this current move of God in spite of its controversial manifestations.

Pastor Arnott invited me to be a major speaker in Toronto at the October 1994 "Catch the Fire" conference for pastors and church leaders. There I addressed three thousand church leaders about Christian pharisaism. I also taught a workshop on the sacramental dimension of revival. A significant foul-up occurred in reference to that workshop. Prior to the conference I called the Toronto Airport Vineyard staff with the titles of my talks and gave the title for the workshop as "The Sacramental Dimension of Revival." However they heard "Liturgical Revival," which was what their theological mindset understood. Thus it was billed. About a dozen pastors showed up, mostly Anglican; the rest of the pastors thought I was teaching something about the proper vestments during revival service!

In the past years I have witnessed many major and some minor revival evangelists. For the most part these revival meetings have been effective and healed those attending. Many marriages have been strengthened, and I have also seen emotional and physical healings. In these revival services the classic charismatic pattern continues: praise music, teaching, witness, and then "ministry time." I have never seen the Lord's Supper or baptism considered as a part of revival.

In fact, some of Howard-Browne's sayings may be taken as *antisacramental*. In his teachings he declares, "Religion is the problem." By this he means that the Christian's tendency to expect religious services to be regular and predictable can obstruct the "divine intrusion" of the Holy Spirit and his transforming presence. That point is valid, but what is dangerous is the unspoken extension that many evangelical and charismatic believers associate with the term *religion*. To them it is the formal observance of sacraments, unvarying liturgy, and priestly vestments. Revivals, by contrast, are free from such encroachments.[22]

I recently taught a series on the history of revivals at a local Vineyard church. This was a vibrant church that preached the evangelical gospel and ministered powerfully with the gifts of the Spirit. The church was full of young families who appreciated its intense worship and contemporary music. Hordes of lovely children romped the halls, squealing in delight. The church's evangelical impetus and theology were inspiring, but the parishioners had no concept of sacramental worship. They had not had a single communion service in the two-year history of their church.

Like so many things in the spiritual life, God honors the heart and intentions of those who love him and authenticates them with power. The classic modern revival pattern, which lacks a conscious sacramental element, has been effective in the church for the last hundred and fifty years. From Charles Finney, Billy Sunday, and Billy Graham to Rodney Howard-Browne, millions have been brought into the kingdom. It is only when one sees the pattern of church revivals *before* the nineteenth century that one understands how central the Lord's Supper was and should be to the rhythm of revival. It is to this pattern that we now turn our attention.

NOTES

1. The type of dream in which one is aware of dreaming is called a lucid dream. Apparently it is a special spiritual state in which one has the power of moral choices, unlike most other dreams where the action and images are unpredictable. The biblical example for this is found in 1 Kings 3:5–9. See the pioneer Christian work by Morton Kelsey, *Dreams: The Dark Speak of the Spirit: A Christian Interpretation* (New York: Doubleday, 1968), and more recently and pastorally useful, L. Savary and P. Berne, *Dreams and Spiritual Growth: A Christian Approach to Dreamwork* (New York: Paulist, 1984).

2. I am using the term *evangelical-charismatic* to designate those churches or groups who are conscious of and practice the gifts of the Spirit (1 Cor. 12), and whose theology has been influenced by evangelical (often Reformed) doctrines. This is a relatively new development, for the original Pentecostals were molded by Wesleyan, not Reformed theology. See Gerald T. Sheppard, "Pentecostalism and the Hermeneutics of Dispensationalism: Anatomy of an Uneasy Relationship," *Pneuma* 6 (Fall 1984): 5–34.

3. For a history of this important parachurch group, see Vinson Synan, *Under His Banner* (Costa Mesa, Calif.: Gift Publications, 1992).

4. Harold Hill, *How to Live Like a King's Kid* (Plainfield, N.J.: Logos International, 1974).

5. Church of God, Cleveland, Tennessee, is the oldest Pentecostal denomination, dating back to 1886. For an excellent short history of this denomination's seminal role in the development of Pentecostalism, see C. W. Conn, "Church of God (Cleveland, Tenn.)," in *The Dictionary of Pentecostal and Charismatic Movements*, ed. Stanley M. Burgess and Gary B. McGee (Grand Rapids: Zondervan, 1988), 197–202.

6. Doug Chatham, "A Pentecostal Church Where the Fire Still Burns Brightly," *Charisma* (December 1984), 20.

7. Jude 23. See O. W. Polen, "The Mount Paran Story," *Church of God Evangel* (Dec. 9, 1974), 23.

8. For a picture of Mount Paran during the 1970s and early 1980s, see Charles Paul Conn, "A Large Church on the Grow," *The Pentecostal Minister* (Fall 1983), 26–29. On Dr. Walker's especially effective ministry to the youth of Atlanta, see Paul Thigpen, "Christian Rock: Is It a Problem or a Gift?" *Ministries Today* 5 (Jan./Feb. 1987): 28–30.

9. See chapter 12.

10. We will discuss the origin of the evangelical "memorialist" theology of the Lord's Supper in chapter 3.

11. For an introduction to the problem of antinomianism, see Gerhard O. Forde, "Fake Theology: Reflections on Antinomianism Past and Present," *Dialogue* 22 (Fall 1983): 246–51. For an evangelical (Reformed) understanding of the problem, see Robert Payne, "Antinomianism and Dispensationalism," *Bibliotheca Sacra* 153 (April-June 1996): 141–54.

12. Robert W. Jenson, "Luther, Lutherans and Antinomianism," *Dialog* 22 (Fall 1983): 246–300.

13. Gertrude Huehns, *Antinomianism in English History: With Special Reference to the Period 1640–1660* (London: Cresset, 1951).

14. Brian Moynahan, *Rasputin: The Saint Who Sinned* (New York: Random House, 1997).

15. For a critical and insightful discussion of the dangers of "altar call" Christianity, see the work by the noted evangelical scholar, Iain Murray, *Revival and Revivalism: The Making and Marring of American Evangelicalism, 1750–1858* (Edinburgh: Banner of Truth Trust, 1994).

16. Paul Walker, "Ten Ways to a Better Life," Tape #90414 (Atlanta: Mount Paran Church of God, 1990).

17. The leading figures of the anticharismatic movement were the authors Dave Hunt and John MacArthur, and the talk radio host and president of the Christian Research Institute, Hank Hanegraaff. I discuss all of these figures in the revised edition of *Quenching the Spirit* (1996).

18. John White, *When the Spirit Comes in Power: Signs and Wonders Among God's People* (Downers Grove, Ill.: InterVarsity, 1988).

19. Perhaps the best single account of the current revival is Richard M. Riss, "A History of the Worldwide Awakening of 1992–1995," which will probably not be printed as a hardcopy book. It contains many direct quotes and documents. It is available through the Internet at http://www.grmi.org/Richard_Riss/history.

20. Guy Chevreau, *Catch the Fire* (London: Marshall Pickering, 1994), and more critically James A. Beverly, *Holy Laughter and the Toronto Blessing* (Grand Rapids: Zondervan, 1995).

21. Since 1995 the Brownsville Church of God near Pensacola, Florida, has become perhaps equally influential in spreading the revival throughout the United States.

22. See "Rodney Howard-Browne's Florida Church Growing Fast," *Charisma and Christian Life* (April 1997), 26.

PART 2

REVIVAL AND
THE LORD'S SUPPER
IN THE REFORMED
TRADITION

THE REFORMERS

ENCOUNTER THE

SACRAMENTS

3

CONCERN FOR THE LORD'S SUPPER

In December 1687, Edward Taylor, Puritan pastor of the frontier town of Westfield, Massachusetts, wrote an impassioned letter to a neighboring minister, Solomon Stoddard. Pastor Stoddard of the Northampton church had opened the Lord's Supper to those in the congregation who did not have a recognizable "experience" of their salvation, although they were baptized and lived publicly decent lives. While this practice was common in Protestant Europe, Taylor was alarmed because such openness was contrary to New England practice.

Among other things, Pastor Taylor believed Stoddard was putting the unregenerate members of his congregation (those who did not have the experience of saving grace in their lives) in mortal danger by having them receive communion (1 Cor. 11:27). He cited as an analogy the biblical story of the death of Uzzah, who died for unlawfully touching the ark of the covenant (1 Chron. 13:7–11). Taylor pleaded with Stoddard:

It is not according to the foundation nor expectation of your church: no, nor these churches here: & therefore can't but be to the great commotion, & disturbance of their peace, & not to their edification. . . . It will be in danger to influence neighbor churches with disturbance; malevolent persons growing audacious. . . . And how grievous this may prove who knows?[1]

In fact, Stoddard's practice struck at the heart of the noble experiment that the Puritans had attempted in the American wilderness. The original founders of the colony wanted to create a "city upon a hill," that is, a true Christian commonwealth for the whole world to admire and imitate. To do this the Puritan churches would be congregations of "visible saints," those who both lived morally and were *truly* Christian. Only these visible saints could vote on church and civil matters and receive the sacrament of the Lord's Supper. With such persons in the helm of church and civil government, surely New England would become the beacon of the world.

Stoddard immediately wrote to Taylor and offered to discuss the matter further with him at their next meeting. He added with determination: "But I judge that it is the cause of God, & am therefore under pressure of Spirit in all regular ways to promote it."[2] We will examine Solomon Stoddard's theology and ministry in the next chapter. At this point it is important to note that both Stoddard's and Taylor's concern over, and devotion to, the Lord's Supper were common to Puritans of the age.

Modern readers do not generally appreciate this. Even many educated Christians think of the Puritans mostly in terms of "hellfire and damnation" sermons, drab clothing, prudishness about sex, and fixation on witchcraft.[3] Nowhere in that cluster of stereotypical ideas (most of which are exaggerated) is there an awareness of the Puritans' intense sacramental piety.

In regard to Taylor, his sacramental devotion was unusual only in that he was a first-rate poet and could express himself in verse:

Hence in this bread, and wine thou dost present
    Thyself, my Lord, celestial food indeed,
Rich spiritual fare soul-food, faith's nourishment,
    And such as doth all saving graces feed,

For which an heaven full of thanks, all free,
Is not too much my Lord to render thee.[4]

REFORMERS VERSUS CATHOLIC
SACRAMENTAL THEOLOGY

This Taylor-Stoddard dispute was not unique among Protestants. The proper meaning and use of the sacraments was one of the driving forces of the Protestant Reformation. When Martin Luther triggered the Reformation (1517) by challenging Roman Catholic practices and doctrine, he was attacking, in great part, an *exaggerated* sacramental system. Medieval Roman Catholicism had evolved into an authoritarian church in which salvation seemed to be offered through priestly manipulation of the sacraments that included "money-for-grace," as in purchased masses said for the dead.

The Catholic liturgy of the Lord's Supper (the mass) was particularly disturbing to the Reformers. Luther and the other Reformers understood from their study of the early church that the Lord's Supper was originally ministered to the Christian community with both bread and wine and was celebrated often. Yet common Catholic practice at the time was to distribute communion to the laity only twice a year, Easter and Christmas, and then only as a wafer of bread.

Ironically, these abuses stemmed from an attempt by medieval theologians to define the meaning of the "real presence" of Christ at the Eucharist. With the official theology of transubstantiation, the bread and wine were understood to be physically the body and blood of Jesus. This physical presence was deemed so grace-giving that the laity did not have to receive the Lord's Supper frequently. Rather, they would "observe" the elevated host during Sunday mass (highlighted by chiming altar bells).[5] Other occasions for observing and venerating the consecrated host were the ritual of benediction and public processions, such as during the Feast of Corpus Christi (i.e., "the body of Christ").

The wineless communions developed out of the logic of priestly convenience, which declared that a body always included some blood, so that reception of wine was unnecessary. This avoided all sorts of problems, such as peasants consuming too much communion wine at the altar (too expensive) or the fuss involved with the problem of spilt wine (dropping Christ's blood on the floor). Anyone who objected to this obviously unbiblical sophistry was rebelling against the Church and was therefore a heretic. In fact, a century before Luther's break with Rome the population of Bohemia and Moravia, following the theology of their martyred John Hus, rose in armed revolt over this very issue. After destroying several crusading armies sent against them by the pope, they forced the Catholic Church to reinstitute the Lord's Supper with wine for the laypeople (1436). The Church did not extend this privilege beyond the Hussite areas.[6]

More centrally, Luther and the other Reformers understood that the Catholic sacramental system had usurped the central role of God's Word in the Christian's life. Luther initially proclaimed that the only real sacrament was the preaching of the Word. He quickly retreated from this extreme position and recognized the "dominical" sacraments, baptism and the Lord's Supper (those sacraments clearly mandated by Christ). He and other Reformers wished to bring the church to a biblical balance of teaching the Word and ministering the sacraments, a balance not easily achieved. History would demonstrate that it is as easy to *under*value the grace and purpose of the sacraments as Catholic practice *over*valued it.

An inherent difficulty in Protestant sacramental theology was that its central theological understanding was based on Paul's (and St. Augustine's) concept of election and predestination. If a person's salvation depended solely on God's decrees in election, then why the sacraments?[7] The Bible itself is unclear about the exact role of the sacraments. Jesus plainly mandated both baptism and the Lord's Supper but did not give reasons *why*.

Protestantism's ambivalence toward the sacraments led to the first great divide in Protestant theology. Martin Luther came to appreciate the need to affirm the real presence of Christ in the Eucharist, but he rejected the Catholic term *transubstantiation* as misleading and too physical. In its place he came to an understanding of Christ's presence *in* the elements, which was termed *consubstantiation*. Yet within two decades Luther was himself challenged by more radical Reformers on the true meaning of the sacraments.

Further, several groups, called Anabaptists, denied the effectiveness of infant baptism and began rebaptizing their adult followers. Some of the Anabaptists were also social radicals. An Anabaptist mob temporarily took over the city of Munster in Germany (1535) and began practicing polygamy and enforcing the sharing of property. Luther railed against them as the worst of heretics, and for the next century the Anabaptist doctrine of adult baptism was associated in the minds of "decent Protestants" with mob rule and radicalism.

A more serious threat to Luther's Reformed sacramental piety came from the ex-priest and zealous Swiss Reformer, Ulrich Zwingli (1484–1531). Zwingli based his sacramental theology on John 6:63 ("the flesh counts for nothing") and on the fact that Jesus *bodily* ascended to the right hand of the Father (Acts 1:10). Therefore, Zwingli reasoned, Jesus' body could not be distributed on earth in communion. He saw the Lord's Supper as an ordinance that Christians must perform out of obedience, not as a grace-giving event.

An acrimonious debate broke out between Luther and Zwingli. The Protestant princes in Germany feared this division would split the Protestant cause and allow the Catholics to divide and destroy Protestantism by force of arms. They persuaded Luther and Zwingli to meet at Marburg castle (1529) to mend their differences. Out of fifteen points of contention between the two Reformers they could compromise and agree on fourteen, but on the meaning of the Lord's Supper no compromise was found. Zwingli held to his "memorial only" view, whereas Luther reaffirmed the real presence of Christ in the sacrament. In a dramatic gesture Luther wrote in large chalk letters on the debating table Jesus' words, "This is my body."

Zwingli did not live long after the Marburg meeting. He was killed in battle against the Catholics in a civil war that broke out in his beloved Switzerland. His radical antisacramental theology remained in the background of Protestant thought but has been a major resource to Protestants when sacramental piety is weakened, as in much of modern evangelicalism.

CALVIN'S SACRAMENTAL THEOLOGY

John Calvin (1509–1564), the theological genius of the Reformation, began writing his famous *Institutes of Christian Religion* after the Marburg castle debate. Like Luther, he desired to affirm the real presence of Christ in the Lord's Supper, but he also wanted to assert the supremacy of the preached Word. He rejected Zwingli's radical anti-sacramentalism for a view that affirmed an active role of the Holy Spirit in the Lord's Supper. Calvin agreed with Zwingli that the Lord's body was presently glorified and at the right hand of the Father. However,

> even though it seems unbelievable that Christ's flesh, separated from us by such great distance, penetrates to us, so that it becomes our food, let us remember how far the secret power of the Holy Spirit towers above all our senses, and how foolish it is to wish to measure his immeasurableness by our measure. What, then, our mind does not comprehend, let faith conceive: that the Spirit truly unites things separated in space.[8]

Thus, according to Calvin, there is a real presence of Jesus in the Lord's Supper, even though it is a spiritual presence, not a physical one. He viewed the Lord's Supper as a major instrument of the Christian's sanctification. In his writings and in his church in Geneva, Calvin stressed the proper preparation for reception of the sacrament, especially in the examination of conscience.[9] But he also criticized Catholic theology for making proper preparation *too* difficult, as in the observance of the whole penitential season of Lent before receiving communion on Easter Sunday:

> Surely the devil could find no speedier means of destroying men than by so maddening them that they could not taste and savor this food which their most gracious heavenly Father had willed to feed them.... Let us remember that this sacred feast is medicine for the sick, solace for sinners, alms to the poor.... For since Christ is given to us as food, we understand that without him we would pine away, and faint — as famine destroys the vigor of the body.[10]

Calvin advised that the Lord's Supper be received weekly at the Sunday service, in conjunction, of course, with the vigorous preaching of the Word.[11]

ENGLISH PURITANISM[12]

The Puritans in England were given their name because they wished to "purify" the Anglican Church of residual Roman Catholic traditions, such as elaborate priestly vestments. They wanted the Anglican Church, which had broken with Rome under Henry VIII, to become more like continental Protestantism. As we have seen in the poetry of Edward Taylor, Puritans were not generally antisacramental as in the Zwinglian tradition. Typically, the famous Puritan pastor Arthur Hildersham said of the Lord's Supper that it was "a principal means that God has ordained for reviving, strengthening and increasing our faith."[13]

As time progressed Puritan theologians made increasing use of the biblical concept of *covenant* to express their sacramental theology. Calvin had suggested this motif, but it was the Puritans who elaborated it. Many Puritans came to understand the sacraments as covenant signs of God's salvation. The issue that triggered this development was the Anabaptists' insistence that infant baptism was invalid. Puritan thinkers, like many early church theologians, saw an analogy between infant circumcision and infant baptism, namely, that both actions brought a child into covenant relationship with God. Nevertheless, as the Anabaptists were quick to point out, many who were baptized as infants did not mature to real Christians. What then was the effect and grace of baptism? The Puritan response varied, but a consensus arose that indeed infant baptism was necessary and that although it did not mediate regeneration (as in Catholic theology), it at least gave a "grace of preparation" for the child to hear and receive the gospel.[14]

Puritan pastors and theologians also gave much thought to the Lord's Supper. They generally followed the theology of Calvin and accepted the traditional position that the Supper was reserved for those already baptized and received into the church. This idea originally arose in the early centuries of church history, when adult conversion to Christianity signified a definite turning away from pagan Roman culture. After baptism, such an individual could receive the Lord's Supper, which proclaimed that he or she was no longer a "learner" of Christian doctrines and morals (*catechumen*) but a member in full standing.

As time went on, the Catholic Church expanded, and no pagans were left in Europe (at least publicly). The official definition of a Christian shifted to that of a baptized person, but the Eucharist was still reserved for those baptized and instructed in Christian doctrine. In the 1600s in England those who wished to become devout Christians and turned away from nominal faith did not come from a pagan culture but were from a more or less Christian one. The catechism (Christian doctrine) was universally known. Conversion usually signified a turning away from nominalism to full commitment to the lordship of Jesus and submission to the gospel.

This being the case, several English Puritan writers noticed that, at times, nominal or weak Christians were moved to become sincere believers by the grace of the Lord's Supper. Thus, they saw in the Supper a potential for its use as a "converting sacrament," that is, *conversion from nominalism*. Among these astute observers was pastor William Prynne (1600–1669), who wrote an influential work with the longish title (typical of the era), *The Lord's Supper Briefly Vindicated and Clearly Demonstrated by Scripture and Other Authorities, to Be a Grace-Begetting, Soul-Converting (as Well as Affirming) Ordinance* (London, 1657).[15]

Prynne's work molded the debate on the Lord's Supper for the next hundred years, both in England and in New England. Other Puritan pastors quickly came to print opposing Prynne and affirmed the more traditional position. Ministers from other traditions joined this sacramental debate. John Humfrey (1621–1719), who began as an Anglican minister but transferred to a Congregational pulpit, followed Prynne's lead in advocating the converting potential of the Lord's Supper. But a majority of Puritan and Anglican pastors did not accept this view and insisted that the Lord's Supper was intended only as a confirming and strengthening sacrament.

THE "CALLED OUT" CHURCH

The Puritans also discerned that the medieval church had lost much of its moral discipline in the process of expansion. That is, because the Catholic Church believed in regeneration through infant baptism, everyone who was baptized became a Christian. Necessarily, every adult was also a Christian and part of the local church, no matter how immoral his or her public behavior or regardless of how infrequently the person attended church. Only rebellion against church authority or heretical beliefs would trigger excommunication. This is far from the biblical pattern where, for example, in Paul's letter to the Corinthians, he excommunicates a man on *moral* grounds (a man who was sleeping with his stepmother; see 1 Cor. 5:1–5).

The Protestants of the Reformed tradition (Calvinists) wanted the church more properly to reflect this New Testament model of a congregation "called out" of the world and subject to moral discipline. Calvin himself was wise enough to realize that not even the New Testament church was free of hypocrites and that the visible church only approximates the true body of Christ. He understood the parable of wheat and the weeds (Matt. 13:36–43) as a warning that only angels could discern with accuracy a saint from a hypocrite.

The New England Puritans were more optimistic that they could form congregations of true saints. They stressed the Scriptures of the New Testament, such as 1 Peter 2:4, which describes the church as composed of the elect. In practice, the Puritan congregations of New England were a hybrid pattern that included everyone in the church proximity as a church attendant and learner (the parish model), but full membership — that is, voting or receiving the Lord's Supper — was restricted to those who could be identified as true saints. Significantly, many English Puritans — such as Richard Baxter, the most famous and respected Puritan pastor of all — saw that the New England attempt at forging a totally pure church was doomed to futility.[16]

EXPERIENCE AS A CRITERION FOR TRUE CHRISTIANS

Calvin was rightfully skeptical of Roman Catholic claims that all baptized persons were Christians. His works stressed election by God as the true criterion of being a Christian. In turn, the signs of being among the elect (but never absolutely knowing) were the internal "witness of the Spirit" and living the fruit of the Spirit.

Puritan authors developed Calvin's insights of the witness of the Spirit into a theology of conversion and its stages. English pastor William Perkins (1558–1602) was the pioneer and perhaps the ablest of those who described the conversion experience. He analyzed many adult conversions and discerned a pattern that began with conviction, often triggered by preaching or religious conversations. The process of conversion then proceeded with a futile search for justification in one's good works and moral life, then a dramatic illumination that such self-righteousness is worthless (Rom. 3–7). This was followed by a period of despair. Finally, with God's grace, the person experienced a sudden lifting of his or her sense of condemnation and despair and received an interior sense of assurance that one's sins were forgiven through Jesus' blood (Rom. 8).[17] Perkins and other Puritans understood this as a typical pattern only and knew that God dealt individually and uniquely with every person. Yet this description of conversion became normative for many Puritans.

John Cotton (1584–1652), another English Puritan, was the person who popularized Perkins's theory of assurance in New England. He came to Boston in 1634 and pastored the influential First Church of Boston. From there he convinced other Puritan pastors that the indispensable mark of a Christian was not only this process of conversion but the sense of personal assurance in God's forgiveness and acceptance as a child of God. For Puritan churches Cotton's understanding of assurance became the mark of a true saint on earth.[18] Thus a person who wished to become a full communicant and voting member of his or her church had to witness to a "conversion experience."

With the new-found analysis of conversion and assurance, the Puritans believed they had the tools to create a new Zion, the perfect heavenly church on earth. They did not realize that what they had done was to go beyond the biblical evidence by creating a universal out of their immediate historical circumstances. Specifically, the type of conversion process demanded by them described a person who was an adult nominal Christian within a semi-Christian society. Although many persons who underwent this conversion experience became truly mature Christians, it is by no means a biblically mandated pattern of conversion.

How, for example, would the gospel come to those born into homes and a culture that was not nominally but deeply Christian, as in New England? The answer was not at all what the Puritan leaders of New England expected. Such children, raised in Christian households where the Scriptures and moral instruction were ever present, mostly did not go through the conversion crises described by Perkins. They were often well-mannered, moral persons who accepted orthodox church doctrines, yet rarely experienced the normative conversion crisis and process. In fact, most of the second-generation children had little passion for the faith and often focused their desires on commerce and material gain.

In 1662 the Puritan Synod met in Boston and adopted a resolution that allowed grown, "unregenerate" children — those who had no experience of conversion but who accepted orthodox doctrines — to baptize their children. This at least made available to the children "preparatory grace" for later conversion, or so it was hoped. Later generations called this compromise "the Half-Way Covenant." The problem was serious, for the passion for Christ and the kingdom that categorized the pioneers and founders of New England Puritanism was not reproducing itself.

NOTES

1. Letter from Edward Taylor to Solomon Stoddard, Dec. 13, 1687, reprinted in Thomas M. Davis and Virginia L. Davis, eds., *Edward Taylor vs. Solomon Stoddard: The Nature of the Lord's Supper* (Boston: Twayne Publishers, 1981), 64. Spelling modernized by author, as are most of the quotations that follow from the seventeenth and eighteenth centuries.
2. Letter from Solomon Stoddard to Edward Taylor, Jan. 4, 1688; see Davis and Davis, *Edward Taylor,* 66.
3. It would take a volume to document the vast distortions about Puritanism that shapes present consensus opinion. The charge of "witch hunting" has been the most persistent and damming. On this issue see the article by David Downing, "The Mystery of Spirit Possession," *Books and Culture* (Jan./Feb. 1997), and Chadwick Hansen's *Witchcraft in Salem* (New York: G. Braziller, 1969). This book is particularly

significant since the author shows through archaeological evidence and other sources that there were indeed substantial numbers of witches and warlocks in New England. "Witch hunting" may have been done with little discernment and tragic results, as the Downing article indicates, but the quest to uproot witchcraft in New England was *not* a crusade against a nonexistent enemy.

4. Edward Taylor, Meditation #105 on Matt. 26:26, "Jesus Took Bread and Blessed It, and Broke It," in Edward Taylor, *The Poems of Edward Taylor,* ed. Donald E. Stanford (New Haven, Conn.: Yale Univ. Press, 1960), 272–73. Taylor considered his poems a personal expression of his piety and thus forbade his heirs from publishing them. They were recovered by accident in 1883, but none saw print until 1937; only recently has the full corpus of Taylor's poems been published. He is now recognized as the greatest of American colonial poets.

5. This may seem incredible to modern readers, who are used to seeing many Catholics receive communion weekly or even daily. The practice of frequent communion for Catholics was established in the nineteenth century and took considerable prodding by the Vatican to achieve.

6. On John Hus, see Matthew Spinka, *John Hus: A Biography* (Princeton, N.J.: Princeton Univ. Press, 1968).

7. E. Brooks Holifield, *The Covenant Sealed: The Development of Puritan Sacramental Theology in Old and New England, 1547–1720* (New Haven, Conn.: Yale Univ. Press, 1974), passim. This book is a masterwork of historical theology.

8. John Calvin, *Institutes of the Christian Religion,* 4.17.10 (available online at www.smartlink.net/~douglas/calvin).

9. Ibid., 4.17.41.

10. Ibid., 4.17.42.

11. Ibid., 4.17.43.

12. The following description of Puritan sacramental beliefs is drawn from Holifield, *The Covenant Sealed.*

13. Ibid., 52.

14. Ibid., ch. 3 ("The Baptismal Debate in England").

15. Discussed in ibid., ch. 4 ("The Lord's Supper: Debate and Devotion").

16. David D. Hall, "Introduction," in *Ecclesiastical Writings* by Jonathan Edwards, ed. David D. Hall (New Haven, Conn.: Yale Univ. Press, 1994), 22.

17. See *William Perkins, 1558–1602, English Puritanist; His Pioneer Works on Casuistry: "A discourse of conscience" and "The whole treatise of cases of conscience,"* ed. and intro. by Thomas F. Merrill (Nieuwkoop: B. de Graaf, 1966).

18. Ziff Larzer, *The Career of John Cotton: Puritanism and the American Experience* (Princeton, N.J.: Princeton Univ. Press, 1962).

SOLOMON STODDARD'S
SACRAMENTAL EVANGELISM[1]

4

Into this situation of stagnant and declining church growth stepped
one of the great figures of American orthodoxy, Solomon Stoddard.
He successfully combined Calvinist preaching with an evangelistic use of the Lord's Supper. The fruit of this combination was
revival in his church and others throughout the Connecticut River
valley.

Stoddard was the child of a prominent and prosperous Boston
merchant, Anthony Stoddard. The elder Stoddard, like many of the
founding Puritans, mixed a talent for business with a passion for the
kingdom. He provided his children with the best education available,
and Solomon was sent off to Harvard College (1658).

There his tutor was Jonathan Mitchell, a Puritan scholar who
tended toward the Anglican tradition of spirituality more than others
at Harvard. He introduced Stoddard to the writings of Anglican and
English Puritans who advocated the Lord's Supper as a converting
sacrament (Prynne and others). Unlike more orthodox Calvinists,
Mitchell told his students to be active in seeking their conversion:
"Lie in the way of the Spirit in the use of the means [of grace]."[2] This

was the message Stoddard needed because like most young men of his generation, he did not yet have that experience.

The young Stoddard was a brilliant student. After receiving an M.A. in divinity he sailed to the Barbados, where he pastored a dissenting church for two years. When he returned from this temporary assignment, he received an invitation to preach at the frontier town of Northampton, along the Connecticut River. The former pastor of the Northampton church had been a rigorous Calvinist. He refused to accept the decision of the synod of 1662 and would not baptize the children of unregenerate parents. He had just died, and the congregation was looking for someone who would baptize children according to the new policy.

Stoddard and Northampton were a perfect match. Within a few months he was installed as pastor and, in addition, married the former pastor's widow, Esther. This was not in any way scandalous in that era since quick remarriage was common. In fact, Puritan literature of the age gloried in tales of widows and widowers remarrying and enjoying renewed marital bliss.

Esther discerned of her new husband that in spite of "his graces of character and manner, he had really no experimental acquaintance with the Gospel."[3] She put her devout friends to pray for his conversion. How Solomon Stoddard came to full conversion and assurance is not known with certainty. However, according to a description from the nineteenth century from an aging relative of Stoddard, he had an experience in 1672 that definitely *did not* follow the Perkins pattern. Solomon was ministering the Lord's Supper to the congregation when

> he caught such a full and glorious view of Christ and his great love for men as shown in his redemptive work, that he was almost overpowered with emotion, and with difficulty went forward with the communion service. By the reason of this peculiar experience of his he was led to think, that the place where the soul was likely to receive spiritual light and understanding was the Lord's table — that there, in a special manner, Christ would be present to reveal himself, in all the fullness of love to the souls of men.[4]

At the beginning of his ministry at Northampton Stoddard was a normal Half-Way Covenant pastor. He baptized the children of the unregenerate but examined those who applied for communion privilege to ensure that they had experienced regenerating grace. Adults in Northampton who could not witness to a converting experience were kept in the "state of education," in that they attended services and received doctrinal instruction, but they could not vote or receive communion.

Stoddard was not happy with this division. In his congregation of about five hundred adults, less than eighty received communion.[5] The system promoted spiritual complacency and pride within the few "visible saints," and low morale and indifference among the majority. In 1677 he rejected this division and simply stopped recording parishioners according to their conversion status in the church registry. Stoddard was not insensitive to the profound issues involved and consulted about this change with his ministerial friends in the Connecticut valley. Many pastors agreed with his bold move, and by 1679 he and seventeen others petitioned for a new synod to discuss the situation. In that same year he published his first pamphlet, entitled "Nine Arguments Against Examinations Concerning the Work of Grace Before Admission to the Lord's Supper." The work was widely circulated and discussed, and in the next synod (1680) Stoddard's position was upheld by majority vote and recommended to other churches.

Even before the synod, Stoddard began his open communions to "all such as do make a solemn profession of their repentance, and are of godly conversation, having knowledge to examine themselves, and discerning the Lord's Body...."[6] By "godly conversation" Stoddard meant living a moral, Christian life, and "discerning the Lord's Body" he understood as the ability to examine one's conscience. In other words, he returned to the classic Reformed practice observed throughout Protestant Europe.

The fruit of Stoddard's break with the restrictive communion policy was that revival did indeed break out in Northampton. That first open-communion year, 1679, eight men and fourteen women came to experience full conversion and assurance, a large number for the relatively small congregation. In comparison, many Puritan churches in New England went for years without a single new conversion. Stoddard's church in Northampton had four other "seasons of grace" (revivals) — 1680, 1683, 1696, and 1712. This was a revival repetition unprecedented in other New England towns.

The argument about "experienced conversion versus historic faith before communion" did not end at the synod of 1680. Increase Mather, the influential Boston pastor (now remembered for his role in the witchcraft trials) joined with Edward Taylor to oppose "Stoddardism." A letter, sermon, pamphlet, and book war broke out between them that lasted most of two decades. Mather rallied most of the clergy in the immediate Boston area to hold on to the full conversion requirement, but Stoddard won over many of the clergy outside of Boston, in part because the Northampton church became known as the evangelistic center of New England.

As the years went on, Stoddard gained increasing fame and respect in New England. In the later years of his ministry he frequently gave the commencement lectures at Harvard, an honor reserved for the most respected pastors of the New England colonies. His opponents called him "Pope Stoddard" in reluctant recognition of the influence he wielded among many of the clergy. This was not due just to his communion innovation but to other aspects of his writings and ministry as well. He advocated, for instance, a modification to the Puritan congregational system that favored more authority to the pastor and oversight by regional synods. However, Stoddard's evangelistic writings, ministry, and preaching were what gained him most attention.

STODDARD'S SACRAMENTAL EVANGELICALISM

Stoddard's evangelistic use of the Lord Supper's cannot be separated from his major goal, which was to preach the gospel and gain converts for the kingdom. Like traditional Reformed pastors, Stoddard affirmed both the primacy and importance of the preached Word. He understood that the preacher had to preach both terror and grace. That is, the sinner must be made aware of his or her sinfulness and of the dangers of dying in an unconverted state, yet be given hope in God's mercy for salvation:

> If sinners don't hear often of judgement and damnation, few will be converted.... They need to be told of the terrors of the Lord.... Reason will govern men in other things; but it is fear that will make them diligently to seek Salvation.[7]

To this end Stoddard's preaching was vigorous and explicit. In a passage that foreshadowed his grandson's later famous sermon "Sinners in the Hands of an Angry God,"[8] Stoddard warned:

> Will it not be dreadful to be filled with the fiery wrath of God; to have every limb of thy body, and faculty of thy soul as full as it can hold of the indignation of the Almighty ... what will you think when the Devil shall lay hold of you to drag you down to hell? How will you cry out when tumbling into the lake that burns with fire and brimstone? What can comfort you in that condition?[9]

Stoddard was a master of evangelistic preaching. He was able to move his hearers emotions and make them desire salvation and seek it in God's grace. That is where the Lord's Supper played its converting role. A person under conviction and seeking salvation would often find the grace of assurance at the Lord's table.

Thus it was in the context of evangelization that Stoddard framed his sacramental beliefs. For him, all the sacraments, including those rites of the Old Testament such as Passover, were designed by God to bring the lost to him. This was especially true of the Lord's Supper:

> This ordinance has a proper tendency to draw sinners to Christ; in this ordinance there is particular invitation to sinners, to come to Christ for pardon; here is an affecting representation of the virtue of Christ's sufferings; here is a seal whereby the truth of the Gospel is confirmed, all which are proper to draw sinners to Christ.[10]

Stoddard's "Sermon on Galatians 3:1" was his mature definition of the belief of the Lord's Supper as a converting ordinance. He was careful in defining conversion:

> Conversion is taken two ways in scripture. Sometimes it's taken for the conversion to the Christian religion, Acts 15:3, declar-

ing the conversion of the Gentiles. And participation in the Lord's Supper is not appointed to work this conversion: but for the building up of them that are already converted to the Christian Religion. Though the Church's celebration of the Lord's Supper is useful to promote other means of conversion to the Christian faith.

But sometimes conversion is taken for a saving turning of the soul unto God, & participation in the Lord's Supper is a means to make up the match between Christ, & the soul.[11]

Addressing his congregation and their disappointment in the declension of piety throughout New England in past decades, Stoddard continued:

You are troubled that the preaching of the word in the country does no more good, truly the Lord may justly deny a blessing to that: because the Lord's Supper is so much neglected, if you will not use all means God may righteously deny his blessing to the means that are used.[12]

Stoddard ended the sermon by exhorting those in his congregation who were reluctant to accept the new way:

Here God is applying the call of the gospel particularly to you, Matt. 26.7,8 here God is testifying to you to the virtue of the blood of Jesus Christ, by these signes he is witnessing that Christ's flesh is meat indeed & his blood drink indeed, here God is setting his seal to the truth of his covenant. & giving you great assurance that if you come to Christ you shall be saved.[13]

We should stress that Stoddard's genius was not in creating new theology. What he said about the Lord's Supper was a paraphrase in New England idiom of what had been said by Prynne and others a generation before. Stoddard's genius was in the *execution* of his communion theology. His preaching and leadership talents united with the graces of the Lord's table to produce consecutive revivals and phenomenal growth of the Northampton church. After his death those churches most influenced by him were the very ones to experience revival in the years of the Great Awakening.

As Stoddard reached his eightieth year, he still possessed a clear mind, but his physical abilities and his capacity to deliver passionate sermons were rapidly declining. With the full support of his congregation Stoddard began searching for an assistant to ease his tasks. In the winter of 1725 the son of a well-known pastor in Boston was called to Northampton on a trial basis but left the following summer for another church. The next year Solomon's young grandson, Jonathan Edwards, was invited to preach for the month of August. Edwards greatly pleased his grandfather and impressed everyone with his brilliant sermons. He was given an official call to become assistant minister at Northampton in November 1726.

For over two years Edwards honed his preaching skills at Northampton as he observed his grandfather's ministry. He had come to Northampton awed by the legend of his grandfather's successful ministry and believing he was stepping into a Puritan heaven of righteousness and perfect Christian love. Edwards's bubble quickly burst. He discovered that even in this evangelical center of Puritanism, the people were divided by the usual political divisions and family feuds common to small-town life.

In February 1729 Solomon Stoddard died "full of years." Thankfully, in the years before his death he and Increase Mather had fully reconciled their theological feud. In fact Mather wrote the preface to Stoddard's *Guide to Christ* (1714). Stoddard was mourned throughout all of New England, even by those who disagreed with his theological "innovations." Young Edwards now stepped into the heavy responsibility of pastoring one of the most important churches in all of New England.

Edwards himself was born in a Puritan parsonage, but unfortunately he had less than happy memories of his father's ministry. The senior Edwards constantly quarreled with his congregation over salary, which was inadequate for his large family, and over the role and prerogatives of his position. Tradition and law had set the duties and responsibilities of an Anglican pastor, but the role of the Puritan (Congregational) pastor in New England was ambiguous, and this often led to disputes.

Jonathan Edwards was a precocious child, developing interests in science and skills in philosophical studies far beyond his age. When he graduated from Yale College at age seventeen, he was head of the class. Jonathan displayed both genius and zeal for all he did, including his spiritual development. As a young man he wrote down his goals for constant improvement.

> 1. Resolved, that I will do whatsoever I think to be most to God's glory, and my own good, profit and pleasure, in the whole of my duration, without any consideration of the time, whether now, or never so many myriad's of ages hence. Resolved to do whatever I think to be my duty and most for the good and advantage of mankind in general. Resolved to do this, whatever difficulties I meet with, how many and how great soever. . . .
>
> 3. Resolved, if ever I shall fall and grow dull, so as to neglect to keep any part of these Resolutions, to repent of all I can remember, when I come to myself again. . . .
>
> 5. Resolved, never to lose one moment of time; but improve it the most profitable way I possibly can. . . .
>
> 28. Resolved, to study the Scriptures so steadily, constantly and frequently, as that I may find, and plainly perceive myself to grow in the knowledge of the same. . . .
>
> 30. Resolved, to strive to my utmost every week to be brought higher in religion, and to a higher exercise of grace, than I was the week before.[14]

JONATHAN EDWARDS HAS SECOND THOUGHTS[15]

From the time Edwards arrived at Northampton he exhorted the congregation to strive for ever higher levels of Christian virtue. He was disappointed that the people of Northampton did not respond to his sermons and come to the same zeal for the gospel he felt. As early as 1733 he began considering in his private notes that perhaps the fenced sacrament of earlier Puritan tradition had the good disciplinary result of forcing people to a higher spirituality.[16]

At this point Edwards was especially concerned with the "creeping Arminianism" of some surrounding towns. Edwards and other orthodox Puritans believed that Arminian "heresy," which stressed humanity's ability to appropriate God's offer of salvation, slighted the sovereignty of God and weakened orthodoxy. To counter Arminianism he held a series of sermons on "justification by faith alone" (winter of 1734–1735). These sermons triggered a dramatic revival, in which many "fainted away" or fell screaming to the ground in terror of damnation. The revival included many of the youths of the town.[17]

Though privately suspicious of the Stoddard practice of open communion, Edwards could not but agree that it had brought many in Northampton to conversion, and he continued to celebrate open communions during the revival years that followed. Edwards recognized the continuity between the revivals led by grandfather Stoddard and the one that took place in his ministry:

> The work that has now been wrought on souls, is evidently the same that was wrought in my venerable predecessor's days; as I have had abundant opportunity to know, having been in the ministry here two years with him, and so conversed with a considerable number that my grandfather thought to be savingly converted in that time; and having been particularly acquainted with the experiences of many that were converted under his ministry before. And I know no one of them that in the least doubts of its being the same spirit, and the same work.[18]

The late 1730s were the high point of Edwards's pastoral career. He was respected and admired locally as ushering in a major revival and skillfully leading many to a full conversion experience. He was also internationally recognized through his writings. He seemed to have assumed his grandfather's mantle of authority while avoiding the hassles of his father's ministry. But from 1736–1741 no further revivals came to Northampton regardless of what he tried, including repeating his initial revival-triggering sermons. Furthermore, he was disappointed that the original revival did not bear long-range fruit:

> The work that went on so swiftly and wonderfully while God appear'd in might & irresistible power to carry it on, has seemed to be very much at a stop in these [valley] towns for a long time, and we are sensible by little and little, more and more declining.
>
> This was caused by among other things, eagerness after the possessions of this life, and undue hearts of spirit among persons of different judgement in public affairs. Contention and party spirit

has been the old iniquity of this town; and . . . has of late manifestly revived.[19]

Most disappointing to Edwards was that the youth of the town began drifting from moral ways. This was aggravated by demographic factors: The town had simply run out of new land to divide among the young men. These sons of the founders had to live in prolonged adolescence, waiting for land to inherit, forced to delay marriage, and thus especially subject to sexual temptations.

Finally, in 1741 revival again came to Northampton, but Edwards had little to do with it. It was sparked by the visit of George Whitefield, the famous revival evangelist (and Anglican priest) who passed through and preached at Northampton for several days. This revival was more intense than the earlier one, and some of the physical manifestations, such as outcries and fainting away, seemed to be getting out of hand. (Edwards termed these manifestations "exercises.") To bring better order to the Northampton congregation, Edwards brought the people to a ceremony of "renewing the covenant" formed on Old Testament models (e.g., Ex. 34:10–17; Neh. 9). With this and with his own pastoral guidance the revival excesses in Northampton quickly abated.

The renewing of the covenant ceremony succeeded in focusing the minds of the Northampton congregation on the fruits of Christian life and away from the revival phenomenon. The covenant was crafted by Edwards to cover what he considered the chief failings of his congregation in regards to factional disputes, commercial self-interests, youthful lusts, and so on. Like his youthful list for improvement, it was a perfectionist's plan for sainthood. Its unintended consequence was to hold an impossible (and demoralizing) standard to the people, one that left no possibility for human frailty.

For example Edwards wanted all gossip and evil-speaking to cease, absolutely!

We will take great heed to ourselves to avoid all violations of those Christian rules, Tit. 3:2, "Speak evil of no man"; Jas 4:11, "Speak not evil of another, brethren"; and II Cor. 12:20, "Lest there be [. . .] strifes, backbitings, wisperings"; and that we will not only not slander our neighbor, but also will not, to feed the spirit of bitterness, ill will, or secret grudge against our neighbor, insist on his real faults needlessly, and when not called to it; or from such a spirit speak of his failings and blemishes with ridicule, or an air of contempt.

We now appear before God . . . solemnly to devote our whole lives to be laboriously spent in the business of religion: ever making it our greatest business, without backsliding from such a way of living; not hearkening to the solicitations of sloth and other corrupt inclinations. . . .[20]

Outside of Northampton, the revival phenomenon was coming under widespread criticism from many quarters.[21] Edwards attempted to defend the revival as a whole by partially agreeing with its critics. That is, he agreed that some revival "exercises" were not from God and should be curtailed. He constructed a discernment theology, partially out of the corpus of Puritan writings on the emotions and manifestations of conversion and partly from his own experiences in Northampton. Edwards concluded that it was the pastor's duty and responsibility to watch over his flock and discern if specific revival manifestations were authentic or not.[22]

After 1742 no further revival came to Northampton. More seriously, the youth, including many deeply affected by the revival of 1741, resumed their less-than-perfect lifestyles. Many partook of "night walks" (i.e., unsupervised courting). More seriously, in 1744 the "bad book incident" shook the social fabric of Northampton. Some youths got hold of a midwifery book that had illustrations and vivid descriptions of women's menstrual cycles and the progress of a pregnancy. This was considered salacious knowledge for males. A few young men who read the work snickered and joked publicly of women's periods.

Edwards exploded with indignation from the pulpit, naming both the truly guilty and those who had merely heard the comments. Many parents were rightfully scandalized by the tactless way Edwards handled the matter. Equally important, he lost the confidence of the Northampton youth, who had been his most loyal followers. Edwards was disappointed in his congregation. They had not upheld the standards of the renewed covenant. He continued to ponder the issue of open communion and the advantages of using the fenced communion as a disciplinary tool.

In 1749 Edwards publicly announced that he would not accept his grandfather's position. Instead, he would henceforth demand the evidence of a conversion experience from those seeking communion. The town was outraged, as many were old enough to remember the dreadful consequences of the older system. Edwards was given an opportunity to explain his position, and he did so in a work entitled *An Humble Inquiry*.[23] In this work he rejected point by point Stoddard's theology of the Lord's Supper as a converting ordinance. He reaffirmed the traditional view that the Lord's Supper is only a seal of conversion. Furthermore, he even rejected the mandate of the Half-Way Covenant (the synod of 1662) and declared he would no longer baptize children of parents not fully converted.

In his analysis of the situation he placed the discernment burden of identifying a truly regenerate Christian from a mere seeker or hypocrite on the pastor.

> The minister, in receiving him to the communion of the church, is to act as a public officer, and in behalf of the public society, and not merely for himself, and therefore is to be governed, in acting, by a proper visibility of godliness in the eye of the public.[24]

The congregation asked two local pastors to critique *An Humble Inquiry*, and both concluded that Edwards was greatly mistaken in his rejection of the open communion. Not unexpectedly the congregation of Northampton voted 200 to 20 to remove him as pastor and to seek someone who would continue the Stoddard practice. Edwards left Northampton in 1750 to the frontier village of Stockbridge. There, with a small mixed congregation of settlers and Indians he had time to compose some of the theological classics for which he is now remembered, such as *The Freedom of the Will*.

Historians have tended to view that Northampton congregation as mistaken, ungrateful, and theologically uncouth. After all, they dismissed the person who was arguably the most creative orthodox theologian of America. From a more detached perspective we can say that he was indeed a tremendous theologian and gift to the church as a whole, but he was also an incompetent pastor who mismanaged his congregation. The two are not exclusive.

Edwards's personality was that of a perfectionist, a virtue in scholarship and critical thinking but not necessarily a positive for a pastor. More specifically, his perfectionism crowded out the pastoral virtue of mercy, by which one understands the failings of others and the fact that many will not progress in their spirituality as quickly as expected. This unfortunate pastoral fault had important and tragic consequences in the history of American revivals. Edwards transformed his personal disappointments (and mismanagement) into general theological principles and rejected the whole Stoddard system.

DISCREDITING THE SACRAMENTAL
MODEL OF REVIVAL

Jonathan Edwards's prestige as theologian of revivals, which grew especially during the nineteenth century, assured that Stoddard's blend of sacramental piety and evangelistic preaching would not be the model of future American revivals. Edwards's theology asserted in precise Calvinist assumptions that revivals are the product of God's sovereign move but also dependent on evangelistic preaching as a precondition. Thus, the Lord's Supper no longer had a role in revival and was again restricted as an ordinance of fully converted Christians, not seekers.

The clergy who welcomed the Great Awakening looked to Edwards's writings as inspiration and as a protection to their critics. These ministers were called the "New Light" party, and it was they and their descendants who led the revivals of the nineteenth century. They accepted Edwards's view that revival occurred by God's sovereign will through evangelistic preaching and that the Lord's Supper had no role in revival.[25]

Today one can drive through America and see church marquees announce "Revival: Monday to Saturday, 7:30, Evangelist J. Jones preaching," or some such announcement. One can be assured that the sign will *not* read, "Communion service Sunday for the new seekers." Solomon Stoddard's revivals were not the last occasions in

American history when the Lord's Supper was an integral part of revival. In spite of Edwards's veto there would be one more, a marvelously glorious "last hurrah" for communion-centered revivals in America. That story begins not in New England but in the hills and glens of Scotland.

Notes

1. A good biography of Solomon Stoddard is not available, and unfortunately, few of his works are in print, a situation that begs the attention of a modern editor. The recent biography of Stoddard, Ralph J. Coffman's *Solomon Stoddard* (Boston: Twayne Publishers, 1978), is a seriously flawed work. It is poorly written, and Coffman attempts to reduce spiritual forces to sociological trends, e.g., witchcraft is formed by "political anxiety," etc. See also the critique by E. Brooks Holifield, "Solomon Stoddard," *Church History* 49 (Summer 1980): 340–41. More helpful have been chapters 1 and 2 of Patricia J. Tracy's *Jonathan Edwards, Pastor* (New York: Hill & Wang, 1979), and the dissertation by Paul Edward Husband, "Church Membership in Northampton: Solomon Stoddard Versus Jonathan Edwards" (Philadelphia: Westminster Theological Seminary, 1990). For Stoddard's theology see the article by Thomas A. Schafer, "Solomon Stoddard and the Theology of Revival," in *A Miscellany of American Christianity*, ed. Henry Stuart (Durham, N.C.: Duke Univ. Press, 1963), 328–61.
2. Coffman, *Stoddard*, 35.
3. Ibid., 60.
4. See I. N. Tarbox, "Jonathan Edwards as a Man; and the Ministers of the Last Century," *The New Englander* 43 (1884): 625–26, cited in Husband, "Church Membership," 139.
5. Coffman, *Stoddard*, 72.
6. Ibid.
7. Cited in Schafer, "Theology of Revival," 341.
8. Available online from the very fine Jonathan Edwards web site: http://www.jonathanedwards.com.
9. Cited in Schafer, "Theology of Revival," 341.
10. Ibid., 340.
11. "Sermon on Galatians #1," cited in Thomas M. Davis and Virginia L. Davis, eds., *Edward Taylor vs. Solomon Stoddard: The Nature of the Lord's Supper* (Boston: Twayne Publishers, 1981), 132.

12. Ibid., 143.

13. Ibid., 147.

14. From another fine Jonathan Edwards website: http://members.aol.com /jonathanedw/Resolutions.html.

15. The following section is based on the recent and thorough scholarship of Patricia J. Tracy, *Jonathan Edwards, Pastor: Religion and Society in Eighteenth Century Northampton*, and David D. Hall, "Introduction," in Jonathan Edwards, *Ecclestical Writings*, ed. David D. Hall (New Haven, Conn.: Yale Univ. Press, 1994; vol. 12 of *The Works of Jonathan Edwards*).

16. Tracy, *Jonathan Edwards, Pastor*, ch. 2, "Preparation."

17. All of this was described in his famous work, *A Faithful Narrative of the Surprising Work of God* (1737), cited in Schafer, "Theology of Revival," 328–61. He reworked this initial booklet in the following years as increasingly sophisticated and detailed descriptions of revivals, revival phenomenon, and theology.

18. As cited in Schafer, "Theology of Revival," 326.

19. Letter from Jonathan Edwards to Benjamin Coleman, May 19, 1737, cited in Tracy, *Jonathan Edwards, Pastor*, 124.

20. Jonathan Edwards, *The Great Awakening*, ed. C. C. Goen (New Haven, Conn.: Yale Univ. Press, 1972), 552–54.

21. On the opposition to this revival, see my work *Quenching the Spirit* (Lake Mary, Fl.: Creation House, 1996), ch. 3, "The Great Awakening Quenched."

22. See especially Edwards's *A Treatise Concerning Religious Affections* (1746). There have been many editions of this classic, and the entire text can be downloaded from the website www.jonathanedwards.com.

23. The full title is *An Humble Inquiry into the Rules of the Word of God Concerning the Qualifications Requisite to a Complete Standing and Full Communion in the Visible Christian Church*, in *Puritan Sage: Collected Writings of Jonathan Edwards*, ed. Vergilius Ferm (New York: Library Publishers, 1953), 451–65.

24. Ibid., 456.

25. Hall, "Introduction," 50.

THE SCOTTISH

COMMUNION CYCLES[1]

5

Like John Calvin, John Knox and the Scottish Reformers wanted a balance of "Word and sacrament" for their new Scottish Reformed church. Their theology followed closely that of Calvin, which affirmed the real, "spiritual" presence of the Lord in the Eucharist. Knox, again following Calvin, sought to reconstruct the Lord's Supper as celebrated in New Testament times. Bread and wine were served on tables to a seated congregation in sufficient quantities to simulate a small meal. The minister said the words of consecration, but the elements were in turn distributed by lay elders to the congregation. The goal was to recreate the atmosphere of a New Testament meal and to get as far away from the priest-centered "sacrifice of the mass" as possible.

Knox wanted weekly communions in contrast to the Catholic practice of twice yearly communion with bread only. Ironically, practicality intervened. The Scottish Reformers could not recruit enough educated candidates or ex-priests to ordain as clergy. Instead, many rural parishes were led by laymen, "the most apt men, that distinctly can read the common prayers and the scriptures,"[2] but these "readers" were not authorized to minister the sacraments or even preach. The few ordained ministers periodically visited the lay-led congregations to preach and minister baptism and communion. Thus unintentionally, the Scottish Reformed Church (Presbyterian) drifted into the Catholic pattern of communion once or twice yearly per congregation.[3]

THE COMMUNION CYCLE

By the 1630s a pattern had developed that served as the perfect vehicle for sacramental piety and recurring revivals. With Calvin's theology of the real spiritual presence as a base and with a new generation of ministers educated and in place, the Lord's Supper was celebrated as a three- or four-day cycle. On Fridays and Saturdays the pastor preached repentance and gave opportunity for public confession. Also on Saturdays small metallic tokens (similar to poker chips) were given those in the congregation qualified for communion — those in good standing in the church.

Sunday was the day for the sacrament. The communion service could be done inside the church on temporary tables that filled the church (fixed pews had not come into use) or outdoors under tents. The tables were set with immaculate white linen. The tokens were deposited with the elders in a special box as a solemn recommitment to lead a Christian life in the coming year. Wave after wave of communicants received the elements to the sound of the congregations singing the Psalms or an elder reading portions of the Bible. The communion service often took all morning, and many communicants had deeply moving experiences at the communion table. One communicant from the 1740s reported: "I cannot express what I met there, I can only say, my soul was filled with rays of divine light & love and I was so full of the gracious presence of God, that I could hold no more."[4] The cycle normally came to an end in the afternoon with a thanksgiving sermon.[5]

Although each parish celebrated the Lord's Supper only once or twice a year, the host church usually invited neighboring parishes to participate — as many as eight or ten congregations. Thus the pious

Scot might attend five to eight communions during the "sacramental season" of summer and fall. Food and lodging was provided by the host village, and since there was little public lodging, the guests crowded every available barn and shed. It was considered a sin to accept money for the food provided, and this was a problem for the poorer regions of Scotland. Some pastors would schedule a parish communion only once every two years to lessen the burden on his people. More prosperous parishes, however, had the luxury of hosting two communions per year.

Like the famous Irish wake, these sacraments were both solemn and festive. Solemnity reigned during the preaching and at the communion table, but there was much festivity in the social interactions at the periods of shared food, ale,[6] and crowded lodging. Courtships were initiated, and friendships were formed or reestablished. Significantly, many unbelievers who came for the social aspects were often convicted and converted during the sacramental cycle. George Wemyss, editor of a popular collection of communion sermons of the era, wrote:

> The great Master of Assemblies is pleased so far to countenance them with his presence and power, that many hundreds, yea thousands in this land, have dated their conversion from some of these occasions.[7]

REVIVAL IN NORTHERN IRELAND[8]

The first noticeable communion-cycle revival took place in Northern Ireland, among a string of churches along the Six Mile River valley from Antrim to Larne on the coast. Scots brought over by the government of James I (1603–1625) had settled this region to counter the possibility of insurgency by the Catholic population. The religious state of these Presbyterian Scottish settlers was deplorable, many being petty criminals and debtors. There were practically no clergy to minister to their spiritual needs.

The situation began to change when James I attempted to enforce Anglican liturgy and practices throughout England, Wales, and Scotland. James forced Parliament to pass the "five articles of Perth" (1621), which was seen by devout Presbyterian and Puritan pastors as a regression to Catholicism. Among other things, the articles mandated the reception of communion in a kneeling posture. To the Scots this was a sure sign that the dreaded concept of transubstantiation and "bread worship" was just around the corner! Scrupulous Presbyterian clergy would not minister communion under these circumstances, and many were harassed or persecuted for their stand. Some fled to Northern Ireland, where they were welcomed to staff the empty pulpits by the local Anglican bishops as "Anglican" clergy — few questions asked. Providentially, King James had little interest in Northern Ireland, so the exiled Scottish pastors could minister communion and preach in their new parishes according to their conscience.

The revival itself began through the combination of human weakness and divine grace. One of the exiled Presbyterian pastors, James Glendinning, settled in the garrison village of Carrickfergus, where he preached to the soldiers and local people. His style was academic and flowery, including many classical references that no one understood. The rumor spread that he was preaching very "learned" sermons — they must be good with all the classical stuff! Another exiled pastor, Robert Blair, came to hear Glendinning's preaching. Blair recorded: "I perceived he did but trifle citing learned authors whom he had never seen nor read. After the sermon I waited on him and communed with him, freely asking him if he thought he did edify that people."[9]

Blair's reproof struck Glendinning to the core, and the humbled pastor went in repentance to minister in the tiny village of Oldstone. There he preached a fiery gospel of human sinfulness and the terrors of hell, with no classical allusions. Under that preaching the Spirit moved among the rough and uncultured settlers. They howled and cried out in despair over their sinfulness. Crowds from the entire Six Mile River valley came to hear the dramatic preaching and see the manifestations.

However, Glendinning did not know how to complete the gospel with the comfort and salvation in Christ. Providentially, yet another exiled pastor, Josias Welsh, came, and he was able to bring forward the preaching to the grace of the cross. Other Presbyterian pastors joined in, and the revival spread to adjoining towns and villages along the Six Mile River valley. The success of the revival went to Glendinning's head, and he became convinced that he possessed the key to interpreting the book of Revelation. Blair again attempted to correct the fiery preacher, but this time he would not listen and in fact left Ireland in search of the "seven cities of Asia."

Meanwhile, the revival preachers began regular teachings in the town of Antrim to serve the whole region. These were held on the last Friday of every month. Large crowds came to take part in the day-long affair. Two teaching/preaching sessions were held in the morning and two in the afternoon. The crowds stayed for further sermons, token distribution, and fellowship on Saturday. On Sunday all descended upon one of the neighboring villages for communion. At times the Spirit of God was so present that the cycle was extended to a Monday thanksgiving service. One eyewitness reported:

> I have known them that have come several miles from their own houses ... and spent the whole Saturday night in several companies, sometimes a minister being with them, sometimes themselves alone in conference and prayer, and waited on the public ordinances the whole Sabbath, and spent the Sabbath night likewise, and yet at the Monday sermon not troubled with sleepiness.... [10]

The more dramatic manifestations were also much in evidence. A participating pastor wrote in 1625:

> I have seen them myself stricken, and swoon with the Word — yes, a dozen in one day carried out of doors as dead, so marvellous was the power of God smiting their hearts for sin, condemning and killing; and some of these were none of the weaker sex or spirit, but indeed some of the boldest spirits. [11]

These were among the first references to the "fallings" that became common in many forthcoming revivals. Jonathan Edwards, the theologian of the Great Awakening, would call the physical manifestations of the fallings, groanings, tremblings, and so on, "exercises." He viewed them as an ambiguous part of revivals. That is, in themselves the exercises could not *prove* the presence of God as they were easily counterfeited, but they were not forbidden by Scripture and *could be* from God.[12] That the exercises, such as a falling or swooning to the ground, *were from God* was indicated if the person proceeded in the conviction to conversion while immobile, as often happened. Two centuries later Pentecostals called this same phenomenon the fallings, "falling under the power." It has recently been given the more dignified name by the famous charismatic theologian Francis McNutt, "resting in the Spirit."[13] At the time of the Six Mile River revival, a full century before Jonathan Edwards wrote, they were little understood.

OPPOSITION

Naturally these manifestations brought controversy, and the revival soon came under pharisaic attack. That is, it was opposed by orthodox clergy who assumed that the manifestations originated from demonic or "soulish" sources and, being unruly, *could not be of God*.[14] The Anglican Dean of Down observed the 1625 outpourings and wrote to his skeptical fellow priests:

> The people in that place are grown in such frenzies that the like is not to be found among the Anabaptist.... So that every sermon, 40 or so people, for the most part women, fall down in the church in a trance, and are (as it is supposed) senseless, but in their fits they are grievously afflicted with convulsions, tremblings, unnatural motions. After they awake they confess that they have seen devils (as who may not see a factious and a cheating devil among them)....[15]

Opposition increased steadily, especially from the Anglican ministers in the area. By 1632 Bishop Echlin, who back in 1623 had gladly welcomed Blair and other Scottish ministers, ordered the same prelates suspended from the ministry and closed the revival meetings at Antrim.[16] He had been under considerable pressure from English authorities to do so. The pretext Bishop Echlin cited was that the Scottish ministers were advocating the necessity of the manifestations for salvation (they were not) and would not conform to Anglican liturgy (that was true, but it had been winked at thus far). The revival clergy scattered, mostly returning to Scotland but leaving behind a revived laity that met in homes and continued the memory of "the sacrament." Later in the 1640s the Presbyterian Church was organized in Ireland, and not being subject to Anglican oversight, the communion cycles resumed.

In Scotland, Charles I (1625–1649) followed his father's aim of imposing Anglican liturgy ("Laud's liturgy") on the Presbyterian Church. Again, this frightened the Scots into thinking they were being forced into the old rituals of Catholicism. Most of the people and clergy resisted in spite of government harassment and persecution. There was insufficient royal control to be effective, with the result that the revival and innovations from Northern Ireland were introduced into Scotland. The Monday thanksgiving service, often the occasion for weddings or baptism, became part of the communion cycle, making the cycle even more popular with the people. Thus even in the times of severe persecution — the period just before the English Civil War (1642–1646) — the communion cycles continued to grow in popularity, and mini-revivals broke out in the villages and towns of the Scottish heartland.

The ministers who were harassed and ousted from their pulpits by the authorities became itinerant preachers and communion ministers, living off the care of the people directly. Their communion cycles were held in the woods or barns, away from the bishop's agents. The authorities called these meetings "coventicles" and considered them hotbeds of rebellion. In 1634 a royal proclamation banned such meetings and mandated that every person receive communion only at their parish church. The decree was largely ignored and merely made Charles I even more unpopular. Eventually the Scottish people rose in rebellion (1638) and later joined with the Puritan forces to oust the king.

An even more severe period of political and religious persecution came decades later, after the Puritan government of Oliver Cromwell was overthrown. During the Restoration years (1660–1685), Charles II was determined to make the Scots into good liturgical Anglicans. The communion cycles were again strictly forbidden, but again they continued as secret meetings, sometimes with armed guards to prevent interference by the king's cavalry.

COMMUNION TOKENS[17]

In the period before the Restoration the communion cycles reached their mature form. In the 1650s it became common to declare the Thursday before the communion Sunday a fast day. Metal tokens became standard and more carefully minted. They were made of lead or some inexpensive alloy, and they were stamped with the initial of the local church, a chalice, or some other simple illustration. Some tokens were minted in heart shape to signify God's love.

The contemporary Christian is likely to view the communion tokens as strange or unbiblical. Indeed, there is no biblical basis for the custom, a fact that critics of the communion cycles often pointed out. Yet the distribution of the tokens as a sign of the communicant's readiness to receive and the depositing of the tokens as a pledge to live a holy life the coming year became a rich and meaningful part of the cycle.

It was John Calvin who introduced the notion of tokens to the Reformed communion liturgy. Ironically, he was known for affirming the principle of *sola scriptura*, that is, that all Christian practices and doctrines must be based on Scripture. Calvin knew of tokens from his wide knowledge of classical literature. Tokens, either paper or metal, had been in circulation since Roman days as a screening device for social and religious occasions. The tokens of the ancient world were sometimes made of small polished and engraved stones (the possible reference point of Rev. 2:17).[18] In 1560 Calvin requested the use of tokens for distribution in his church in Geneva. He intended them as an instrument by which the pastor could control who did and who did not receive communion and thus prevent its reception by the ignorant or unrepentant parishioners. The Geneva council rejected the idea. However, Calvin was the spiritual leader also of the French Protestant Church and through his correspondence got the French Huguenots to accept the use of tokens.[19]

Knox and the Scottish Reformers, like the French Protestants, made the tokens a normal feature of the Reformed communion service.

By the end of the seventeenth century the tokens were an inseparable part of the Scottish communion cycle. They signified that the possessor had been examined by a church elder, had demonstrated adequate knowledge of the catechism, and could recite the Lord's Prayer, the Ten Commandments, and the Apostles' Creed. Possession of the token also signified that the local minister knew the communicant was living a godly life.

The requirement that a person pass a catechism-based examination kept some persons away from communion, including some who through extreme poverty were illiterate. A more biblically based restriction referred to persons who had disputes with their neighbors and were not reconciled (Matt. 5:23). Thus Saturdays were used not only for repentance and confession but also for public *reconciliation* among quarreling parties. The pastor who knew of feuding and unreconciled parishioners could deny tokens just on that basis. Thus the number of participants at the table was always significantly less than the whole congregation.

The communion service itself was never as liturgically set as in some of the more traditional branches of Christendom. For instance, the exact form and words of consecration were never mandated, although 1 Corinthians 11:23–26 was usually chosen. A simple ritual of sermon, consecration, and psalm singing developed. Holy utensils were purchased just for the service. These included the silver or pewter flagons to hold wine, cups for the drinking of the wine, and platters to hold the loaves. These items were often the most expensive objects a church would own. The table linens and the napkins to cover the bread during the service were of the finest quality and were bleached, washed, and ironed with meticulous care.

The communion cycle took place in late summer or early fall, the "sacramental season." Pastors coordinated with each other so that nearby villages celebrated together. There were agreements between servants and masters as to how many communion cycles the servants could attend, this being the only holiday period of the year for the poor and the only time outside of Sundays when they did no labor.[20]

If the communion season was an occasion for festivity for some, it was also an especially demanding time for ministers. A famous pastor wrote of the communion season in 1729:

> Our communions in the country are all crowded in the summer time, and what by my work at home, and assisting my neighbors from May to September, I am generally overburdened.... Perhaps I may have about three hundred of my own charge who are allowed to partake, and yet we will have a thousand, sometimes eleven or twelve hundred at our tables.[21]

PREACHING THE WORD OF REPENTANCE

Preaching for the communion cycle was so extensive that it took several preachers to accomplish the task. There were sermons on Friday afternoons and evenings, most of Saturdays, and an "action" sermon just before communion. The fast was usually set for Thursday sunset to Friday sunset. The sermons on Friday stressed the need for repentance, often with Joel 1:14 as the central Scripture:

> Declare a holy fast;
>   call a sacred assembly.
> Summon the elders
>   and all who live in the land
> to the house of the LORD your God,
>   and cry out to the LORD.

Saturdays continued the repentance motif with a careful explanation of the Ten Commandments as they applied to individual life. Ministers would stress human sinfulness and unworthiness to receive the great sacrament:

> You are naturally unfit for this ordinance; naturally you have neither habitual nor actual preparation, being dead in sins and trespasses, leprous, loathsome, carnal, and earthly-minded. Wherefore we must be quickened and purified, before we can hold communion with a holy God.[22]

Paul's warning in 1 Corinthians 11:27–32 was understood as literally true and a threat to those who might receive carelessly (we noted this earlier in the Puritan debate on open communion). The most famous of Scottish communion preachers, John Willison of Dundee, listed thirteen dangers of receiving the sacrament unworthily, some of which were:

> If you do not sanctify and prepare yourselves, God will come and do wonders of judgment, wonders of wrath among you. 1. He may inflict bodily diseases, as 1 Cor. xi. 30. 2. He may send untimely death. 3. He may smite with desertion from God. 4. He may send darkness of the mind. 5. He may smite with deadness and impenitency on the heart. 6. With decaying and withering on the gifts and graces.... [23]

These preparatory sermons stressed inner cleansing through careful examination of consciences. Special attention was given to sins that defile the mouth, such as evil-speaking about others, gossip, cursing, and so on. The mouth had to be cleansed before it could eat the communion bread! Preparation also extended to the externals, such as proper dress (Ex. 19:10–11), which had to be clean and the person's best, though not pretentious or showy. In an era when the poor went barefoot much of the time, shoes and stockings were always worn to church. Often these were cleaned and wrapped in kerchiefs and donned as the person approached the church.

On Sunday there was one more sermon just before the communion service. It was called an "action sermon." It summoned the token-holders to receive communion and encouraged those not having tokens to make themselves ready for a future occasion. After all the repentance talk, here were detailed the benefits of the Lord's table, including adoption as children of God, peace and strength for spiritual struggles, and most importantly, forgiveness of sins:

> Here [at the table] is pardon of sins sealed to a believer.... Here you get Christ's blood, which was shed for many, for the remission of sins. Here we clasp about a crucified Christ as the propitiatory sacrifice for our sins, accept him as the Lord of our righteousness; and thus we receive the remission of sins.[24]

Psalms were sung as one wave after another took their seats at the linen-covered tables and received the elements. Psalm 24 was a favorite, for it summarized the work of repentance and the achievement of righteousness in Christ:

Who shall ascend onto the hill of the LORD? Or who shall stand in his holy place?

He that hath clean hands, and a pure heart; who hath not lifted up his soul unto vanity, nor sworn deceitfully.

He shall receive the blessing from the LORD, and righteousness from the God of his salvation. (Ps. 24:3–5 KJV)

JOHN WILLISON: THEOLOGIAN
OF THE COMMUNION CYCLES

We have already cited John Willison of Dundee (1680–1750). He was dean and theologian of the Scottish communion revivals.[25] His writings, dating from 1716 to 1747, were republished many times, and a few have continued in circulation in Scotland even to this day. Willison had a special heart for the young. Among his writings were catechisms for children and young persons,[26] and even a catechism designed to help mothers with the religious instruction of their children. He also wrote devotional and polemical works and was noted in his day as one who called Scotland out of its moral laxity.

Willison was an orthodox Presbyterian who expressed his faith as a passionate sacramentalist. In fact, a majority of his works deal with sacramental issues, such as proper preparation for communion or meditations on the Lord's Supper. In his sermons he often lapsed into the question-and-answer format of the catechism. Note in the following passage from one of his sermons:

Quest. What is meant by taking this [consecrated] bread? Ans. It is the accepting of Christ as he is offered to us; a receiving the atonement, approving of it, consenting to it, coming up to the terms on which the benefit is proposed to us. It is an accepting of Christ's grace, and submitting to his government. Believing on Christ is expressed by taking and receiving him. . . .

Quest. What is meant by eating this bread? Ans. It signifies our feeding by faith upon Christ and his benefits, which is done by our believing the report concerning Christ and his purchase, and making a particular application of Christ and his benefits unto our soul, and their various necessities and exigencies. And particularly this eating signifies, 1. Our union with Christ. 2. Our satisfaction and complacency in him. 3. Our receiving strength and increase in grace from Christ.[27]

Willison was also one of the early hymn writers of the English language. At the beginning of the eighteenth century churches in the English-speaking world sang only the biblical psalms in dreadful, overly literal translations.[28] This was unfortunate and almost incomprehensible, seeing that Martin Luther, the first great Reformer, wrote scores of stirring hymns — including the famous "A Mighty Fortress Is Our God." However, the Lutheran hymn tradition did not cross over to the English or Scottish Reformations, and the earlier Catholic practice of singing the Latin Psalms was simply upgraded to an English text.

It was Isaac Watts (1674–1748) who composed the first popular English hymnals, *Hymns and Spiritual Songs* (1707), followed in 1719 with *Psalms of David Imitated in the Language of the New Testament*. These hymnals became popular with the Dissenting Churches but were forbidden in Anglican services as a radical and unscriptural innovation. The Watts hymnbooks made possible others, including the hymns of Willison and those by John and Charles Wesley (see ch. 11).

Willison's *One Hundred Gospel Hymns* was the first major Scottish hymnal. His hymns were meant to be sung during the entire sacramental cycle. Most were poetic meditations on Christ's death and suffering, but six were written to be sung during the communion distribution. Among them was Hymn IV, "The Lord's Table":

Come here, admire Christ's love to us,
    That gives his Flesh for Food;
And Drink to us he doth provide,
    By pouring out his Blood.

This Food doth Life unto the Dead,
    Health to the Sick impart;
This Drink revives the fainting Soul,
    And melts the frozen Heart.

What Folly is't for men to starve,
Or feed on Husks like Swine;
When Christ calls to a Table spread,
To feast on food Divine![29]

Just how seriously the Scottish Presbyterians came to "feast on food Divine" is demonstrated in the story of the greatest revival event of Christian Europe in the eighteenth century, which took place in a village a few miles east of Glasgow.

NOTES

1. The best single book on the Scottish Presbyterian sacramental revivals is Leigh Eric Schmidt, *Holy Fairs: Scottish Communions and American Revivals in the Early Modern Period* (Princeton, N.J.: Princeton Univ. Press, 1989). It is well written and makes for an exciting spiritual narrative. Schmidt represents a new type of academic scholar who takes religious experiences seriously and does not marginalize them as abnormal psychological states.
2. Mary McWhorter Tenny, *Communion Tokens: Their Origins, History, and Use* (Grand Rapids: Zondervan, 1936), 27.
3. George Burnet, *The Holy Communion in the Reformed Church of Scotland* (Edinburgh: Oliver & Boyd, 1960), ch. 1, "From Mass to Communion in the Reformed Era."
4. Anonymous participant in the Cambuslang sacrament, 1742 (see next chapter), cited in Schmidt, *Holy Fairs*, 161–62.
5. For a modern, practical rendition of this liturgy, see David A. Ramsey and R. Craig Koedel, "The Communion Service—An 18th Century Model," *Journal of Presbyterian History* 54 (Summer 1976): 203–16.
6. These communions took place two centuries before the evangelical temperance movement, and moderate consumption of alcoholic beverages was considered normative for all social occasions. Drunkenness was the sin, not drinking wine or ale.
7. Schmidt, *Holy Fairs*, 45.
8. The following account is drawn from the monograph by W. D. Bailie, *The Six Mile Water Revival of 1625* (Belfast: Presbyterian Historical Society of Ireland, 1976).
9. Ibid., 7.

10. Ibid., 13. The modern reader may not realize that for some, "several miles" could mean a walk of twenty miles (ibid., 14).

11. Marilyn J. Westerkamp, "Enthusiastic Piety — From Scots-Irish Revivals to the Great Awakening," in *Belief and Behavior: Essays in the New Religious History*, ed. Philip R. Vandermeer and Robert P. Swierenga (New Brunswick, N.J.: Rutgers Univ. Press, 1991), 70.

12. Jonathan Edwards, *Religious Affections* (1743), part 2, esp. section iii.

13. Francis McNutt, *Overcome by the Spirit* (Old Tappan, N.J.: Fleming H. Revell, 1990).

14. All revivals spawn opposition, directed by traditionalists among the clergy who cannot discern the Spirit of God moving within the "enthusiasm" and disorder of revival (see my *Quenching the Spirit*).

15. Cited in Bailie, *Six Mile*, 18.

16. Ibid., 14; on opposition from dissenting clergy, see pp. 16–17.

17. The following section is based on the work of Tenny, *Communion Tokens*.

18. "To him who overcomes, I will give some of the hidden manna. I will also give him a white stone with a new name written on it, known only to him who receives it."

19. Tenny, *Communion Tokens*, 17. Tokens continued in use among the Reformed French community until the 1840s.

20. The Reformers saw Christmas and Easter as "Catholic" inventions not warranted by Scripture, and these holidays were not recognized by the Reformed churches. One of Schmidt's main points is that the Reformers dismantled the Catholic holiday system without replacing it with anything, much to the loss of the common person. The Reformed liturgical year became just one Sunday after another. The communion cycle then became, quite unintentionally, a replacement for the Catholic holidays (see *Holy Fairs*, passim).

21. Tenny, *Communion Tokens*, 50.

22. John Willison, "A Preparation Sermon Before the Sacrament," 422, as cited in John Willison, *A Balm of Gilead . . . Likewise, Sacramental Meditations and Advices* (Edinburgh: J. Pillans & Sons, 1819), 408–9. This book was a compound edition of several of Willison's works; the first edition of *Sacramental Meditations and Advices* was published in 1747.

23. Ibid., 423.

24. John Willison, "Action Sermon," as cited in *Balm of Gilead*, 427.

25. There is no modern biography of Willison, but a doctoral dissertation provides much information about him; see Stephen Albert Woodruff III, "The Pastoral Ministry in the Church of Scotland in the 18th Century" (University of Edinburgh, 1965).

26. A sample of Willison's *The Young Communicant's Catechism* (c. 1813) can be downloaded from the following website: http://members.aol.com/RSISBELL/young1./html.

27. John Willison, "A Lecture, on 1 Cor. xi. 17. to the end," included in *Balm of Gilead*, 408.

28. A short account of the eighteenth-century hymn revolution is given in "The Golden Age of Hymns," *Christian History* 10/3 (1991) (entire issue).

29. John Willison, *One Hundred Gospel Hymns, in Memory of Redeeming Love, and the Death and Sufferings of the Lord Jesus Christ for Perishing Sinners* (Dundee: H. Galbraith, 1767), 30–31.

Triumph and Opposition

at the "Cams'lang Wark"

6

With the "Glorious Revolution" of 1688 the last of the Stuart kings was driven out of the United Kingdom and the very Protestant William of Orange, from the Netherlands, assumed the crown. The Scottish Presbyterians were released from any further persecution or attempt to make them "liturgically correct" Anglicans. With the new freedoms, the years between 1688 and 1750 saw the communion cycles reach their flowering, with sacramental occasions of five thousand participants becoming common. The largest and most famous of the sacramental cycles was the one held at the village of Cambuslang (five miles from Glasgow) in 1742.[1]

For several years prior to that date, the people of Cambuslang had experienced a steady stream of awakenings and conversions under the evangelical preaching of its minister, William McCulloch. A servant girl in the McCulloch household recalled:

> At a communion occasion, when I saw some young folk coming to my master [Pastor McCulloch] about their soul concerns ... I wondered what it was that affected them ... next year, 1739, when the communion came about, something of a concern about my soul revived in me....[2]

McCulloch mobilized faithful intercessors within the parish's "societies of prayer" to pray for revival. Such societies were common at the time. They had been introduced in the 1670s by an Anglican minister (and ex-Lutheran) Anthony Horneck. They were similar to modern home fellowships but were more formal in organization and worship than today's groups. Often the groups had written agreements and careful regulations as to the conduct of their members. Cambuslang had several such societies, and they were now focused on praying for revival.

McCulloch raised the expectancy of his parishioners by reading from the pulpit news items about the revival led by the Anglican evangelist and priest George Whitefield. He also publicly read Jonathan Edwards's account of the revival at Northampton, *A Faithful Narrative* (1737). One Cambuslang villager described how McCulloch had exhorted the unsaved during the winter of 1741–1742:

> At the close of the Sermon, the minister [McCulloch] charged us to go home to a retired place, and fall down upon our bended knees before God, and with all possible earnestness, as for life, to beg of him his Holy Spirit to renew and change our hearts and natures, and take no comfort in any thing worldly, till we got it.[3]

Under this type of preaching many in the parish were newly awakened. In January 1742, revived parishioners petitioned for a midweek prayer and sermon service. Also, persons from nearby villages were coming to Cambuslang and being converted. The Sunday service at Cambuslang was packed to overflowing, and after the service the pastor's manse was filled with persons under conviction and seeking McCulloch's advice and direction. All of Scotland knew that Cambuslang was in revival. By the middle of the year so many pilgrims came that McCulloch organized *nightly* sermons to serve the visitors. Preachers from nearby churches came both to observe and to lend a hand at the blossoming revival.

George Whitefield had preached throughout Scotland during 1741, with an especially effective ministry in Glasgow. McCulloch corresponded with him, and when Whitefield again came to

Scotland in June of 1742, he agreed to come to Cambuslang for its summer sacrament the week of July 6. McCulloch coordinated with local churches and prepared for a large turnout. Two preaching tents were set up so that the people could be close to at least one preacher. These were set at the end of a ravine near the Cambuslang church, which formed a natural amphitheater. It was hoped that perhaps ten thousand might come, double the normal maximum of the time.

In fact, about thirty thousand persons descended on Cambuslang from all over Scotland and England. Whitefield showed up on the Tuesday of his assigned week and preached three times to large crowds. He then left, but he returned to preach the Saturday sermon. Whitefield wrote to a friend:

> It far out-did all that I ever saw in America.... Mr. M[cCulloch] preached after I had ended, till one past in the morning, and then could scarce persuade them to depart. All night in the fields, might be heard the voice of prayer and praise.[4]

Along with a dozen other ministers McCulloch and Whitefield distributed the elements on Sunday to over 1,700 communicants. Whitefield stayed Monday and preached again with special effect. He wrote to his revivalist friend John Cennick, "[There were] thousands bathed in tears. Some at the same time wringing their hands, others almost swooning and others crying out."[5] McCulloch estimated that at least five hundred persons were converted during this communion cycle.[6]

That Monday one of the principal minister-celebrants of the communion, Dr. Webster of Edinburgh, suggested another sacrament soon. Although this was unprecedented, Whitefield, McCulloch, and others agreed. Another communion cycle was set to culminate on Sunday, August 15. The crowds were duly informed, and those qualified scrambled to get another round of tokens.

The crowds that came for the August communion cycle were even larger, estimated at between thirty and fifty thousand. This was an incredible number of people, seeing that the total population of Glasgow at the time was less than eighteen thousand. Three thousand received communion, with perhaps another thousand, who could not get tokens, watching tearfully from the sides. The Sunday communion began at 8:30 A.M., and the last bread and wine were served at sunset. Whitefield stayed all day and preached after communion until 10:00 P.M. The Monday sermons drew another large crowd, including twenty-four ministers; many of the older ones had endured persecution, banishment, and torture at the hands of the king's agents.[7]

REVIVAL AT KILSYTH

Revival spread in 1742 from Cambuslang and Glasgow northeast to Kilsyth, nine miles from Glasgow. James Robe served there as minister from 1713 to 1753. Like McCulloch, Robe's preaching emphasized regeneration, but nothing dramatic happened until news of the Cambuslang awakening came to his parish. The societies of prayer in Kilsyth were the first to feel the wind of revival. During May his preaching was causing manifestations of conviction, and by July two hundred parishioners had been awakened and were in the various stages of conversion. Robe and many from his church went to Cambuslang for further revival and communion. Robe was deeply suspicious of the manifestations and instructed his elders to remove any person who cried out during his services. But when Whitefield came to his parish and preached to a crowd of about ten thousand in late July, nothing could stop the howls and screams of conviction.[8] Robe was in constant attendance to the awakened, guiding and praying them through the stages of conversion.

Pastor Robe and many in his congregation attended the August communion at Cambuslang. There, McCulloch suggested to Robe that he sponsor a public sacrament later that fall. Robe dismissed the idea as impractical (it would be too cold, nor was there enough time to organize it), but a trusted elder suggested he do it anyway. So Robe changed his mind and announced a sacrament for the first Sunday of October. In spite of the cool weather, large crowds came, and 1,500 received the sacrament. Though not as great as Cambuslang, it showed that the revival of 1742 was not just a single event. In fact, concurrent with the revivals at Cambuslang and Kilsyth the revival spread to other parts of Scotland. Prayer societies increased dramatically in number and power as persons came under conviction and sought the consolation of Scripture and prayer. Throughout Scotland many households returned to the custom of family prayer.

Yet it must be said that the high point of the revival was the sacramental season of 1742. Strong opposition by some elements of the clergy, both Presbyterian and Anglican, took a toll on the public's opinion of revival (see below). After 1742 the sacramental cycles drew fewer crowds, and the manifestations were much less apparent. The numbers at the communion table declined as well. For instance, the sacrament at Cambuslang in 1743 drew 2,000 communicants, in 1744 about 1,500, and in 1745 about 1,300.[9]

DOCUMENTING THE REVIVAL[10]

Pastor McCulloch wished to document how the communion-cycle revival affected the people in his parish. To this end he carefully interviewed and recorded the experiences of 108 parishioners, young and old, male and female, who communed during the summer of 1742. He had planned to publish these interviews in an effort to encourage revival elsewhere and to answer the mounting criticism.

The interview manuscript went 1,200 pages. McCulloch then invited fellow revival ministers to look at the text and edit out anything that might be improper or controversial. As a result, the project never made it to print. What the lay narratives recorded and what the revival friendly ministers planned to edit out speak volumes about the difficulties that Reformed theology had in dealing with the spiritual manifestations and experiences of revival.

We should recall that the Reformers had forged Protestant theology in opposition to the abuses of Catholic medieval practice. They found monastic spirituality, with its emphasis on contemplative prayer and on experiences of visions and revelations, particularly dangerous. In fact, most of the Reformers wrote off the whole idea of visions and revelatory spiritual experiences as "mysticism" and not proper to the current "church age." The Word of God had been given to human beings in the completed Bible, and further revelations ceased after the death of the last apostles. This is the Reformed doctrine of cessationism. Thus, spiritual experiences such as visions and messages from the Lord were a snare of the devil or the product of an overheated imagination. Unfortunately, it was John Calvin, the most important of the Reformed theologians, who formulated the strongest cessationist doctrine.[11]

This theology of cessationism had created a division between minister and laity. The ministers learned cessationism as part of their theological studies. The devout layperson, however, who read only the Bible, the catechism, and perhaps a few devotional books, did not learn it directly. Although cessationism was a powerful and important doctrine, it never became part of the catechism. In the course of the communion cycle, with its meditations on Christ's sufferings, private prayer time, and the graces of the communion itself, many persons experienced the very spiritual events that orthodox theology claimed had ceased.

For example, one of McCulloch's parishioners was a young woman, Catherine Cameron, not quite twenty when she was interviewed for the planned anthology.[12] Brought up in a devout and well-to-do home, she came to have her first spiritual experience at fourteen at a sacrament cycle in a nearby village. There she was "much in weeping & trembling, and a desire to have an interest in Christ." Up to this point all of Catherine's experiences were common to the well-understood conversion process and in proper cessationist order.

But things became more complex. In 1742, Catherine attended the sacrament at Barony, near Cambuslang. She had spent the whole week in careful preparation, including fasting and much private prayer. She went to several other sacraments nearby. At the first Cambuslang sacrament she experienced a sure sense of Jesus' mercy (assurance). But her most significant sacramental occasion was the second sacrament of Cambuslang (August 1742). On Tuesday night during her vigil, she "was so ravished by the love of Christ that night that I could sleep little, and all next morning and day I was in the same frame: and saying as the spouse of Christ, my beloved is mine & I am his. . . ."

On Sunday, when she sat down at the Lord's table, she burst out in tears of penitence and gratitude; and when she took the cup, she heard Christ tell her, "My blood is sufficient to wash away all thy sins." After communion she spent the rest of the day singing psalms and praying, and "every now & then I behooved to rise, and take another view of my Lord's Table." The whole communion scene filled her with heavenly joy:

> I cannot express the joy with which I was filled, in the time the tables were serving, and I could not endure to look down to the earth, but look'e up — mostly to heaven, & thought, I heard Christ speaking to me from thence and saying, Arise my love, my fair one, and come away: And I saw him, as it were, reaching down his hand, & drawing me up to himself. . . .[13]

In the following years Catherine remained steadfast in her devotions and, on several communion occasions, had visions of the Lord and of the gates of heaven. These visions were, of course, contrary to cessationist doctrine.

Naturally, not all who devoutly followed the communion cycle experienced such visions. One woman from Cambuslang reported conversion experiences during the 1742 communion cycle that would win the approval of any Protestant minister:

> I went out to the fields by my self for prayer, & there falling down, while I was earnestly pleading, That the Lord might give me a clearer sight & more affecting sense of evil of my sins as dishonoring to him. . . . The Lord was pleased accordingly to give me the desire of my heart in that manner, & more than I ask'd or could think of. For I . . . was made to see my sins especially . . . & was made spiritually & in the most evident manner by faith to look as it were thro' his pierced side into his heart, & see it filled with Love to me. . . . [14]

The majority of spiritual experiences reported in McCulloch's interviews fell between these two examples. Most significant in the interview manuscript are the side annotations and bracketed sections intended for suppression. These followed the ministers' cessationist theology. Experiences like those of Catherine Cameron's were bracketed out, as were others that plainly spoke of direct visions or of hearing the Lord's voice (called "locutions" in Catholic theology). By contrast, those experiences that were phrased more indirectly, such as "I sensed the Lord say ..." were acceptable for publication.

In any case, even the sanitized manuscript never made it to the printer. We can only speculate that perhaps the ministers could not fully agree on the boundaries of proper spiritual experiences. Another factor that may have influenced the decision not to publish was the mounting opposition to the communion cycles by traditionalist and antirevivalist factions within the Presbyterian church, who sneered at the "enthusiasm" of the revival.[15] Indeed, the opponents of revival were mounting an aggressive propaganda campaign against the cycles.

THE OPPOSITION TRIUMPHANT[16]

As we noted, opposition to the communion cycles had been constant since their institution in the 1630s, mostly from clergy in the Anglican Church. One Anglican critic wrote in 1712 that the Presbyterian ministry had erred in allowing the communion cycles: "They not only allow, but encourage, on these occasions, such rendevouzes of the promiscuous rabble." Further, this rabble was prone to enthusiasm, that is, "illuminations and raptures."[17]

There were also splinter groups within the Presbyterian Church of Scotland that opposed the cycles. One group, known as the "Seceders" because they split off from the main Presbyterian Church when it compromised to conform to Anglican liturgy, saw the communion revivals at Cambuslang and Kilsyth as unwarranted by Scripture and "delusions of Satan."[18] Another fundamentalist splinter, the "Cameronians," believed themselves as the only true remnant of Christendom and attacked the communion revivals with a pamphlet entitled "The Declaration, Protestations and Testimony of the Suffering Remnant of the Anti-Popish, Anti-Lutheran, Anti-Prelatick, Anti-Whitefieldian, Anti-Erastian, Anti-Sectarian True Presbyterian Church of Christ in Scotland."[19] Even within the Cambuslang parish Pastor McCulloch had to face opposition from a disgruntled parishioner who disliked the revival and brought a constant stream of harassing litigation against his pastor.[20]

Until the middle of the eighteenth century opposition to the communion cycles had been largely ineffective. But the very success of the Cambuslang-Kilsyth revivals triggered the most serious, sustained, and effectively destructive opposition by two very different groups. One was an anonymous pamphleteer who signed himself as "Blacksmith" (probably an Anglican priest); the other was Scotland's most famous and beloved poet, Robert Burns. Both authors demonstrated a turn towards Enlightenment Christianity, which was a radical turn away from the doctrines of classical Christianity and Calvinism and toward a "reasonable" interpretation of Christianity. This form of Christianity denied, for instance, the miracles of the Bible, predestination, or the real presence of Christ in the sacrament. It eventually descended into full-blown Deism within a generation.[21]

Blacksmith's writing, a pamphlet entitled "A Letter from a Blacksmith to the Ministers and Elders of the Church of Scotland," appeared first (1759). The author was appalled by the revival preachers who worked up "the mob to the highest pitch of enthusiasm" and who brought "the weak and ignorant to the very brink of downright madness."[22] He saw the communion cycle as similar to superstitious Catholic practices (always a serious charge for a Protestant to make):

> In Scotland they run from kirk to kirk and flock to see a sacrament and make the same use that the Papists do of their pilgrimages and processions, that is indulge themselves in drunkenness, folly and idleness.[23]

Because the communion cycle attracted both the devout and the unconverted, there was always some excess drinking and sexual immorality amidst the crowded lodgings and festive atmosphere. Blacksmith, like most of the communion-cycle critics, exaggerated this for his polemical purpose: "I have seen scenes that had much more of the fury of the bacchanalia, than the calm, serious, sincere devotion of a Christian sacrament." He added, "I would not choose a wife that often frequented them, nor trust a daughter too much among those rambling saints. . . ."[24]

Blacksmith wanted a communion service without the physical manifestations or spiritual experiences ("enthusiasm") that accompanied so many of the communion cycles. He proposed that a new liturgy be created to restrict the "barbarous" outpouring of emotions and bring solemnity to the sacrament. In his opinion, the sacrament had to be taken out of the hands of the populace and placed fully under the control of "prudent" (i.e., nonrevival) ministers.

Blacksmith's pamphlet touched every chord of clerical fear and desire to escape the accusation of "enthusiasm." It was reprinted many times in Scotland and England, and even in Ireland and the American colonies. With each printing it gained more and more influence among the clergy, who increasingly agreed that the Lord's Supper ought to be guarded from "enthusiastic" extravaganzas.

The much-loved poet Robert Burns was an improbable but most effective ally of the antirevival clergy. He was born into a pious Presbyterian family in rural Scotland. Although he celebrated the loves, virtues, and struggles of rural Scottish life in his poetry, he did not understand or share their piety. As a young man Burns had turned away from the orthodox faith and accepted the skepticism then astir in philosophical and literary circles. His rebellion against the faith of his childhood turned to disdain. He wrote of the pious Christian:

But I gae mad at their grimaces,	But I go mad at their grimaces
Their sighan, cantan, grace-proof faces,	Their sighing, cantan grace-proof faces
Their three-mile prayers, an' hauf-mile graces,	Their three-mile prayers, and half-mile graces,
Their raxan conscience,	Their stretched [elastic] conscience,
Whase greed, revenge, an' pride disgraces	Whose greed, revenge, and pride disgraces
Waur nor their nonsense.[25]	Worse than their nonsense.

Burns first witnessed a communion cycle in the town of Mauchline as a young man, when he was already predisposed to view the event through the distortions of Enlightenment ideology and disdain for orthodox faith. His famous satirical poem about the communion cycle, "The Holy Fair," is a powerful example of Burns's awesome wit and poetical talent. It pictures the communion cycle as a meeting of hypocrites and small-minded fanatics (the orthodox

Presbyterians), with licentious youths who take advantage of the social setting of the cycle to indulge their passions.

The lads an' lasses, blythely bent
   To mind baith soul and body,
Sit round the table, weel content,
   An' steer about the toddy:
On this ane's dress, an' that ane leuk,
   Ther're making observations;
While some are cozie i' the neuk,
   An' formin assignations
     To meet some day. (xx)

The lads and lasses, faces downward
   To mind both soul and body,
Sit round the table, well content,
   And stir about the ale:
On this one's dress, and that one's look,
   They are making observations;
While some are cozy in the corner,
   And forming assignations
     To meet some day. (xx)

The preachers are fanatics, who preach hellfire and damnation to an ignorant crowd willing to accept any evidence as a miraculous sign. In one stanza as the preacher describes hell:

Whase ragin flame, an' scorching heat,
   Wad melt the hardest whun-stane!
The half-asleep start up wi' fear,
   An' think they hear it roarin;
When presently it does appear,
   'Twas but some neebor snorin
     Asleep that day. (xxii)

Whose raging flame, and scorching heat,
   Would melt the hardest whinstone!
The half-asleep start up with fear,
   And think they hear it roaring;
When presently it does appear,
   It was but some neighbor snoring
     Asleep that day. (xxii)

Interestingly, Burns did not describe the communion service itself; perhaps he never had interest in it, or perhaps the authentic piety universally found there did not fit his "enlightened" perspective.

The defenders of the communion cycle responded with their own verses, labeling Burns as a tool of infidelity (Deism).

> So! zealous Robin, stout an' fell
> True Champion for the cause o' Hell
> Thou beats the Righteous down pell mell
>   Sae frank an' frothy.[26]

The defenders further pointed out that charges of sexual immorality were vastly overstated and that those who received communion modeled Christian virtue for the unconverted, who would be immoral with or without the communion cycles.

Sadly, the combination of Blacksmith and Burns produced the knockout blows that ultimately killed the communion cycles in Scotland. This did not happen all at once, but by the 1800s the towns no longer sponsored communion cycles. Even the clergy interested in revival had no theology to justify the stream of visions and "exercises" that occurred during the cycles. The communions were "reformed" into quarterly communion services held inside the church. Communion was distributed in the pews, in the new style of tiny individual glasses that became popular all over the orthodox world during the nineteenth century. Each parish held its own services, and the cross-parish visitations that produced the crowds and festive atmosphere stopped. These reformed services were somber and in "decent order," and of course the visions and the manifestations ceased. Revivals such as that of Cambuslang also ceased.

Among the saddest consequences of the Blacksmith-Burns assault on the communion cycle was the fact that their view became the consensus opinion of even orthodox writers of Scottish history.[27] During the Victorian period (1850–1914) many orthodox Christians turned to total abstinence as normative for the Christian life and looked back on the ale and wine drinking of the cycle as proof that its critics were correct. The communion revivals were viewed as an "immature" stage of Scottish Reformed Christianity.

In the years that it took to extinguish the communion cycles and replace it with the "reformed" liturgy, many of the devout prayed for a new outpouring of the Spirit. They would pray, "Come again, as at Cambuslang!" Those prayers were answered, but not in Scotland; rather, it happened across the ocean, where Scottish colonists had populated in large numbers the frontier of the newly independent United States of America. To that frontier revival we will now turn our attention.

NOTES

1. Described in detail, but with some reticence as regard to revival manifestations, in Arthur Fawcett, *The Cambuslang Revival: The Scottish Evangelical Revival of the Eighteenth Century* (London: Banner of Truth Trust, 1971).

2. Ibid., 100.
3. Ibid., 105.
4. Cited in Schmidt, *Holy Fairs*, 114.
5. Fawcett, *Cambuslang*, 117.
6. Ibid., 115.
7. A common torture used to coerce the Presbyterian ministers during the height of persecution was to press the hands under a vice-like device until all the bones were crushed.
8. As we will see, it was John Wesley who taught Whitefield not to quench the manifestations (see ch. 10).
9. Fawcett, *Cambuslang*, 166.
10. The following section is based on the splendid section of Schmidt's *Holy Fairs*, ch. 3, "The Mental World of Pastors and Peoples," one of the best in his excellent work.
11. I trace the development of this destructive theory in my *Quenching the Spirit*, chs. 4–8.
12. Her story, and all of the following quotations, are from Schmidt's *Holy Fairs*, 118–22.
13. For another case study of a visionary experience that was bracketed out, this one by a young man named Alexander Bilsland, see Fawcett, *Cambuslang*, 148–49.
14. Schmidt, *Holy Fairs*, 138.
15. "Enthusiasm" was the smear word of the eighteenth century, much like "fanaticism" is today.
16. The prime sources for this section are again Schmidt's *Holy Fairs* (ch. 4, "The Autumn of the Sacramental Season") and the useful but excessively sociological view of Marilyn Westerkamp, *Triumph of the Laity: Scots-Irish Piety and the Great Awakening, 1625–1760* (New York: Oxford Univ. Press, 1988), ch. 4, "Piety Against Reason.".
17. Schmidt, *Holy Fairs*, 170.
18. Fawcett, *Cambuslang*, 163.
19. Cited in ibid., 163.
20. Ibid., 164–65. How little things really change!
21. On the stages of the "Enlightenment" and how it affected Christian thought, see the masterwork by Peter Gay, *The Enlightenment: An Interpretation* (New York: Alfred A. Knopf, 1973).
22. [Blacksmith], "A Letter from a Blacksmith to the Ministers and Elders of the Church of Scotland" (1759). Many editions were printed in England, Scotland, and America. Cited in Schmidt, *Holy Fairs*, 180.

23. Cited in Henry F. Henderson, *Religion in Scotland* (Paisley: Alexander Gardner, 1921), 228.

24. Cited in Schmidt, *Holy Fairs*, 180.

25. Cited in Schmidt, *Holy Fairs*, 172 (cited here is an accompanying version in modern English).

26. Cited in Schmidt, *Holy Fairs*, 178.

27. See, for example, George B. Burnet, *The Holy Communion in the Reformed Church of Scotland* (Edinburgh: Oliver & Boyd, 1960).

The Second Great Awakening (1797 – 1805): Scottish Communions in America[1]

7

All throughout the seventeenth and eighteenth centuries people from Scotland and Northern Ireland emigrated to the American colonies. From 1728 to 1768 one-third of the Protestant population of Northern Ireland left for the American colonies. In some counties of the Virginia and Pennsylvania frontier Scottish and Scot-Irish immigrants made up a majority of the population.[2] Scottish Presbyterian churches were established in every American colony. These congregations recreated the communion cycle of the home church, and although the Blacksmith and Burns criticisms were known, they were much less influential in the new world than in Great Britain.

THE BOOTH BAY REVIVAL

We have a splendidly detailed record of one revival that took place at the predominantly Scottish Presbyterian church located in Booth Bay, Maine, from 1767 through 1770. Records were carefully kept by the clerk of the church, John Beath.[3] The fishing community here had been recently founded, but the church there had no pastor. The people called John Murray from Ulster (1742–1793) to be its minister. He was a member of the prorevival faction and arrived at Booth Bay early in 1767.

From the beginning Murray proved an effective and enthusiastic evangelist and revivalist. He "conversed with every one, old and young, separately, and one by one, concerning the state of their souls and the great work of salvation."[4] He organized prayer societies in the settlements around Booth Bay and initiated a Monday night prayer and teaching program. He then established a program of catechism instruction so that everyone, young and old, would be instructed in the church's essential doctrines.

New awakenings began by the winter of 1767. In order to ensure that the people would not stop coming to church during the frigid Maine winter, Murray imported an iron stove from Boston, which he placed in the church (a bold innovation for that time). In early spring Murray announced plans to gather the church for a sacrament. It would be open to Christians of local churches who could prove they were in good standing. John Beath, the scribe of Booth Bay, commented on this aspect of Presbyterian theology:

> Presbyterians believe there is but one visible Church of Christ on earth; therefore particular churches are not so many distinct bodies, independent of, and unconnected with each other, but so many apartments of the same house. . . .[5]

A local elder was given the task of examining those persons from nearby churches who wished to receive a token for the sacrament. Those within the Booth Bay congregation were carefully questioned by Pastor Murray in regard to their knowledge of Christian doctrine, their understanding of the sacrament, and the work of grace in their souls. The latter was not a demand for specific experiences as in Puritan churches but an inquiry for indications of a grace-led life.

Murray then requested a freewill offering for the necessary communion utensils. Sufficient money was raised to purchase cups, flagons, and platters of the "best hard metal" (pewter) as well as the necessary linens. The sacrament was set for the second week of April. In a fishing area such as Booth Bay, a post-harvest date was not relevant.

Murray's communion cycle was somewhat abbreviated, but it included all the elements of the Scottish sacraments. The Sunday before the communion the church was filled to overflowing to hear Pastor Murray explain the sacrament and the need for careful preparation. Wednesday was set as a dawn-to-dusk fast, and Saturday was given over to a review of the Ten Commandments and public repentance, followed by token distribution. Beath gives a careful description of the Saturday service, which must have been identical to many in the mother country.

> Before the delivering of these tokens he [Murray] called us to join in solemn prayer in which the covenant was again renewed; and the particular ascension gifts and graces earnestly sought that might be needful and suitable to every case; after which a short exhortation was given, in the time of which the communicants were desired to come up one by one & receive their tokens from his hand, and then return to their seats again; during the distribution, he continued the exhortation, which being finished the service was concluded by a Psalm, and the congregation dismissed with a blessing.[6]

The number of communicants at the first sacrament, less than two hundred, was not large by the standards of Scotland. The effects of the communion cycle were, however, dramatic. Beath records:

> The whole of the Winter a very unusual seriousness and solemnity appeared amongst the generality of the people here, accompanied with an insatiable desire after the word . . . but nothing very remarkable of public nature until the sacrament, then there were such symptoms of the powerful and special presence of God of grace as every one might discern and we can never enough be thankful for; it was a solemn, sweet and glorious season; many of God's children were filled with the joys of the Lord and many poor souls brought to see their need of the Savior they had shamefully neglected. . . .
>
> The effects [of the revival] were evident the ensuing week and on the next Sabbath . . . the Pastor at the call of several of the neighboring towns, undertook a visit to them on the Gospel errand . . . during the space of two weeks which his tour took up, he preached every day; and the work of God was glorious, every day

it appeared that someone awakened ... many were obliged to cry out, in their distress, some were clearly brought out into the light of the gospel ... religion became the conversation of all companies; the voice of opposition was struck dead ... the pastor's lodging were then daily crowded with poor wounded souls, that knew not what to do ... and great companies would retire to the woods to sing hymns of praise, so that one might almost all the time hear the wilderness ringing hosannas. ... The Wednesday exercises were also greatly blessed, especially on the young people. ...[7]

The season of revival lasted three years, transforming the area of Booth Bay into one of the most pious areas in New England, but because of difficulties in communication and the thinness of the population it did not spread. In 1781 Pastor Murray accepted a call from a church in Massachusetts, where he remained until his death in 1793. He is remembered in American history mostly for the important part he played in rallying the Patriot cause. During the Revolution the British placed a price on his head, but he survived to see the nation birthed and established under its new constitution.

THE COMMUNION CYCLE IN THE GREAT AWAKENING

The Scottish Presbyterian ministers (immigrant or first-generation native) were a major element of colonial Presbyterian clergy during the First Great Awakening (1737–1743). Unfortunately, that Awakening itself produced a bitter dispute among the clergy over the "exercises" and their relation to revival. Those who favored the revival and accepted its exercises as a necessary part of revival (following the theology of Jonathan Edwards) were called the "New Light," while those who deemed the exercises as mysticism and "enthusiasm" were called the "Old Light."

Among the most prominent New Light ministers was Samuel Blair (1712–1751), who led several Pennsylvanian frontier congregations into revival during the Great Awakening. Unlike Pastor Murray, who ministered revival at the beginning of his ministry, Blair preached an evangelical gospel for a decade with little observable effect. In 1739, however, there was a dramatic effusion of the Holy

Spirit on his church, and many were convicted and converted. During the awakening in his church Blair discovered a way to discern who was truly converted. He noticed how the communicants responded to receiving the Lord's Supper, whether it was just an exercise in obedience or a truly moving experience. He also saw, like Solomon Stoddard earlier (ch. 4), that persons under conviction and condemnation often found release and assurance at the Supper.[8]

Besides Blair, many other Scottish Presbyterians, including the Tennant family, were important leaders of the Great Awakening. William Tennant Sr. founded a log college on the Virginia frontier in 1735 and educated American-born Presbyterians in the theology and traditions of Scottish Presbyterianism. The Tennant students — including son Gilbert, who later became the famous itinerant preacher — were prepared for the "exercises" of revival through the cherished memory of Cambuslang and knowledge of the revival theology of Jonathan Edwards.

After 1743 the Eastern colleges became centers of opposition to the Great Awakening. It was left to the Tennants and several other log colleges to educate a new breed of prorevival, New Light ministers. Though their facilities were crude in comparison to Yale and Harvard, they produced a surprisingly well-educated clergy who practiced the Scottish communion cycle wherever they ministered.[9]

The New Light had some successes in continuing the Great Awakening, especially in rural Virginia and the Carolinas, but for the most part the Awakening, of which so much was expected, faltered by 1744. It was stymied by internal disputes, nondiscerning revivalists, and virulent opposition from the established clergy.[10] Perhaps worse, many of the orthodox Puritan and congregational churches that had resisted revival drifted into Unitarianism and Deism.

RELIGION IN THE NEW NATION

Many contemporary Christians have romantic notions of the colonists during the American Revolution as a God-fearing and Christian people. In actuality, the period from about the 1750s to 1800 was a time of deep spiritual decline, in which the anti-Christian philosophy of Deism came close to becoming the national religion.[11] The writings of the French writer and philosopher Voltaire and the Americans Ethan Allen and Thomas Paine were immensely popular. These "enlightened" writers hated denominational Christianity and believed the Bible full of superstitious and incredulous miracles. A Christian student who arrived at the University of North Carolina in 1796 wrote home:

> In North Carolina and particularly in that part of the state that lies east of us, everyone believes that the first step which he ought to rise into respectability is to disavow as often and as publicly as he can all regard for the leading doctrines of the Scriptures. They are bugabares very well fitted to scare the ignorant and weak into obedience of the law; but the laws of morality and honor are sufficient to regulate the conduct of men of letters and cultivated reasons.[12]

Not surprisingly, morals were in rapid decline, with alcoholism a scourge — women of the era often put whiskey in children's bottles to keep them quiet. Significantly in 1800, Thomas Jefferson became the first Unitarian (Deist) president of the United States. It seemed to many Christians that the new nation had irrevocably turned its back on the God of the Bible.[13]

The percentage of believing, orthodox Christians around 1800 may have been no more than 17 percent of the population, with most of the rest as nominal Christians, Deists, or agnostics — a sad comment on the Puritan attempt to create a Christian commonwealth in the new world.[14] The Christian remnant understood the peril of the times, however, and many believers and churches from every denomination were praying for a new outpouring of the Spirit.[15]

THE SECOND GREAT AWAKENING AS SCOTTISH PRESBYTERIAN SACRAMENT

Immediately after the end of the American Revolution, a local but seminal revival broke out at the Presbyterian Hampden-Sydney College in Virginia. This revival refreshed the Presbyterian Church of the state and allowed the denomination to grow there at a time when other churches were losing members to disinterest and Deism.

In 1790 James McGready, son of Scot-Irish parents and graduate of a Presbyterian log college, passed through Virginia and was touched by the Hampden-Sydney revival. He continued to Gilford county in North Carolina, where he settled and discovered that his preaching seemed to have taken on a new anointing. He was definitely a "son of thunder," who denounced horse racing, gambling, and cockfighting and drew vivid pictures of the torments of the damned. McGready was detested by the Deists, and the local young toughs grew tired of his jeremiads. Expressing their displeasure, a crowd trashed McGready's church and threatened him in a blood-ink letter. McGready thought it prudent to accept an invitation to pastor three congregations on the Kentucky frontier in the Cumberland Gap area.

He arrived in 1796 to pastor the churches of the Red River, Muddy River, and Gasper River area. Several of his New Light minister friends, including Barton Stone, also moved to the Kentucky frontier churches to serve the growing population. McGready saw that the spiritual atmosphere in the frontier was even worse than in North Carolina. Indeed, many of the frontiersmen were fugitives from justice, who found the lawlessness of the frontier to their liking.

The fiery pastor immediately set the church faithful on a course of prayer for revival. He drew up a covenant with those in his congregations who agreed to be prayer intercessors. They promised to use one Saturday a month for prayer and fasting for revival, locally and nationally. They also agreed to spend a half hour Saturday evening and Sunday morning in prayer for the same purpose. McGready resumed his jeremiads against the vices of frontier society and added to his previous list dishonest bargains, cursing, Sabbath-breaking, and disregard for the Bible. McGready also preached that the sinner could use the "means of grace," such as prayer and Bible study, to seek conversion — almost an Arminian position.[16]

Revival began during the communion cycle celebrated in July 1799 at the Red River church. A deep spirit of solemnity and conviction spread in the area. The August sacrament at Gasper River Church, now pastored by John Rankin, also turned into revival, as did the September sacrament at Muddy River. McGready, Rankin, and McGee (all prorevival Presbyterians) ministered together in these sacraments and formed the core leadership for what was to come next.

The sacramental season of 1800 was one of continuous revival. People were convicted and cried out in despair, and the ministers were kept busy leading them through the stages of salvation. The Gasper River Church sacrament of July was especially significant. Pastor McGready invited nearby Methodist and Baptist churches to attend, but he also suggested that they bring their supplies and camp out for the communion cycle. He understood that the resources of his frontier community were limited, and they could not offer hospitality in the usual Scottish way.

People came from over a hundred miles. They brought wagons, carriages, or simply pieces of canvas for tents. The tents and wagons were arranged in a hollow square in an open field, with two preaching stands and communion tables in the center. Perhaps five thousand people attended. During Saturday evening the "camp resounded with cries; and the ministers spent the night in passing from one group to another."[17] The communion service followed the usual pattern of solemnity and joy.

Thus began the first "camp meeting" in modern history. The revival exercises appeared with great force, including the usual fallings and outcries, but also prophetic exhortations by young children (Matt. 21:16) and bodily movements called the "jerks." Peter Cartwright, the famous frontier Methodist evangelist, described this exercise:

> No matter whether they were saints or sinners, they would be taken under a warm song or sermon, and seized with a convulsive jerking all over, which they could not by any possibility avoid. . . . I have seen more than five hundred persons jerking at one time. . . . To see those proud young gentlemen and young ladies, dressed in their silks, jewelry, and prunella, from top to toe, take to the jerks, would often excite my risibilities. The first jerk or so, you would see their fine bonnets, caps and combs fly. . . .[18]

Revival spread among the frontier churches of Kentucky that summer, with hundreds awakened and converted. In addition, the

Methodist and Baptist preachers became full partners in both preaching and administering the sacrament.

The frontier was electrified by news of the events. Revival began to occur in normal Sunday services by the spring of 1801 as the faith and expectancy of the communities increased. The sacraments consistently attracted large crowds. One at Concord in June under Pastor Barton Stone drew four thousand. Another at Pleasant Point drew eight thousand, with over two hundred and fifty persons struck down. In June, at Indian Creek, ten miles from Lexington, ten thousand came to the sacramental cycle. An unsympathetic eyewitness wrote about the preaching on that occasion:

> The clergyman rises and introduces the solemn service; takes a text as a motto; commences a vociferous and passionate address . . . an individual to your right (may be converted or unconverted person) is taken with the exercise, of which you were notified with a shriek . . . a circle collects around the individual, and commences singing, and then praying, and then exhorting. Another is seized to your left, another in front, which soon spreads over the whole extent of the congregation. . . . The clergy now leave the stand, spread over the congregation, and converse with the exercised, and exhort, as occasion may offer. This scene was exhibited, day and night, without intermission, as long as the meeting lasted. There was no regular intermission for eating and sleeping.[19]

AMERICA'S CAMBUSLANG: CANE RIDGE

McGready's communion cycle at Gasper River inspired the Rev. Barton Stone, of a small Presbyterian congregation in northern Kentucky, to announce a public sacrament for August of the next year (1801) at his congregation at Cane Ridge.

Stone was born in 1772 into a poor frontier Presbyterian family.[20] As a young man he could not accept Calvin's doctrines of predestination and the total depravity of the human race. Providentially, he visited his brother in Georgia, there encountered the Methodists, and stayed to teach at a local Methodist school for a year. He found Methodist theology, with its accent on human freedom to accept

God's grace, much more to his liking. He received a license to preach from the Methodists.

Stone then itinerated along the frontier and preached several times during 1798 at Cane Ridge. The good Presbyterians of Cane Ridge liked his preaching so well that they called him to take charge of their church in spite of his inability to affirm allegiance to the Westminster Confession — the standard confession of the Presbyterians. Stone attended several of the communion cycles in the summer of 1800 and became an advocate for the revival.

In August 1801, perhaps as many as 30,000 poured in and set up camp at Cane Ridge.[21] All social classes attended, from the governor of the new state of Kentucky to plantation slaves. The pious came for the communion, and the Deists, skeptics, and backsliders came to see and laugh at the "exercises" and enjoy the refreshments — just as in the Scottish cycles. There was precious little entertainment in the frontier of the 1800s, and none wanted to miss the show.

Dozens of preachers exhorted and preached simultaneously from several pulpit stands. The Spirit fell on believer and unbeliever alike. The exercises came to full bloom: weeping and groaning by sinners, the jerks, rolling on the ground, dancing to unheard music, visions, child prophecies, and holy laughter in the saints.[22]

Child exhortations triggered many conversions. Children as young as five boldly harangued unbelievers to seek Christ. One seven-year-old girl preached from her father's shoulders until fatigued. As she lay her head on her father's to rest, an observer suggested, "Poor thing, she better get some sleep." The girl roused and said: "Don't call me poor, for Christ is my brother, God my father, and I have a kingdom to inherit, and therefore don't call me poor, for I am rich in the blood of the Lamb."[23]

The fallings especially took a heavy toll. The curious, the cynics, and the Deists fell to the ground in droves. The Rev. John Lyle, another Presbyterian minister at the Cane Ridge sacrament, wrote in his diary:

> We began to talk and pray for those that were fallen down, and a deist fell, son to widow.... He had said just before he would not fall so for a thousand dollars and that he did not believe in heaven, hell

or the devil. Shortly after two of his cousins fell. He lay speechless for an hour or two, then spoke and said he had been ridiculing the work before he fell and said he wanted to seek Christ.[24]

At the communion table the exercises were greatly subdued. Two ministers wept while serving the tables, and many experienced spiritual visions, but the more physical exercises stayed at the outer ring, away from the communicants.[25]

Monday did not end the cycle. Visitors kept on coming, so ministers continued to preach until Thursday, when the crowds finally dissipated. The days and nights were filled with extemporaneous preaching, singing, and praying. Hundreds experienced conversion.

The dozens of communion-camp meetings of 1801 all across the frontier solidified the camp meetings as a Christian institution. The Methodists and Baptists were the first to copy the Presbyterian pattern and adopt it for their own use. Camp meetings spread east until every part of the new nation was covered by them.

Unlike Scotland, the critics did not triumph. Of course there were the usual pharisees, who claimed the communion-camp meetings were the devil's invention.[26] But two factors preserved the course of the revival. First, the writings of Jonathan Edwards on revival and the exercises were widely known and gave the New Light party a theological edge. Second, the power of the established seminaries and antirevival clergy was much less in the United States than in Great Britain and Europe. The antirevival literature fell flat, and the camp meetings spread to become a normal summer event.[27] In fact, by 1805 perhaps five hundred summer camp meetings — Baptist, Methodist, Presbyterian, and mixed camps — were organized throughout the nation, with the South having an especially heavy concentration.

FRUIT OF REVIVAL, DEATH OF DEISM

In January 1801, less than six months after revival had swept the Kentucky frontier, George Baxter, president of Washington Academy in Virginia, traveled through the region and noted a remarkable change in the morals of the people:

I found Kentucky the most moral place I had ever been in; a pro-
fane expression was hardly heard; a religious awe seemed to per-
vade the country; and some deistical characters had confessed that
from whatever cause the revival might originate, it certainly made
people better. . . .[28]

The Second Great Awakening destroyed American Deism as a
major factor in American religious life. The touch of God that
revival gave to thousands upon thousands made a lie out of the Deist
claim that the supernatural and God's direct intervention in human
affairs were myths and humbug. Orthodox theology, with its trust in
the veracity of Scripture, quickly became the predominant expression of American Protestantism, especially in the South.[29] Thomas
Jefferson's dream of separating the supernatural from religion
became irrelevant and obsolete. Jefferson himself took little notice
of the revival as he struggled with the weight of presidential responsibilities. He died a Diest even though Deism itself was fading
among his countrymen.

CHANGE AND DECLINE

About 1805 the revival began to change in ways that ultimately
diminished its effectiveness. The Baptists took on camp meetings as
a revival institution and for a season stressed immediate baptism right
in the camps to seal conversion (Acts 2). But this sacramentalism did
not extend to the Lord's Supper, which declined in popularity at their
camps. The Methodists introduced their own sacramental form of
the "love feast" to the camp meetings, and with other changes the
focus on the Lord's Supper declined (see ch. 11).

What happened to the camp meetings among the Presbyterians
after 1805 is particularly tragic.[30] The frontier revival brought special
stresses and novel opportunities that the more traditional clergy could
not handle. The New Light ministers wanted to take full advantage
of the moment and accelerate evangelism. They saw how the
Methodists were making great strides with lay exhorters — that is, zealous laymen with little formal education but who knew the Bible and
basic doctrines. They wanted a similar group for Presbyterians.

However, the Old Light demurred, upholding the standards of their denomination that had always prided itself in the education of its clergy. They also feared that uneducated exhorters would bring excesses and loose "enthusiasm" in the church. The Old Lighters and many of the moderates wanted ministerial candidates to undergo normal theological education, even if only at log colleges, and were reluctant to accept lesser ministerial stages such as exhorter. As a compromise, the position of catechist was created as a local teacher of religious instruction, but that person could not preach.

This was not enough for the revival clergy. The Cumberland Presbytery, under the control of the New Light revivalists, went ahead and licensed young men who could preach but did not know Latin or Greek and otherwise fell below standard educational requirements.

In 1806 a commission established by the larger Kentucky Presbytery found that many of the persons licensed by the revivalists not only had inferior education but denied basic Presbyterian doctrines, especially predestination. This was true, since the revivalists had discovered that preaching that humankind was free to accept God's universal offer of salvation was easier to understand than the subtleties of the Calvinist doctrine of predestination. The commission sought to review and, if need be, invalidate many of the Cumberland licenses.

The New Light revivalists refused to accept such disciplinary measures and formed, in effect, an independent denomination, continuing the work of revival on the frontier with great results. James McGready, the revivalist most credited with sparking the Second Great Awakening, refused to join the new group. Like most centrists, including Jonathan Edwards, he was unsuccessful in mediating a compromise, and the two sides drifted further apart.[31]

In fact the Cumberland Presbytery, as the new denomination was first labeled, had great success on the frontier and preempted the traditional Presbyterians in what would later become the American heartland. Other denominations came out of New Light revivalists. Barton Stone (Cane Ridge) and others formed a loose association of revived churches that disavowed creedal statements. They believed that orthodoxy could be protected best by adhering to Scripture alone, through the guidance of the Holy Spirit. Thus the "Restoration Movement" was formed, which eventually birthed the Church of Christ, the Disciples of Christ, and the Christian Church.[32]

Many Old Lighters saw these events as a recipe for future heresy and destruction. Their suspicions were heightened when John Rankin and Richard McNemar, both prominent New Light revivalists, became Shaker converts and publicists.[33] The Shakers came on the scene as the revival was reaching its peak. They promised "exercises" every day in the form of their ecstatic dancing and hand-clapping and claimed to be a new and final revelation of Christianity.

As a result, even moderate Presbyterians retreated from the summer communion cycles and camp meetings. They accepted the reforms of the communion service advocated by their trans-Atlantic brothers in Scotland. American Presbyterian communities turned to an in-church quarterly communion with none of the revival exercises that so frightened them.

Significantly, within another fifty years most Presbyterian preachers were no longer preaching the real presence of Christ in the Lord's Supper and had adopted the Zwinglian view of the sacrament as only a memorial. This drift was highlighted by a controversy that arose with the publication of one of the most famous books of nineteenth-century Protestantism, John W. Nevin's *The Mystical Presence* (1846). This work attempted to call Protestants, and especially Presbyterians, back to the Reformed doctrine of the real spiritual presence of Christ in the Lord's Supper. Nevin's book was challenged and rebuked by Charles Hodge, who occupied a chair at Princeton University and possessed enormous prestige. The Nevin position was also attacked from Union Theological Seminary in Richmond, Virginia, where Professor Robert Dabney referred to Nevin as mystic-minded and boldly affirmed that Calvin's sacramental theology was an "impossible theory." He affirmed the Zwinglian view as Protestant sacramental orthodoxy.[34]

Presbyterians have never been united in their sacramental theology. However, the Nevin-Hodge-Dabney controversy shows how easily the theology of the real presence is lost when the connection with the experiential dimension of the sacrament is decried as "enthusiasm" and "mysticism." Under the reformers' program Presbyterian churches came to "decency and order," but they lost the type of experience that happened to Catherine Cameron at Cambuslang. A great opportunity for American Presbyterians to affirm the Reformation quest for a balanced, yet powerful mix of Word and sacrament slipped away.

NOTES

1. There is an abundance of excellent published and web sources on the Second Great Awakening. The best overall presentation is Paul K. Conkin's *Cane Ridge: America's Pentecost* (Madison: Univ. of Wisconsin Press, 1990), which is similar to Schmidt's *Holy Fairs* in approach and thoroughness. Other excellent works include James R. Rogers, ed., *The Cane Ridge Meeting-House* (Cincinnati: Standard, 1910); Catherine C. Cleveland, *The Great Revival in the West, 1797–1805* (Chicago: Univ. of Chicago Press, 1916); and Ernest Trice Thompson, ed., *Presbyterians in the South: Volume I, 1607–1861* (Richmond: John Knox, 1963). Many of the eyewitness documents of the Second Great Awakening are available from the web site of the "Restoration Movement," at www.mun.ca/rels/restmov/restmov.html.

2. Thompson, *Presbyterians*, ch. 3, "In the Back Country."

3. These are reprinted in their entirety by Thomas C. Pears, ed., "Seasonal Records of the Presbyterian Church of Booth Bay, 1767–1778," *Journal of the Presbyterian Historical Society* 16 (1935): 203–40, 243–88, 308–55. The revival at Booth Bay is also described in Schmidt, *Holy Fairs*, 70–73.

4. Pears, "Seasonal," 232.

5. Ibid., 235.

6. Ibid., 245.

7. Ibid., 249–51.

8. Samuel Blair, *A Shortened Faithful Narrative of the Late Remarkable Revival of Religion in the Congregation of New Londondery and Other Parts of Pennsylvania* (Philadelphia: William Bradford, 1744), 27ff.

9. Note the sacramental sermons by the Tennants found in A. Alexander, ed., *Sermons and Essays by the Tennants and Their Contemporaries* (n.p.: Presbyterian Board of Publication, 1855).

10. See ch. 4. Jonathan Edwards believed that the Great Awakening was aborted by the excesses of its undisciplined fringe, an interpretation that has become standard. My own work shows that perhaps a more important factor was the effective opposition of the antirevival pharisees of the orthodox churches. See my *Quenching the Spirit*, ch. 3, "The Great Awakening Quenched."

11. See Cleveland, *Great Revival*, ch. 1, "The Religious Condition of the West Prior to 1800."

12. Thompson, *Presbyterians*, 126.

13. To the surprise of most Christians of the era, the Jefferson presidency did not result in a lawless reign of terror, as in Deist France. In fact, Jefferson's administration proved somewhat bumbling but also fruitful to the expansion of democratic ideals. This was a case study of divine providence using an unbeliever for good. Note the similarities with Abraham Lincoln, who also disliked denominational Christianity; see Mark Noll, "The Struggle for Lincoln's Soul," *Books and Culture* (Sept./Oct. 1995), 3–7.

14. Roger Finke, *The Churching of America, 1776–1990: Winners and Losers in Our Religious Economy* (New Brunswick, N.J.: Rutgers Univ. Press, 1992).

15. John Boles, *The Great Revival, 1787–1805: The Origins of the Southern Evangelical Mind* (Lexington: Univ. Press of Kentucky, 1972), ch. 3, "The Theory of Providential Deliverance."

16. Thompson, *Presbyterians*, 132.

17. Ibid., 134.

18. Peter Cartwright, *The Autobiography of Peter Cartwright* (New York: Abingdon, 1956), 45.

19. Thompson, *Presbyterians*, 136.

20. Stone's autobiography can be downloaded in its entirety at http://www.mun.ca/rels/restmov/texts/bstone/barton.html.

21. Estimated numbers vary greatly. All crowd estimates are only guesses. Note the recent controversies as to how many attended the African American "Million Man March" of 1996 and the later Washington Promise Keepers prayer rally.

22. Thompson, *Presbyterians*, 137.

23. Conkin, *Cane Ridge*, 95.

24. Cleveland, *Great Revival*, 187.

25. Conkin, *Cane Ridge*, 92.

26. The major pharisee of the Second Great Awakening was Adam Rankin, whose work, *Review of the Noted Revival in Kentucky* (Washington: John Israel, 1802), claimed all the exercises, including the spontaneous praise songs of the camps, were demonic inspirations.

27. Richard Carwardine, "The Second Great Awakening in Comparative Perspective: Revivals and Culture in the United States and Britain," in *Modern Christian Revivals*, ed. Edith L. Blumhofer and Randall Balmer (Urbana: Univ. of Illinois Press, 1993), 84–100.

28. Thompson, *Presbyterians*, 138.

29. Boles, *Great Revival*, passim.

30. The following account is taken largely from the fine discussion of the post–1805 period found in Thompson, *Presbyterians*, ch. 10, "Frontier Schisms."

31. John Opie Jr., "James McGready: Theologian of Frontier Revivalism" *Church History* 34 (December 1965), 445–56.

32. The Restoration churches are represented on the web by one of the best Christian websites, filled with many eyewitness accounts of the Second Great Awakening and other documents: www.mum.ca/rels/restmov/index.html.

33. The full text of Richard McNemar's work, *The Kentucky Revival, or A Short History of the Late Extraordinary Out-Pouring of the Spirit of God, in the Western States of America, Agreeably to Scripture — Promises, and Prophecies Concerning the Latter Day: With a Brief Account of the Entrance and Progress of What the World Call Shakerism, Among the Subjects of the Late Revival in Ohio and Kentucky; Presented to the True Zion-Travelers, as a Memorial of the Wilderness Journey* (1808), can be downloaded with less trouble than it costs to say the full title at: http://www.mun.ca/rels/restmov/people/rmcnemar.html. McNemar's work is most interesting as it gives an excellent firsthand account of the Second Great Awakening, as well as a picture of his descent into cultism.

34. E. Brooks Holifield, "Mercersburg, Princeton, and the South: The Sacramental Controversy in the Nineteenth Century," *Journal of Presbyterian History* 54 (Summer 1976): 238–57.

PART 3

REVIVAL AND SACRAMENTAL SPIRITUALITY IN THE WESLEYAN TRADITION

"MAD GRIMSHAW'S"

METHODICAL ANGLICANISM

8

WHITEFIELD'S FAMOUS SERMON

In October of 1756 George Whitefield, the most famous preacher of
the Great Awakening, came to the northern English town of Haworth
to preach at the local Anglican church, St. Michael's. Thousands
came to hear the "great itinerant," many walking from long distances.
Unlike other preaching engagements where Whitefield was unwel-
come by the local clergy, here he had been invited by the rector,
William Grimshaw, and given the pulpit. Revival had been going on
at St. Michael's under its rector since 1742. This parish was one of
the few that had fully embraced the Wesley brothers' "methodical"
form of revived Anglicanism.

The crowds filled St. Michael's and overflowed into its courtyard,
especially on communion Sundays. Even after expansion St.
Michael's could not contain the crowds. In a bold stroke, Grimshaw
built a special preaching scaffold outside one of the church's narrow
windows. There, with the window open, he or a guest preacher could
stand and be heard by the thousand or so persons packed inside the

church as well as the two or three thousand standing outside in the courtyard.

The Wesley brothers had preached often from this wooden scaffold, but on this chilly overcast October Sunday, it was Whitefield who stood to address the expectant crowd. In his youth Whitefield had wanted to become a famous actor and had demonstrated great talent in this field. However, after his conversion he forsook the stage for the pulpit but brought to the pulpit all of his acting talents and flair. To the thrill of eighteenth-century audiences on both sides of the Atlantic, he acted out the parables, dramatized the plight of the condemned, and preached the gospel with a histrionic style never before seen.[1] The biographer of Lady Huntingdon, one of the great Christian ladies of the era, describes the scene of the famous sermon Whitefield gave that Sunday:

> Mr. Whitefield mounted the temporary scaffold to address the thousands spread before him, he was observed to engage in secret prayer for a few seconds. Then casting a look over the multitude, elevated his hands, and in an energetic manner implored the divine blessing and presence. With a solemnity peculiarly his own, he announced his text — *"It is appointed unto man once to die, and after death the judgment."* After a short pause, as he was about to proceed, a wild, terrifying shriek issued from the center of the congregation.... Mr. Grimshaw hurried to the spot, and in a few minutes was seen pressing through the crowd towards the place where Mr. Whitefield stood. "Brother Whitefield (said he, with the energy which manifested in the strongest manner the intensity of his feelings, and the ardor of his concern for the salvation of sinners), you stand among the dead and dying — an immortal soul has been called into eternity — the destroying angel is passing over the congregation...." After the lapse of a few moments, Mr. Whitefield again announced his text. Again a loud and piercing shriek proceeded from the spot where Lady Huntingdon and Lady Margaret Ingrham were standing. A shrill of horror seemed to spread itself over the multitude when it was understood that a second person had fallen victim to the king of terrors. When the consternation had somewhat subsided, Mr. Whitefield gave indications of his intention of proceeding with the service.... All was hushed — not

a sound was to be heard — and a stillness, like the awful stillness of death, spread itself over the assembly, as he proceeded in a strain of tremendous eloquence to warn the careless, the Christian sinner, to flee from the wrath to come.[2]

William Grimshaw, Improbable Pastor

The great revival that took place at St. Michael's in Haworth was not something one would have predicted from Grimshaw's family heritage or youth. The Grimshaws eked out a living in the northern English town of Bridle as tenant farmers. William's illiterate parents were not religious. Young William (born 1708) attended the local "free schools," where he did exceptionally well and eventually received a scholarship to Cambridge University. There he proceeded to follow a career path for ordination into the Anglican clergy. This was not due to a divine call to ministry or felt piety. Rather, it was one of the few avenues available to a laboring-class young man that ensured middle-class status and income. He graduated from Cambridge as a normal (and nominal) Christian cleric, knowing Latin, Greek, Hebrew, and the history and doctrines of the church, but believing in little.

Ordained in 1732 and sent to minister in the parish of St. Mary's in Todmorden, Northern England, he settled into a comfortable routine. He was an avid huntsman and fisherman and a first-rate cardplayer. An observer reported: "He refrained as much as possible from gross swearing, unless in suitable company, and when he got drunk, would care to sleep it out before he came home."[3]

None of this was scandalous to his contemporaries. He at least *lived* in his parish and performed *most* of the duties of a parish priest. This cannot be said of many of the other Church of England clergy at the beginning of the eighteenth century. In fact, the era was one of the low points of the Anglican Church, brought on by the politics of the preceding century.

As brilliant and fruitful as Puritan theology was at the hands of Owens, Edwards, Stoddard, and others, Puritan rule in England proved a disaster. After the Puritans triumphed over the Royalists in the English Civil War, Oliver Cromwell assumed the dictatorship of the nation (1649) and attempted to force the Puritan vision of righteousness over Great Britain. Theaters were shut down, Sabbath restrictions expanded, and strict public morality was enforced with coercive force. The result was not unexpected: The English people overthrew the Puritans as soon as Cromwell died and brought back the monarchy (1660). The Puritan period was remembered mostly for its repression and for its "enthusiastic" sects, such as the Levelers and Diggers, who combined social radicalism with an utter disregard for church tradition. The people of the Church of England were ready for a less intense and a more traditional form of Christianity.[4]

The abuses of the Anglican Church under the earlier Stuart kings reemerged. Puritan pastors, no matter how pious and effective, were removed from their pulpits. The more prestigious and lucrative clerical posts (including those for bishop) were bought and sold. Many positions were filled with amoral and absentee clerics, who had little interest in religious affairs or the care of their people. Naturally, there was a profound decline in the morals and spirituality of the nation.

The Glorious Revolution of 1688 imported a new sovereign, William of Orange. This resulted in political reforms and the permanent establishment of the constitutional monarchy. Spiritually, however, the situation for the Anglican Church did not improve; in fact, it declined even further. Some of the more devout Anglican clergy could not accept the legality of the new sovereign and refused to swear allegiance to William. These "nonjurors" were thrown out of the Anglican Church. Among these was William Law, whose work *A Serious Call to the Devout Life* (1729) has become a classic of Christian spirituality.

Thus the Anglican Church within thirty years lost the best of its "Reformed" wing, the Puritan pastors, and squeezed out the most dedicated members of its "Catholic" wing, the nonjurors. The classic Anglican attempt to be a *via media*, a middle way between Catholicism and Reformed Christianity, became a parody of itself. Instead of drawing from the *best* of both camps, Anglicanism settled into a passionless middle with the *faults* of both camps.

Religious instruction among the general populace was especially poor. John Wesley noted in his early travels in Great Britain:

> I do not mean they are ignorant of Christ. Many of them can say both the Lord's Prayer and the Belief [Apostles' Creed]. Nay, and some, all of the Catechism; but take them out of the road they have learned by rote and they know no more (nine in ten of those with whom I conversed). . . . [5]

Grimshaw's Conversion

Thus, when William Grimshaw began his career as Anglican priest, no one found his lack of devotion and piety strange. His conversion from nominalism to an ardent and orthodox faith came in stages. Early on as curate in St. Mary's, he noticed how a woman was consoled after the death of her infant son through the Eucharist. This triggered a conviction as to his own lack of faith. In 1735 he married a woman he deeply loved, but she soon became ill and died. This caused profound grief, but also deep reflection on evil and the lost state of humankind. Interrupting a prepared sermon with an unusual silence, he blurted out: "My friends, we are all in a damnable state, and I scarcely know how we are to get out of it!"[6]

The answer came to him shortly. At the home of a friend he chanced to touch one of many books on a shelf, and before he even knew its author or title he was hit by an unknown light and "uncommon heat flashes."[7] He turned to the title page and discovered it was John Owen's classic work on justification. Another wave of heat and light hit him. He took this as a divine sign to read the book. He discerned correctly. Before he completed its introduction, he understood that justification by faith and imputed righteousness was the key to his spiritual search. Quickly, he reread St. Paul's epistles, and there he found the peace and faith he so longed for. This began a transformation to one of the most dedicated and effective pastors England has ever known.

After his conversion Grimshaw was called to a larger parish, St. Michael's at Haworth (1742). He found a new anointing and power in his preaching. John Wesley was to exclaim on hearing him preach: "An Israelite indeed. A few such as him would make a nation tremble. He carries fire wherever he goes."[8] His preaching ministered to the simple laborers and farmers of his parish, yet kept the attention of the finer classes. For example, his comment on the promises of Psalm 48 included "they who have this God for theirs, shall never want a pound of butter for eightpence, or three pints of milk for a ha'penney as long as they live."[9]

St. Michael's was soon ablaze with revival fire. Grimshaw wrote to a friend:

> Our dear Lord was pleased to visit my parish. A few souls were affected under the word, brought to see their lost estate by nature, and to experience peace through faith in the blood of Jesus. My church began to be crowded, insomuch that many were obliged to stand out of doors. Here, as in other places, it was amazing to hear and see what weeping, roaring, and agonies many people were seized with the apprehension of their sinful state, and the wrath of God.[10]

Not only did people come to Grimshaw from distant parishes, but he went out to the people. He became a particularly effective visitation pastor. Mirroring what John Wesley was to do during the Bristol revival (see chs. 9–10), Grimshaw set up prayer societies in the outlying villages where he would visit and preach on a regular schedule.

He was especially noted for his sick-bed visitations. Often he would assist the dying with the practical help of will writing in addition to spiritual consolation and prayers. He also visited the dying unconverted, attempting to snatch the soul from Satan's clutches even at the last moment. On one occasion, when the door to the deathbed patient was not open to him, he stood outside and shouted: "If you will not come to church to hear me, you shall perish with the sound of the gospel in your ears!"[11]

Grimshaw possessed a sense of humor and delight in practical jokes that was quite unlike the more proper Wesleys and uncommon to devout Anglican priests. On one occasion a young lady in Haworth was seduced by a man who had promised her marriage but reneged.

Grimshaw dressed up as the devil (tail and all) and "appeared" to the terrified seducer to claim him for eternity. The man fled in terror, repented, and married the woman. Not surprisingly, the rector of Haworth was called "Mad Grimshaw" by the locals.[12]

Grimshaw was a forceful pastor in the rough style of his era, who combined the duties of school teacher, sheriff, and truancy officer with that of pastor. One Sunday visitor to Haworth passed an ale house and saw "several persons making their escape out of it, some jumping out of it, some jumping out of the lower windows, some over a low wall." The visitor was alarmed, thinking the house on fire, but he was told there was no emergency, only that those inside had seen the parson coming to round up his more reluctant parishioners.[13]

In another incident a parishioner from an outlying village reported to Grimshaw that young toughs regularly came and disrupted their Bible meetings. Grimshaw came to the next meeting unannounced:

> Being a man of athletic sinew, he managed to impel them [the toughs] by degrees further and further up the passage ... when, with one desperate effort of strength and violence, he forced the whole gang into the room and into the light. He instantly shut the door, took from under his great coat a horse-whip, dealt round its utmost virtue on the astonished clowns till his vigorous arm was tired, then fell on his knees in the midst of them, uttering in a loud imperative tone, "Let us pray."[14]

There were no further disturbances from the young toughs.

GRIMSHAW THE SACRAMENTALIST

Besides being a forceful pastor and superb preacher, Grimshaw was a dedicated Anglican sacramentalist. When he first came to St. Michael's, he rounded up all the unbaptized in his parish, young and old, and ensured their baptism. He was especially concerned in preparing the youth for confirmation. Later, he also imitated Wesley's custom of yearly covenant services to rededicate parishioners to the Lord (see ch 10).

Most of all, Grimshaw's monthly communion services were special and attracted participants from many neighboring churches and visitors from faraway (a cause of some tension with unrevived churchmen of the area). The services had an air of spontaneity to them that marked the presence of the Spirit. He "did not confine himself to the old dry form of words, but from the fullness of his heart he broke out in the most lively, pious, and animating exhortations, and enlivened the whole service with hymns."[15] The distribution of the elements at the communion rail was itself marked by a Spirit-inspired spontaneity. At times he would touch the communicants affectionately on the ear and encourage them, "And for thee too, Tommy."[16] At other times the communion distribution was momentarily stopped for a spontaneous prayer, a hymn, or an exhortation. A contemporary observer wrote of the communion services at Haworth: "There has scarce been a dry eye among the communicants whose number was seldom short of a thousand."[17]

St. Michael's as Prophetic Witness

What Grimshaw achieved at Haworth and the Yorkshire circuit of preaching stations and village societies fulfilled the dream of the Wesley brothers for a reformed and revived Anglicanism. Grimshaw was neither a brilliant scholar nor a profound theologian. But here at St. Michael's was the union of devout preaching *and* sacramental worship that defined the true Anglican *via media* between Catholicism and Protestantism. Here was a dedicated orthodox Anglican pastor, leading a congregation in revival and love of the Lord, all of which took place where the sacraments and the *Book of Common Prayer* were faithfully observed. Salvation by faith alone was preached from the Haworth pulpit, but the people lived a spirituality that honored and observed the "means of grace" (prayers, Bible reading, fasting, etc.) outlined in the liturgical rhythm and rites of the *Book of Common Prayer*.

John and Charles Wesley spent their energies and lives in attempting to bring the Anglican Church to a standard like that of St. Michael's. They failed in that quest. They were unheeded prophets, spurned by most of the clergy as "enthusiasts" and Puritanical fanatics. Less than half a dozen parishes in all of the United Kingdom went the way of Grimshaw's methodical Anglicanism.

Yet all of this gets ahead of our story, which really began half a century prior to the Haworth revival in the sleepy seaside parish of Epworth, on the north coast of England, where parish life was under a particularly devout Anglican clergyman named Samuel Wesley.

Notes

1. The relationship between Whitefield's histrionic ambitions and his ministry is treated in the controversial work by Harry S. Stout, *The Divine Dramatist: George Whitefield and the Rise of Modern Evangelicalism* (Grand Rapids: Eerdmans, 1991).
2. A. Crossley Hubert Seymour, *The Life and Times of Selina, Countess of Huntingdon* (London: William Edward Painter, Strand, 1844), 1:265–66.
3. Arnold A. Dallimore, *George Whitefield: The Life and Times of the Great Evangelist of the Eighteenth-Century Revival* (2 vols.; Westchester, Ill.: Cornerstone, 1979), 1:312.
4. See the discussion of this point in W. Stephen Gunter, *The Limits of "Love Divine": John Wesley's Response to Antinomianism and Enthusiasm* (Nashville: Kingswood, 1989), 119–20.
5. John Wesley, *The Journal of the Rev. John Wesley, M.A.*, ed. Nehemiah Curnock (London: R. Culley, 1909–1916) — a standard work, hereafter cited as *JWJ*. The quotation is from October 20, 1739.
6. Frank Baker, *William Grimshaw, 1708–1763* (London: Epworth, 1963), 44.
7. Ibid.
8. John Wesley, *The Letters of the Rev. John Wesley, M.A.*, ed. John Teleford (London: Epworth, 1931), 4:160.
9. J. Horsfall Turner, *Haworth: Past and Present* (Brighouse, Eng.: Jowett, 1879), 70.
10. Baker, *Grimshaw*, 61.
11. Turner, *Haworth*, 13.
12. Frank Baker, "'Mad Grimshaw' and His Covenants with God," *The London Quarterly and Holbourn Review* 28 (1958): 211–15, 271–78. Inexplicably, this imaginative and effective rite was never accepted into the Anglican *Book of Occasional Services*.

13. Turner, *Past and Present*, 59.
14. Ibid., 71.
15. Baker, *Grimshaw*, 92.
16. Ibid., 180.
17. John C. Bowmer, *The Sacrament of the Lord's Supper in Early Methodism* (London: Dacre, 1951), 194.

The Origins of
Wesleyan Spirituality

9

The Anglican Holy Remnant

Among the approximately 13,000 Anglican parish clergy in the United Kingdom in the 1700s, not all were nominal or looking only for a comfortable living. In fact, the church was graced with a remnant of faithful pastors and bishops who managed to live and minister the gospel in that spiritually dark era. Some faithful Anglican clergy labored as scholars and teachers, continuing the revival in patristic studies that was rediscovering the riches of the early church. On the lay level, many parishes had independent Anglican "societies," where parishioners came together for prayers and devotion. These societies multiplied in the first decades of the eighteenth century, encouraging a core of faithful and pious laypersons. Significantly, the prayer societies received no opposition from the hierarchy since they focused on personal piety and had no reform agenda.

THE WESLEY FAMILY[1]

Among the faithful remnant was Samuel Wesley, rector of the Anglican parish of Epworth in Lincolnshire, on the north coast of England. He was among the most effective and conscientious pastors of his generation. Samuel and Susanna, his wife, were raised in Dissenting homes but became Anglicans by conversion. In spite of the corruption of the Anglican church, they saw in the records of the early church an episcopal structure and sacramental worship missing in the Dissenting churches but present in Anglicanism.

The Dissenting churches, including the Puritan congregations now outside of the Anglican church and other denominations such as Presbyterians, Baptists, and Quakers, remained uncorrupted by the established system of forced tithing and privileges. Their congregations prayed earnestly for a fresh revival in the realm. Many of the people in Epworth were Dissenters, either Baptists or Quakers, and saw Samuel Wesley as a turncoat. Some of them demonstrated less than Christian charity and took it upon themselves to make life difficult for the Wesleys through verbal insults at the marketplace, vandalism of their property (such as ruining their garden), or loud demonstrations in front of the parsonage.

Samuel Wesley did not respond in kind. Rather, he focused on the practice of a high church and faithful Anglicanism: constant house-to-house visitation, regular religious instruction, punctual twice-weekly prayer, and celebration of the Lord's Supper monthly (the norm at the time was quarterly). He formed a religious "society" for the parishioners' spiritual development. In his study Samuel read and appreciated the writings of the church fathers as well as the more modern Catholic mystics, and at the same time he developed a distrust for continental Calvinism.

Susanna was not only a person of prayer but active in parish life as leader of the women. John Wesley later recounted how his mother had led an impromptu revival:

> Our family devotions were held not only for us but for the servants as well. Devotional meetings were frequently held in the rectory kitchen on Sunday evening. When my father was away my mother took charge. Once when my father was in London . . . some mem-

bers of the congregation joined our meetings. At first there were thirty or forty but by the time my father returned the attendance had reached more than 200.[2]

The Wesley children were raised strictly, and Christian instruction was foremost in the education of each child. The parsonage burned down when John Wesley was a small child. When John became trapped by the flames, a servant pulled him out unscathed at the last second. Susanna believed that John's deliverance was a sign that he was destined to special service for the Lord. She took meticulous care to ensure his religious development, and their relationship was close all of their lives. As a gifted student, John made great progress in both his religious and secular studies and went on to Oxford University.

OXFORD AND THE HOLY CLUB

When John arrived at Christ Church (college) in 1720, Oxford was in a period of decline. It was considered "backward" in comparison to the more "forward-looking" Cambridge. Ironically, this was spiritually fortuitous insofar as the predominant theology at Cambridge was the spiritually poisonous Deism. Oxford continued in its traditional orthodoxy and in its accent on the church fathers, always a key part of the Anglican *via media*. However, Oxford was by no means a center of spiritual revival. Rather, it manifested a complacent orthodoxy. Like the rest of the Church of England, the faculty and students disdained passion or "enthusiasm" in religion.

As a serious and conscientious student, John Wesley completed his B.A. degree in 1724 with honors and decided to follow his father into a clerical career. Unlike William Grimshaw, who chose the priesthood for its secure livelihood, John had dedicated considerable prayer to this step and felt a call to Anglican orders.

As he labored towards his M.A. degree, he deepened his studies in the church fathers. At the same time he paid attention to the heritage of Anglican divinity, including the Puritan writers of the previous century. By 1725 he received his M.A. from Oxford but continued to study for his ordination into the priesthood. On the eve of ordination his mother, who had advised him on spiritual matters all the while, wrote: "I would heartily wish you would now enter upon a strict examination of yourself, that you may know whether you have a reasonable hope of salvation by Jesus Christ."[3] In this quote we can detect that the Wesley family understanding of salvation was closer to the Catholic understanding than to the Reformed. That is, a Christian needed to contend for his or her salvation continuously in "fear and trembling" (Phil. 2:12) and never be assured of one's spiritual destiny.

Wesley's diligent scholarship bore fruit in 1726 when he was elected by the faculty as "fellow" (instructor) at Lincoln College, another college within Oxford. This was a secure position that gave him a modest but steady income. It also gave him the right to preach in any church in the king of England's dominion, a privilege that later would be important. As fellow, Wesley lectured on Greek, logic, and philosophy. Receiving ordination to the priesthood in 1728, John took a leave from Oxford to help his elderly father as assistant rector at Epworth.

In the meantime, Charles Wesley, five years younger than John, arrived at Christ Church to begin his undergraduate studies. He and three other students banded together for mutual encouragement and met three or four evenings per week to study together, read the Greek New Testament, and pray.

In 1729 John Wesley was recalled to Oxford as tutor. John visited his brother's evening fellowship and found it delightful. He quickly became its leader and acted as spiritual director for the group. In 1730 William Morgan, one of the original founding students, started visiting the sick and the imprisoned at the local jail, and the Wesley brothers adopted this as their ministry also. Others joined the group, and they began going to holy communion weekly at the university chapel, a practice most unusual for the time. All this aroused suspicion, as their piety seemed to smack of enthusiasm and perhaps renewed Puritanism. Morgan wrote to his father:

> Almost as soon as we made our first attempts this way, some of the men of wit in [the College of] Christ Church ... between mirth and anger, made pretty many reflections upon the Sacramentarians,

as they were pleased to call us. Soon after, their allies ... changed our title, and did us the honor of styling us The Holy Club.[4]

"The Holy Club" became increasingly intense in its spiritual focus. John Wesley shepherded the group in the "means of grace," including prayer, mutual confession, sharing of spiritual trials and experiences, fasting, frugal living, and frequent communion. Membership was never large, averaging about fifteen and reaching a high of twenty-seven, and included a few nonstudents from the town of Oxford.

THE HOLY CLUB AS SCHOOLHOUSE
OF CHRISTIAN SPIRITUALITY

John Wesley directed the members of the Holy Club towards a study of the classics of Christian spirituality, including the Catholic mystics. John Wesley's favorite was Thomas à Kempis's famous work, *The Imitation of Christ*, but the readings in the Holy Club included many others, ancient and modern, including the writings of the contemporary Anglican nonjuror William Law.

John Wesley's attitude towards Christian mysticism was ambiguous. He admired the fact that this tradition produced individuals who manifested heroic charity and purity of life. Yet there were certain unscriptural aspects of this spirituality, as the Reformers had noted. Wesley found extreme penitential asceticism, such as the self-flagellation practiced by some monks, suspect; he also had reservations about the tradition of the solitary monk living a life of prayer away from any and all social intercourse. Once he commented, "The gospel of Christ knows of no religion but social; no holiness but social holiness."[5]

John studied the stages of spiritual development as codified by the Spanish mystic St. John of the Cross. These stages consisted in (1) awakening (when the person feels a desire to follow the gospel); (2) purgation (when through the spiritual disciplines of prayer, fasting, confession, etc., the grip of sin is broken); (3) illumination (when the seeker receives a special grace of understanding Scripture and discerning spiritual realities); (4) the "dark night of the soul" (a special period of testing when prayer is "dry" and the felt presence of God disappears); and finally (5) perfection (when the person, filled with grace, can live in continuous prayer and be free of sin).

While many in the Reformed and evangelical tradition have viewed the attainment of this type of perfection as impossible and a mystical delusion, Wesley saw much of this Christian mystical literature as a valid description of the road to holiness, though he also came to understand the danger in viewing these stages as a form of "works righteousness" rather than signs of God's increasing grace. Specifically, Wesley believed the "dark night of the soul" was an unnecessary and unbiblical stage, a deceptive form of the works-righteousness error of Catholic theology.[6]

Into this discussion came John Clayton, who joined the Holy Club in 1732. His specialty was the Eastern church fathers. Under his direction, John Wesley and others in the club were guided to a study of the writings of such early devout Christians as Macarius of Egypt. Unknowingly, the writings attributed to Macarius were dependent on Gregory of Nyssa (c. 337–394), the greatest of the Eastern fathers.[7] The Macarius-Nyssa theology stressed perfection as the goal of the Christian life but had a more biblical understanding of perfection than later Catholic mystics. For Gregory, perfection was a continuous process in which the Christian proceeded from "glory to glory" (2 Cor. 3:18) in an endless grace-empowered increase of love. Gregory's theology was also less extreme in its asceticism than later Western Catholic theology. In fact, Gregory was a married man.[8]

Members of the Holy Club experimented with various forms of the spiritual disciplines. Among them was a young man named George Whitefield, who came from an impoverished middle-class family. He was at Oxford as "servitor," a student scholarshiped to the university in exchange for being a personal servant to a wealthy student. Whitefield took the spiritual disciplines more seriously than others, wearing only old, threadbare clothing and fasting to the point of thinness and weakness. He was called the "odd fellow" by the other Oxford students. The issue of fasting became a matter of great controversy as one of the club's members, William Megan, became sick and died. Although he suspended fasting a year before he died, the rumors were ruthless that the Holy Club had caused his death.

A hostile reporter of the period wrote of the Holy Club:

> They imagine they cannot be saved if they do not spend every hour, nay minute, of their lives in service of God. And to that end they read prayers every day in the common jail, preach every Sunday, and administer the sacrament once every month. They almost starve themselves to be able to relieve the poor and buy books for their conversion.... They fast two days a week, which has emaciated them to that degree that they are fearful of sight.... They rise every day at five of the clock, and till prayers, which begin at eight, they sing psalms, and read some divinity. They meet at each other's rooms at six of the clock five nights in the week, and from seven to nine read a piece of some religious book.[9]

It was for the Holy Club that John Wesley developed his sermon "Duty of Constant Communion." It was researched in response to questions from its members as to the position of the early church on the frequency of communion. Wesley was led by the evidence to believe that the early Christians received communion *every* time they gathered for worship, and he urged the Holy Club to imitate them with communion once a week. Years later (1788), while he was reviewing his sermons for publication, he added these words as a preface:

> The following discourse was written above five-and-fifty years ago, for the use of my pupils at Oxford. I have added very little, but retrenched much.... But, I thank God, I have not yet seen cause to alter my sentiments in any point which is therein delivered.[10]

AMERICAN ADVENTURE

John Wesley believed he was called to be a missionary to the Indians, and in 1736, he, Charles, and several others from the Holy Club went off to the recently founded colony of Georgia. They hoped that such heroic measures would help "save their souls." In spite of Governor Ogelthroup's best intentions, the spiritual state of the colony was like a nominal parish in England, namely, dreadful. Charles, hurriedly ordained in preparation for the American journey, began a parish ministry at the village at Fort Federica. He became mired with local controversies and, discouraged and ill with dysentery, returned to England. John stayed in Savannah, but he soon discovered he had no gift in evangelizing the Indians, and they had little interest in hearing the gospel.

The most significant event of John and Charles Wesley's American adventure, however, took place not in Georgia but on the high seas, on their way to America. On board ship, the Wesley brothers noticed a group of German Moravians. They displayed unusual Christian virtue and meekness even under ridicule and abuse. They cared for others and did much of the ship's dirty work, as in attending to the sick. The ship ran into violent weather, but in the midst of the storm John Wesley saw that the hymn-singing Moravians kept a perfect calm and joy:

> Here was now an opportunity of trying whether they were delivered from the spirit of fear, as well as from that of pride, anger and revenge. In the midst of the Psalm wherewith their service began, the sea broke over, split the mainsail in pieces, covered the ship and poured in between the decks, as if the great deep had already swallowed us up. A terrible screaming began among the English. The Germans calmly sung on.[11]

The ship did not go down. John Wesley sought the Moravians out and discovered that the source of their peace was their sincere faith, and specifically their experience of assurance. That is, they had experienced a grace by which they came to a deep, unshakable understanding that the atoning blood of Jesus was theirs forever. This experiential understanding of being a true, born-again Christian gave them fearlessness in face of death and a great boldness in witnessing. While in Georgia John Wesley kept in contact with the Moravians, who had settled close to Savannah. Witnessing their "love feasts" and an ordination service, John wrote of the ordination service:

> The great simplicity, as well as solemnity of the whole, almost made me forget the seventeen hundred years between, and imag-

ine myself in one of those assemblies where form and state were not, but Paul the tent-maker or Peter the fisherman presided, yet with the demonstrations of Spirit and power.[12]

GEORGIAN PARISH

In Georgia John was both a meticulous Anglican pastor and a bold innovator. He knew he was in a missionary situation, where he had to go beyond the accepted norms of the Church of England. He modeled his ministry after the Epworth parish and what he learned from the Holy Club. A Lutheran pastor from the period observed: "He performs the duties of Christianity very earnestly, and visits his people industriously, and is well received by same."[13]

John founded a prayer society, but added hymn singing and extemporaneous prayers to its customary activities (both of which he had learned from the Moravians).[14] He raised up several women to do sick-bed visitations. These women he called "deaconesses," although they were not ordained (something far beyond accepted Anglican practice at the time).[15]

Within a year of his arrival he had dramatically increased church attendance, and morals of the colony were greatly improved. In fact, a revival had started among the young people of Savannah. In words reminiscent of Jonathan Edwards's description of the youth revival in Northampton, Wesley recorded:

> We observed the Spirit of God to move upon the minds of many children. They began more carefully to attend the things that were spoken both at home and at church, and a remarkable seriousness appeared in their whole behavior and conversations.[16]

Yet before his second year in Georgia ended, John Wesley was on a ship fleeing the colony. This was the result of his own social and romantic clumsiness. He fell in love with a charming eighteen-year-old, Sophia Hopkey, but he had difficulty expressing his emotions. When he finally proposed marriage, the young woman was being courted by another, more articulate suitor, and she rejected Wesley's proposal. In a neurotic response, the spurned Wesley refused Sophia

Holy Communion. This was a public declaration of a person's unworthiness to receive the sacrament. Her family was rightfully outraged and brought a legal suit that Wesley avoided by leaving the colony.[17]

Many of Wesley's biographers claim that his Georgia mission was a failure, but they miss one important point. It succeeded in bringing renewal to the spiritual life of the colony and created a devout, sacramental congregation in Savannah. It may not have been a full-blown revival of the type manifested later in Bristol, but the active presence of the Spirit could be discerned in the growing church community. It was this Savannah congregation that served as the home base for George Whitefield's later successful colonial tours.[18]

On the long voyage back to England (1738), John took the time to translate Moravian hymns from German into English. When he returned to the London area, he did "supply" preaching there and at Oxford. One preaching invitation was particularly fruitful in an unexpected way. On his way from London to Oxford, he read Jonathan Edwards's seminal work on revival,[19] *A Faithful Narrative of the Surprising Work of God* (published 1737). In that work Edwards described the progress of revival at his congregation in Northampton, including the description of the strange "exercises," such as the fallings, howlings, and other physical manifestations that gripped many in his congregation. This prepared Wesley for what would happen in his own ministry.

THE FETTER LANE SOCIETY

Back in London, John Wesley cultivated new Moravian contacts. He, his brother Charles, and a Moravian missionary named Peter Bohler founded a joint Anglican-Moravian society, named after its address, Fetter Lane (May 1738). The Wesley brothers attracted a devout following, which continued the quest of the previous Holy Club at Oxford, but with some Moravian innovations, such as the rite of the love feast. John spent part of 1738 visiting the Moravian community in their main center at Herrnhut, Germany.

John Wesley came back with mixed feelings about what he saw. He was impressed by their devout lifestyle, which included prayer night-watches, concentrated Christian education for all children, and the rite of the love feast. Also, he observed the Moravian small-group fellowships, called "bands." These bands were segregated according to sex and age, which facilitated mutual confession and correction without undo embarrassment. Nevertheless, Wesley was wary of the adulation that the Moravians gave Count Zinzendorf, founder of the denomination, and sensed a spirit of religious pride, elitism, and secrecy in the community.[20]

Back at the Fetter Lane Society, Wesley and the others celebrated their own Moravian-style love feasts. The love feast was an attempt to re-create the celebration mentioned in Jude 12 and 1 Corinthians 11:33.[21] Current research on the matter indicates that the original Lord's Supper included two components, the "giving thanks to God" (from which the term *Eucharist* is derived) and a full meal, the *Agape* meal ("love feast"). By the time Paul was writing to the Corinthian church, some separation was developing between these two elements, and thereafter all segments of the church adopted the division, with the Eucharist gaining increasing prominence and the Agape losing its importance until being completely phased out by the eighth century.[22] Thus, in a sense, the love feast may be considered a forgotten half of the Lord's Supper, though a lesser half.

The Moravian rite was a meal of biscuit and water (to distinguish it from the Lord's Supper), followed by a witness session of God's grace and work among themselves. During one that took place in January 1739, Wesley recounts:

> About three in the morning, as we were continuing insistent in prayer, the Power of God came mightily upon us, insomuch that many cried out for exceeding joy, and many fell to the ground. As soon as we were recovered a little from that awe and amazement at the presence of his majesty, we broke out with one voice, "We praise thee, O God, we acknowledge thee to be the Lord."[23]

ALDERSGATE EXPERIENCE

After his return to London and the Fetter Lane Society, John had his famous Aldersgate experience (May 1738). On this occasion Wesley visited another prayer society, and Martin Luther's preface to his commentary on the Epistle of Romans just happened to be read. Wesley felt his heart "strangely warmed" by the reading. He experienced a profound assurance of God's mercy and forgiveness through Jesus Christ. He too now had experienced what the Moravians held as foundational to the Christian life.[24] He understood at a deep level that his salvation was not dependent on his constant attempts to please God, but that he was once and for all accepted.

But not all went well at Fetter Lane. Philip Henry Molther, another Moravian missionary, arrived and began propagating the doctrine of "stillness," that is, being mentally still in worship before the Lord. This has always had a place in Christian prayer as a way of listening to God's voice. However, Molther was preaching an extreme form (later rejected by the Moravians themselves) that implied total passivity on the part of the believer. Through stillness the believer was supposed to receive the experience of assurance of God's forgiveness and his or her position as a child of God. Any impatience or actions not directed by an inner voice during the stillness was considered as "striving" (works) and weak faith.

Molther went on to assert that the sacraments, church attendance, and Bible reading as normal Christian activities were unnecessary, even a hindrance to stillness. Moreover, the "ordinances [sacraments] are not means of grace, there being no other means than Christ!"[25] Echoing earlier New England doctrine, he asserted that the sacrament of the Lord's Supper should not be received until the individual Christian experienced unquestionable "full assurance." Thereupon several devout believers withdrew from Holy Communion out of doubts as to whether they had indeed received this full assurance.

As a person who had practiced and encouraged sacramental worship all his life, John Wesley found this teaching strange. Both brothers began to notice how subtly destructive these doctrines were to the spiritual life of some — some of those who experienced full assurance developed spiritual pride. The Wesleys found inspiration in a woman of great faith who resisted the current trends at Fetter Lane and who had herself come to a deeper sense of faith at the communion rail. The lady told John Wesley:

I know the life which I now live, I live by faith in the Son of God, who loved me, and gave Himself for me; and He has never left me one moment, since the hour He was made known to me in the breaking of bread.[26]

The Wesleys were suspicious of the stillness doctrine and its anti-sacramental implications. They saw the possibility of the Moravians becoming an *antinomian,* Quaker-like sect, where faith is divorced from action and normal duties.[27] But John Wesley, now heavily involved in the Bristol revival (see below), delayed taking definitive action at Fetter Lane as he carefully considered the situation and consulted with his brother. Yet as he went back and forth from Bristol to Fetter Lane, the spiritual climate of the society steadily declined into a state of paranoia and accusation as to who had full assurance. The doctrine was manifesting its fruit.

The Moravian party at Fetter Lane continued to descend into the type of antinomianism that Luther, with his biting satire, had railed against two centuries earlier:

> But it is no use — we are so secure, without fear and concern; the devil is far from us, and we have none of the flesh in us that was in St. Paul and of which he complains in Romans 7. . . . No, we are heroes who need not worry about our flesh and our thoughts. We are sheer spirit, we have taken captive our own flesh together with the devil, so that all our thoughts and ideas are surely and certainly inspired by the Holy Spirit, and how can he be found wanting? Therefore it all has such a nice ending — namely, that both steed and rider break their necks.[28]

In the meantime, John Wesley's experience with the revival converts in Bristol showed him that the Christian means of grace such as prayer, Bible study, small-group fellowship, and receiving the Lord's Supper were important in moving a person under conviction toward full conversion, and ultimately assurance (see below).[29]

Finally, in July 1740, after several confrontations with the Moravian leadership, the Wesley brothers withdrew from Fetter Lane. They had attempted to reason with the leaders and preached to the group about the duties of church attendance and sacramental observance. Of the sixty or so members of that society, only nineteen went with the Wesley brothers. They relocated to an old foundry in London, which became the headquarters of Methodism in the following years. John Wesley's sermon "The Means of Grace"[30] was composed specifically as an antistillness teaching. It was a sermon preached many times in the following years, as the stillness issue lingered in Moravian and other circles for some time. Charles paralleled John's sermon with several hymns that defended the means of grace from stillness suspicions. In one he wrote:

> Why did my dying Lord ordain
>   This dear memorial of His love?
> Might we not all by faith obtain,
>   By faith the mountain of sin remove,
> Enjoy the sense of sins forgiven,
>   And holiness, the taste of heaven?
>
> It seem'd to my Redeemer good
>   That faith should here His coming wait,
> Should here receive immortal food,
>   Grow up in Him Divinely great,
> And fill'd with holy violence, seize
>   The glorious crown of righteousness.
>
> Savior, Thou didst the mystery give,
>   That I Thy nature might partake;
> Thou bidd'st me outward signs receive,
>   One with Thyself my soul to make;
> My body, soul, and spirit join
>   Inseparably one with Thine.
>
> The prayer, the fast, the word conveys,
>   When mix'd with faith, Thy life to me;
> In all the channels of Thy grace
>   I still have fellowship with Thee:
> But chiefly here my soul is fed,
>   With fullness of immortal bread.[31]

The Wesleys' withdrawal from the Fetter Lane Society was a defining moment of Methodism. Through their contact with the Moravians, they were challenged to evaluate and ultimately affirm the biblical truth (and Reformed doctrine) that the only basis of the Christian life was trust in the atonement of Christ through grace alone. Both brothers also experienced the joy of personal assurance.

However, after their personal experiences of assurance, the Wesleys had to deal with the fruits of the exaggerations of this biblical truth by way of Molther's stillness-antinomian doctrine. The Wesleys' practical resolution of the classic dilemma between faith and works was a brilliant synthesis that is clearly biblical, but often not held in sharp focus. A person *comes* into a saving relationship with God "by grace alone," yet *proceeds* in the life of discipleship through the "means of grace." Both stages are *grace*-based. This biblical balance can be disrupted easily, either by stressing works and moral law as the basis of salvation or disdaining the means of grace after initial entry into the kingdom. The Wesley brothers, having worked through this understanding, were now in an ideal position to forge a movement that reflected their balanced insight — and sorrowful experience at Fetter Lane.

Circumstances now in motion propelled the Wesley brothers into the midst of revival. Ironically, the key leaders of the revival that broke out in the 1730s and 1740s did not come out of the Dissenting churches, which prayed for it. Rather, it came from within the Anglican church itself, the most self-satisfied denomination in Great Britain![32]

After Aldersgate, John found new power and freedom in his sermons. Providentially, he was forced one Sunday to preach without notes or preparation (a radical and unusual mode at the time). To his amazement he did quite well and in fact had a strong anointing on his message. John Wesley's schedule was filled with preaching engagements in churches, private societies, private enterprises, and prisons in the London area. Revival was breaking out wherever he preached. He wrote to Zinzendorf: "The word of the Lord runs and is glorified. . . . Great multitudes are everywhere awakened and cry out."[33] Even at this stage some revival phenomena were occurring during Wesley's preaching, such as instant conversions, visions, and healings.[34] Even greater revival was occurring in Bristol.

NOTES

1. Northwest Nazarene College has developed a *terrific* Wesleyan website —
   "The Wesley Center for Applied Theology" — at http://wesley.nnu.edu/.
   This contains *all* of John Wesley's sermons and many other Wesleyan
   documents, also back issues of the *Wesleyan Theological Journal*, one of
   the finest academic and biblically orthodox journals of Christendom, and
   many other items.
2. Cited in Robert Tuttle Jr., *John Wesley: His Life and Theology* (Grand
   Rapids: Francis Asbury, 1978), 44–45.
3. V. H. H. Green, *The Young Mr. Wesley: A Study of John Wesley and
   Oxford* (New York: St. Martin's, 1961), 67.
4. Ibid., 160.
5. Frank Baker, *John Wesley and the Church of England* (Nashville: Abingdon, 1970), 29.
6. On Wesley's view of mysticism, see the recent book by Robert G. Tuttle Jr., *Mysticism in the Wesleyan Tradition* (Grand Rapids: Francis
   Asbury, 1989).
7. Major John G. Merritt, "'Dialogue' Within a Tradition: John Wesley
   and Gregory of Nyssa Discuss Christian Perfection," *Wesleyan Theological Journal* 22 (Fall 1987): 92–94.
8. There is a website dedicated just to Gregory of Nyssa and his writings:
   http://www.bhsu.edu/artssciences/asfaculty/dsalomon/nyssa/home.html.
9. Green, *Young Mr. Wesley*, 168.
10. "Duty of Constant Communion," Sermon #101.
11. JWJ, Jan. 25, 1736.
12. JWJ, Sept. 28, 1738.
13. Baker, *John Wesley*, 43.
14. Henry D. Rack, "Religious Societies and the Origins of Methodism,"
    Journal of Ecclesiastical History 38 (October 1987): 583.
15. Baker, *John Wesley*, 355 n. 41.
16. JWJ, May 29, 1737; see also *Letters*, 1:222.
17. Romantic incompetence was part of the legacy of the Holy Club.
    Whitefield had similar problems. It stems from an ascetic theology of
    sexuality and love taught at the Holy Club. They believed that roman-
    tic love was idolatrous and had no place in the true Christian life. See
    Harry S. Stout, *The Divine Dramatist: George Whitefield and the Rise
    of Modern Evangelicalism* (Grand Rapids: Eerdmans, 1991).

18. Charles H. Goodwin, "John Wesley: Revival and Revivalism, 1736–1768," *Wesleyan Theological Journal* 31 (Spring 1996): 172–78.

19. He would also read prodigiously while on horseback, pointing the horse on its way and letting the reins slack.

20. Richard Steele, "John Wesley's Synthesis of the Revival Practices of Jonathan Edwards, George Whitefield and Nicholas Zinzendorf," *Wesleyan Theological Journal* 30 (Spring 1995): 164.

21. For a brief and lucid presentation of the history of the love feast in Christian worship, see Paul Miller "Let Us Break Bread Together," *Touchstone* 8 (September 1990): 29–33. This article includes suggestions for a present-day liturgy of the love feast.

22. For an excellent review of modern biblical research on the New Testament church's practice of the Lord's Supper, see John L. Boyle, "Practice of the Eucharist in the New Testament," *Worship* 44 (May 1970): 289–91, and Myles M. Bourke, "New Testament and the State of the Liturgy," *Worship* 44 (March 1970): 130–42.

23. *JWJ*, Jan. 1, 1739.

24. Henry D. Rack, in his exhaustively researched biography of John Wesley, *Reasonable Enthusiast: John Wesley and the Rise of Methodism*, 2d ed. (London: Epworth, 1992), insists that Wesley's Aldersgate experience was not as profound a severance of his spirituality and theology as is often pictured. Earlier historians have pictured a radical dichotomy between Wesley the "Catholic" before Aldersgate, and Wesley the "Evangelical" after his experience. In fact, Wesley remained sacramentalist all his life, though he later dropped a few high-church doctrines (see, e.g., pp. 145–55). See also my discussion in ch. 11.

25. *JWJ*, Nov. 4, 1739. It is not unusual for Christians who view experience as superior to Scripture to discard sacramental spirituality. It happened to the Quakers and to some early Pentecostals. See Charles Edwin Jones, "Antiordinance: A Proto-Pentecostal Phenomenon?" *Wesleyan Theological Journal* 25 (Fall 1990): xxx.

26. *JWJ*, Nov. 10, 1739.

27. The strong part that fear of antinomianism played in John Wesley's theology is well documented in the excellent study by W. Stephen Gunter, *The Limits of "Love Divine": John Wesley's Response to Antinomianism and Enthusiasm* (Nashville: Kingswood, 1989).

28. Martin Luther, *Against the Antinomians*, in *Luther's Works*, vol. 47, *The Christian in Society*, ed. Franklin Sherman (Philadelphia: Fortress, 1971), 119.

29. For John Wesley's understanding of the means of grace, see his Sermon #16, "The Means of Grace," which was written specifically to counter the "stillness" doctrine at Fetter Lane.

30. Sermon #16.

31. Eucharistic Hymn 65, cited in John R. Tyson, ed., *Charles Wesley: A Reader* (New York: Oxford Univ. Press, 1989), 279–80. Tyson's anthology and introductory notes do a masterful job in locating Charles Wesley's role in the Wesleyan revival. See also Jim Townsend, "The Forgotten Wesley," *Christian History* 10/3 (1991): 6–8.

32. This irony is pointed out by John Walsh in "'Methodism' and the Origins of English-Speaking Evangelicalism," in *Evangelicalism: Comparative Studies of Popular Protestantism in North America, the British Isles, and Beyond, 1700–1990,* ed. Mark A. Noll, David W. Bebbington, and George A. Rawlyk (New York: Oxford Univ. Press, 1994), 20–37. George Whitefield became one of the greatest preachers of all time, John Wesley probably the greatest church organizer of all time, and Charles Wesley probably the greatest hymn writer of all time. All three were Anglican priests who never left their denomination. The concept that the Holy Spirit delights to surprise the church with ironic and unexpected events is elucidated in the masterful work by Peter Hocken, *The Glory and the Shame* (Guildford, Eng.: Eagle, 1994).

33. Cited in Goodwin, "John Wesley: Revival and Revivalism," 179.

34. Ibid., 180.

THE WESLEY BROTHERS'
ACCIDENTAL REVIVAL

10

THE CALL FROM WHITEFIELD[1]

In March 1739 George Whitefield wrote his former mentor from the Holy Club, John Wesley, describing the exciting revival that was occurring in Bristol. The crowds at his meetings were running as high as twenty thousand. However, since he had other commitments and had to leave soon, he wondered whether Wesley would come to Bristol and continue the preaching.

Wesley was reluctant to go, as he knew that open-field, itinerant preaching as Whitefield was doing was against canon law and offensive to many in the Anglican church. Furthermore, there was the practical matter that the revival had begun among the unchurched coal miners of Bristol, the most lawless and dangerous area of England — something like the south Bronx. Charles Wesley advised against going, seeing that the probability of death by mugging was high. The Wesleys and the members of Fetter Lane prayed over the matter and finally drew lots to settle the question (another Moravian practice, in imitation of Acts 1:26). The oracle said "go."

John therefore went, reaching Bristol on Saturday, March 31, 1739, and watched Whitefield preach out of doors the following day:

> I could scarce reconcile myself at first to this strange way of preaching in the fields, of which he set me an example on Sunday; having been all my life (till very lately) so tenacious of every point relating to decency and order, that I should have thought the saving of souls almost sin if it had not been done in a church.[2]

Whitefield left on April 2, and the same day Wesley preached his first outdoor sermon to a crowd of three hundred. He was astonished at his effectiveness and soon was preaching to much larger crowds. His core messages were that nominal Christianity was not enough and that every person needed to be "born again" through repentance and trust in Jesus Christ for salvation.[3]

THE "EXERCISES" IN THE WESLEYAN REVIVAL

As John Wesley preached in the following days and weeks, the crowds were deeply moved, and many responded by fainting away, bursting out in desperate cries, or shaking with fear — in other words, the "exercises" that Wesley had read about in Jonathan Edwards's *Faithful Narrative*. The preaching tours of 1739 through 1741 were the most phenomena-laden of Wesley's long preaching career. Hardly a preaching meeting took place without persons in the crowd falling under some exercise. Wesley, aware of the criticisms of "enthusiasm" his preaching was drawing, was quick to note instances where the hand of God could be discerned from self-delusion or fraud:

> We understood that many were offended at the cries of those on whom the power of God came; among whom was a physician, who was much afraid there might be fraud or imposture in the case. Today one whom he had known many years was the first (while I was preaching in Newgate) who broke out "into cries and tears." He could hardly believe his own eyes and ears. He went and stood close to her, and observed every symptom, till great drops of sweat ran down her face and all her bones shook. He then knew not what to think, being clearly convinced it was not fraud nor yet any nat-

ural disorder. But when both her soul and body were healed in a moment, he acknowledged the finger of God.[4]

Toward the end of that first Bristol revival, Whitefield returned for a week of preaching with Wesley. Whitefield had major reservations about the exercises and did his best to limit outbursts in his meetings. Wesley and Whitefield talked over the issue, with Wesley affirming that the exercises were a normal part of true revival, although not to be encouraged in any way (the Jonathan Edwards position). Whitefield was unconvinced. From Wesley's *Journal*, note how the Lord educated Whitefield:

> But the next day he [Whitefield] had an opportunity of informing himself better: for no sooner had he begun (in the application of his sermon) to invite all sinners to believe in Christ, than four persons sunk down close to him, almost at the same moment. One of them lay without either sense or motion; a second trembled exceedingly; the third had strong convulsions all over his body, but made no noise, unless by groans; the fourth, equally convulsed, called upon God, with strong cries and tears. From this time I trust, we shall all suffer God to carry on His own work in the way that pleaseth Him.[5]

Some Wesleyan historians maintain that the exercises were a manifestation of an initial emotion-driven and perhaps immature stage of ministry. This is simply not true. The exercises (the fallings, screams, and even holy laughter) continued to break out all throughout Wesley's long life and in the revivals of other Methodist preachers.[6] The revival at Everton in the 1750s produced as many phenomena as his early Bristol and Newcastle meetings. Whereas Wesley's early preaching resulted in cries of anguish from unbelievers who suddenly came to conviction for their sin, in the Everton revival there was some conviction but also holy laughter, as the Spirit refreshed those who were already believers but needed a measure of heavenly joy in their life.

> ... a thin, pale girl, weeping with sorrow for herself and joy for her companion. Quickly the smiles of Heaven came likewise on her, and her praises joined with those of the other. I also then laughed

with extreme joy; so did Mr. Blackwell [the local Methodist leader] (who said it was more than he could bear); so did all who knew the Lord. . . .[7]

REVIVAL AS A "HOLY CLUB"

Nevertheless, the success of the Methodist revival was not due to its exercises, but rather to the *fruit* it bore in terms of converted and discipled Christians and ultimately a transformed society. This came about not because of sudden dramatic moments of spiritual experiences but through the graced hard work of organizing and discipling the Methodists in the "means of grace" that followed the anointed sermons. From the beginnings of his itinerant ministry at Bristol, John Wesley was the consummate church planter and mass spiritual director. Whitefield and other itinerants of the Great Awakening had gone from one town to another and allowed the local clergy to finish the work of the convert's integration into church life. Behind this was their assumption that those predestined into the Christian life would also be led to church fellowship, so that the evangelist's duty was solely to give a clear presentation of the gospel.

John Wesley held no such assumptions. His Arminian theology, which stressed the role of free will in appropriating God's grace, gave him a broader sense of the evangelist's responsibility for follow-up work. This was reinforced by his understanding of the "stages" of the Christian life, borrowed and modified from Roman Catholic spirituality. To Wesley, every Christian had to go through the stage of "awakening," but this now included an understanding of the necessity of being "born again." The Christian life then proceeded in sanctification (purgation) by way of the "means of grace," and the ultimate goal was "perfection," or a life so filled with God's grace and love that sin no longer plagued the believer.

In contrast to Whitefield and the Calvinist evangelists, John usually ended his sermons by an invitation to those who were "seriously interested in fleeing the wrath of God" to meet for further instruction. The meeting place was often the humble home or barn of a local supporter. Wesley first preached in Bristol on the second of

April 1739, and two days later, "in the evening three women agreed to meet together weekly, with the same intention as those at London — viz., to confess their faults one to another, and to pray one for another, that they may be healed."[8] In other words, the stage of "purgation" would begin. Later the same evening another band, this one of eight men, was organized.

At the follow-up band meetings Wesley gave instruction and exhortation and offered prayers. He had an eye for spotting persons of spiritual maturity and leadership potential. These he appointed as temporary leaders and further instructed them on guiding the new band. Many of the early band leaders were no more educated than the majority of his underclass listeners. Some had taken part in the earlier prayer societies and had experience in prayer and the disciplines of the spiritual life. Wesley, though educated to the highest standards of the Anglican priesthood, understood the primacy of the born-again status of the believer over formal education.

As it turned out, Wesley's ignorant "exhorters" (lay leaders) became the butt end of countless jokes, cartoons, and plays from secular and religious critics. They were, however, often superb and anointed pastors to their neighbors in the English underclass and peasantry. Like the Moravian bands, Wesley's groups were of six to twelve people of the same sex who met weekly. Among the duties delegated to the bands were visitation of the sick (which women often performed, as John had learned in Georgia) and relief to the poor.

Few of the early Methodist were of the middle or upper classes. But by heroic sacrifice, pence by pence, they were able to gather money to help those even poorer than themselves. One of Wesley's band leaders brought several bands together to make relief money more easily collected, and these became "classes." This grouping became another rung of the Methodist societies, which proved especially helpful for the teaching of basic Christian doctrine, exhortation, and hymn singing.[9]

Hymn singing served two purposes for the Methodists. As for all Christians, hymns were a form of worship, but they were equally an important means of theological education. This was especially important for the first-generation Methodists, most of whom came from the unchurched and illiterate industrial underclass or peasantry. Many had not even received the minimum catechism instruction that was the right of every person in England.

John Wesley, writing the preface to the 1780 *Hymnbook*, expressed his concern that the hymnal not be so large as to be too expensive for the Methodist societies, yet "it is large enough to contain all the important truths of our most holy religion . . . to illustrate them all, and to prove them both by Scripture and reason."[10] An example of the theological instruction given in the Wesley hymns is "Hymn 750," written by Charles. This particular hymn taught the doctrine of the Trinity and was intended to counter the growing popularity of Unitarianism:[11]

> Hail, Holy Ghost, Jehovah,
> Third in order of the Three;
> Sprung from the Father and the Word
> From all eternity!
>
> Thy Godhead brooding o'er the abyss
> Of formless waters lay;
> Spoke into order all that is,
> And darkness into day. . . .
>
> Thy power through Jesus' life displayed,
> Quite from the virgin's womb,
> Dying, his soul an offering made,
> And raised him from the tomb.
>
> God's Image, which our sins destroy,
> Thy grace restores below;
> And truth, and holiness, and joy,
> From thee their fountain flow.[12]

Although John Wesley was a superb hymn translator and did write a few original hymns, it was Charles who was the poetic genius of the family and wrote the overwhelming bulk of the Wesleyan hymns. Altogether he wrote over eight thousand hymns, some of which are only now coming to light. Charles wrote his hymns anywhere and everywhere, including while on horseback, just as his brother read and edited books. The main Wesleyan hymnal, *A Collection of Hymns, for the Use of the People Called Methodists*

(1780), became both a worship resource and theological primer of the Methodists. It also became one of the most influential hymnals of the English language.[13]

The other key element of the Methodist's beginning years was the brothers' constant itinerancy. This included both preaching and pastoral direction to the bands and classes. Charles was an itinerant until he married (1749) and settled down to parish work and hymn writing. John Wesley never ceased his itinerancy and traveled a quarter million miles on horseback, crisscrossing Great Britain in specific regional patterns known as "circuits." He was concerned principally with the development and maturation of his local leaders, but in almost cult-leader terms, he regulated the discipline and life of all the members of the Methodist societies (as he had done at the Holy Club). For example, one of his journal entries reads:

> I met with the [Norwich] society at seven, and told them in plain terms that they were the most ignorant, self-conceited, self-willed, fickle, untraceable, disorderly, disjointed society that I knew. . . . And God applied it to their hearts, so that many were profited; but I do not find that one was offended.[14]

Some societies lost half their membership after a Wesley visit because the people were not meeting Wesley's high standards of comportment! It is well to remember that this was not excommunication from a church but rather dismissal from a voluntary society within a church, where it was plain to all that the rules were obeyed or dismissal occurred.

In spite of these rigorous standards, Methodism grew at a steady rate that at the time seemed moderate, but over time, like compound interest, proved wondrously fruitful. One revival historian has observed:

> Methodism was as much a missionary movement as a revival. It was sustained and refreshed by countless sudden, almost pentecostal movements of glory and transformation as the Spirit came down at a prayer meeting or a love feast. . . . But the main cause of growth lay in patient, persistent evangelism in a myriad of dingy villages and seedy back streets. Much of the movement's success lay in quiet recruitment along networks of kinship and friendship, through little cottage meetings. . . .[15]

At the beginning John Wesley permitted his band leaders to *witness* to their own spiritual experiences but not to *preach* any biblical text, following the rule of the Anglican Church. In 1741 a band leader in London broke the rule and began preaching. John rushed back to the English capital to rebuke and silence him. Again, Susanna Wesley intervened, telling her son: "Take care what you do with respect to that young man, for he is surely called of God to preach as you are."[16] The son relented. Thus was born the greatest of the Methodist innovations, the lay preacher.

This is not to say that the Methodist preachers were all ignorant or that the ill-educated preachers and exhorters stayed that way. The Wesley brothers constantly urged them, along with all Methodists, to higher levels of Christian education. John Wesley produced for his societies a multivolume anthology of the Christian classics called *The Christian Library* — think of a *Reader's Digest* edition of the great works of Christianity. In order that his exhorters and laypersons could have access to solid biblical exegesis, he composed and published a work called *Explanatory Notes to the New Testament*. John described his work as

> not principally designed for men of learning . . . much less for men of long and deep experience in the ways and word of God [ordained ministers]. . . . But I write chiefly for plain, unlettered men, who understand only their mother tongue, and yet reverence and love the word of God.[17]

His preachers at a minimum could read and knew the Bible well, and by reading Wesley's published sermons, the Minutes of the Society (a form of catechism), and *The Christian Library* they acquired a working theology that was certainly more evangelical and orthodox than much of the philosophical theology of the universities.[18]

METHODISM AS ANGLICANISM

In the first decade of the Wesleyan revival there was no thought of separation from the Anglican Church. Wesley intended Methodism to be a "society" of preachers and devout laypersons within Anglicanism as the earlier generations of prayer societies. He was careful to prohibit any band or class meeting during normal Anglican worship times. He urged his followers to attend regular Anglican services, and especially communion, as frequently as possible (see ch. 11). The sacraments were ministered only by ordained Anglican clergy.

A contemporary Methodist scholar has compared early Methodism to the Catholic charismatic renewal of the 1970s and 1980s. Charismatic Catholics attended normal Sunday worship services but met midweek for extra charismatic prayer meetings and hymn singing and went to special teaching or fellowship events. Nevertheless, they were loyal to their Catholic hierarchy and theology.[19]

This analogy is good for the first decade of Methodism, though it suffers from some limitations. Unlike the previous generation of prayer societies within the Anglican Church, Methodists allowed non-Anglicans into fellowship. Many Dissenters found renewal within Methodist societies, so that loyalty to the Anglican Church was never as steady at the lower ranks of Methodism as the Wesley brothers imagined or wanted. Within two decades there was tremendous pressure from the rank and file to separate from Anglicanism and ordain their own clergy. Many found that the reception of the sacraments from immoral or Deist clergy offensive. The brothers, however, held to the historic theological position that the grace of a sacrament did not depend on the spiritual status of the minister.

During the several crises about staying or separating from the Church of England, it was Charles who steadfastly insisted on remaining within the Anglican Church. John was more open to separation after the 1770s. He resisted ordaining his preachers to enable them to administer the sacraments until he was forced to do so for the newly independent United States (1784). Even then no formal break took place between the Methodist societies and the Anglican Church until after both brothers had died.

PERFECTIONISM AS UNIVERSAL CHRISTIAN GOAL

The Wesley brothers were enveloped by controversy in all the years of their ministry. Part of this was due to the fact that they were at core

Arminian in their belief whereas the majority of orthodox Protestants of their generation were of the Calvinist persuasion. This divide not only separated the parties on the issue of predestination and free will, but it also affected the doctrine of Christian perfectionism.

As we have seen, the theology of perfectionism developed in the early church by church fathers such as Gregory of Nyssa and was elaborated in Catholic mystical theology. Martin Luther was suspicious of Christian mysticism and was especially opposed to the concept of perfectionism.[20] He believed that Christians were fated to remain under the dominion of some sin during their life on earth (cf. his interpretation of Rom. 7). Calvin was more optimistic as to the possibility of achieving a sanctified life, but in general later Reformed theologians drifted toward the Lutheran position.

Thus when the Wesley brothers began preaching, they included the notions that salvation was available to all (contrary to the Calvinist doctrine of double predestination) and that every Christian had a possibility of becoming a fully sanctified person. This raised a maelstrom of opposition. Their colleague George Whitefield became their chief theological opponent on these issues. Whitefield had realized the futility of his earlier ascetic extremism and became a staunch Calvinist. Until his death in 1770 Whitefield and the Wesley brothers maintained a public and private debate on these issues, which is a model of Christian discourse.[21] Both parties held their opinions strongly and believed that the other side was in *serious* error. Still, their relationship was of Christian love and reconciliation. In fact, Whitefield, who knew he was in poor health, requested that John Wesley preach his funeral, and Wesley did so in a gracious sermon.[22] After Whitefield's death (1770) the theological controversies between the Calvinists and Wesleyans became more acrimonious and were never resolved.

John Wesley had formulated his idea of Christian perfectionism, or as he called it "perfect love," during his controversy with the Moravians. By November 1739 he had written the first draft of his sermon "Christian Perfection."[23] Wesley believed that the grace of "perfect love" occurred when habitual sin was overcome and every temptation parried. Like Gregory of Nyssa, he believed that "how much soever any man hath attained, or in how high a degree soever he is perfect, he hath still need to 'grow in grace,' and daily advance in the knowledge and love of God his Savior."[24]

Wesley's doctrine of perfection had enormous pastoral repercussions. It elevated the standard of holiness for the dedicated Christian layperson to that which was formerly reserved for cloistered monks and nuns. The miner, the grocer, the blacksmith, and the farmer could all aim for and achieve "perfect love" by attending to one's normal civil pursuits and the normal "means of grace" of daily prayer and Bible study, midweek band meetings, and the sacraments. Regardless of its ultimate truth, the doctrine of perfectionism acted as a motivational engine for the Methodist movement. We now turn to what part the sacraments played in the path to "perfect love."

NOTES

1. In interpreting the initial Wesley revival, I am especially indebted to the relevant chapters in Ronald A. Knox's classic work *Enthusiasm: A Chapter in the History of Religion* (New York: Oxford Univ. Press, 1961); Richard Steele, "John Wesley's Synthesis of the Revival Practice of Jonathan Edwards, George Whitefield and Nicholas Zinzendorf," *Wesleyan Theological Journal* 30 (Spring 1995): 154–72; and Henry H. Knight III, *The Presence of God in the Christian Life: John Wesley and the Means of Grace* (Metuchen: Scarecrow, 1992).

2. *JWJ*, Mar. 31, 1739.

3. See especially Wesley's early sermons "The Almost Christian," #2, and "Awake, Thou That Sleepest," #3.

4. *JWJ*, May 30, 1739.

5. *JWJ*, July 7, 1739.

6. Ronald Knox in his *Enthusiasm* stresses this point in various places.

7. See *JWJ*, May 30, 1759, for a long account of revival at Everton, cited by Wesley from reliable eyewitnesses. See also *JWJ* entry for July 14, 1759, which includes another instance of uncontrolled laughter as well as a warning that some laughter may be demonic in origins.

8. *JWJ*, April 4, 1739. The reference is to being healed in spirit, i.e., salvation.

9. For a detailed account of the class meeting and its importance in the Wesleyan revival, see David Lowes Watson, *The Early Methodist Class Meeting* (Nashville: Discipleship Resources, 1985).

10. Frank Whaling, ed., *John and Charles Wesley: Selected Prayers, Hymns, Journal Notes, Sermons, Letters and Treatises* (Classics of Western Spirituality; New York: Paulist, 1981), 175. This magnificent volume is still in print; it belongs in the library of every minister of the Anglican or Methodist traditions.

11. Barry E. Bryant, "Trinity and Hymnody: The Doctrine of the Trinity in the Hymns of Charles Wesley," *Wesleyan Theological Journal* 25 (Fall 1990): 64–73.

12. [Charles Wesley and] John Wesley, *A Collection of Hymns, for the Use of the People Called Methodists* (London: Wesleyan-Methodist Book-Room, 1889).

13. Timothy Dudley-Smith, "Why Wesley Still Dominates Our Hymn Book," *Christian History* 10/3 (1991): 9–13.

14. *JWJ*, Sept. 9, 1759.

15. John Walsh, "'Methodism' and the Origins of English-Speaking Evangelicalism," in *Evangelicalism: Comparative Studies of Popular Protestantism in North America, the British Isles, and Beyond, 1700–1990*, ed. Mark A. Noll, David W. Bebbington, and George A. Rawlyk (New York: Oxford Univ. Press, 1994), 33–34.

16. Shelby Sansbury, "Susanna Wesley: Pioneer in Faith," see the website http://www.asburyfirstumc.org/links.

17. Cited in Henry H. Knight III, "John Wesley: Mentor for an Evangelical Revival," *Wesleyan Theological Journal* 32 (Spring 1997): 181–82.

18. Things have not changed much in two hundred years!

19. Howard A. Snyder, *The Divided Flame: Wesleyans and the Charismatic Renewal* (Grand Rapids: Francis Asbury, 1986). See ch. 2 (above) for my personal participation in this common pattern.

20. On Luther's ambiguous view of Christian mysticism, see Bengt R. Hoffman, *Luther and the Mystics* (Minneapolis: Augsburg, 1976).

21. On Whitefield's specific response to Wesley's sermon "Free Grace," see his open letter to Wesley, dated August 9, 1740. The full text of this response is available on the Internet at www.gty.org/~phil/wesley.htm.

22. Sermon #53, "On the Death of the Rev. Mr. George Whitefield."

23. Sermon #40, "Christian Perfection." On the dating of the events see Timothy L. Smith, "Wesley and the Second Blessing," *Wesleyan Theological Journal* 21 (Spring/Fall 1986): 137–38. On Whitefield's rebuttal to Wesley's doctrine of perfectionism see Timothy L. Smith, "George Whitefield and Wesleyan Perfectionism," *Wesleyan Theological Journal* 19 (Spring 1984): 62–85.

24. "Christian Perfection," 1.3.

The Sacramental Dimension of the Wesleyan Revival

11

Methodist Devotion to the Lord's Supper

In April 1781 John Wesley was in Manchester, and on the first Sunday of that month he ministered to the local Methodist society:

> I began reading prayers at ten o'clock. Our country friends flocked in from all sides. At the communion was such a sight as I am persuaded was never seen at Manchester before: eleven or twelve hundred communicants at once. . . .[1]

This type of large communion service, reminiscent of the Scottish holy fairs, was common to Methodism under the Wesleys, especially after the 1740s. In 1756 a young man, son of an aristocratic Swiss family, observed John Wesley minister Holy Communion to a large crowd of London Methodists. He was awed at the scene, but his analytical mind also saw the service could be improved, and he wrote Wesley a letter, part of which read:

> As the number of communicants is generally very great, the time spent in receiving is long enough for many, I am afraid, to feel their devotion languish, and their desires grow cold, for want of outward

fuel. In order to prevent this, you interrupt, from time to time, the service of the table, to put up a short prayer, or to sing a verse or two of a hymn; and I do not doubt but many have found the benefit of that method. But, as you can spare very little time, you are obliged to be satisfied with scattering those few drops, instead of a continual rain. Would not that want be easily supplied, Sir, if you were to appoint the preachers who may be present to do what you cannot possibly do yourself, to pray and sing without interruption, as at a watch night?[2]

The correspondent, John Fletcher, would go on to become an Anglican priest and John Wesley's right-hand man and designated successor. John Wesley considered Fletcher's suggestions and introduced hymn singing and organ music during the distribution of the elements, one of the many Methodist innovations that passed on to other denominations.[3] What is interesting about his letter is the picture it gives. Like Grimshaw at Haworth, Wesley was not reluctant about stopping for spontaneous prayers or hymns at the altar. Certainly the occasion was solemn, but it was also liturgically flexible.

Fletcher had refused ordination through the Swiss church (Reformed) because he could not subscribe to the rigorous Calvinist doctrine of predestination. He found in Wesley's understanding of free will precisely what was lacking in the older Reformed theology. He also shared the Wesley brothers' devotion to and love of the Eucharist. This was typical of the Methodist leadership as a whole, as shown in an incident that occurred when Fletcher was at the home of a friend, Mr. Ireland:

> We were about to take our leave when Mr. Ireland sent his footman into the yard with a bottle of red wine and some slices of bread upon a waiter, we all uncovered our heads; which he [Fletcher] had no sooner done but he handed, first the bread to each, and lifting up his eyes to heaven, pronounced these words, "the body of our Lord Jesus Christ which was given for thee, preserve the body and soul unto everlasting life." Afterwards, handling the wine, he repeated in like manner, "the blood of our Lord Jesus Christ . . . etc." A sense of the Divine presence rested upon us all, and we were melted into a flood of tears.[4]

THE WESLEYS' THEOLOGY OF THE LORD'S SUPPER

It might be argued that the original name of the Holy Club, the "Sacramentarians," was more appropriate for the early Methodist movement. Evelyn Underhill, the famous Anglican theologian of spirituality, described the early Methodist movement as essentially a Eucharistic revival.[5] That may be an overstatement, but certainly the Wesley brothers led in stressing the value of sacramental worship in both their theology and life. In the brothers' view sacraments had a primacy among the means of grace, and the Lord's Supper a primacy among the sacraments.[6] Charles wrote:

> Glory to him who freely spent
> His blood, that we might live,
> And through this choicest instrument
> Doth all his blessings give.
>
> Fasting he doth, and hearing bless,
> And prayer can much avail,
> Good vessels all to draw the grace
> Out of salvation's well.
>
> But none, like this mysterious rite
> Which dying mercy gave,
> Can draw forth all his promised might
> And all his will to save.
>
> This is the richest legacy
> Thou hast on man bestow'd:
> Here chiefly, Lord, we feed on thee,
> And drink thy precious blood.
>
> Here all thy blessings we receive,
> Here all thy gifts are given,
> To those that would in thee believe
> Pardon, and grace and heaven.[7]

So esteemed was the Lord's Supper in the Wesley brothers' spirituality that an entire book of hymns was created, *Hymns on the Lord's Supper* (1745), to give the Methodists varied and appropriate hymns for their sacramental occasions. Not well known today, these 166 hymns formed one of the greatest works of Eucharistic devotion ever produced in Christian literature. The hymns were composed by Charles, but John edited them and supervised their theological content. The relative oblivion of the *Hymns on the Lord's Supper* may be due to the fact that modern Methodists are not nearly as sacramental as their first-generation forefathers, while the Anglicans and Episcopalians have considered the Wesleys as Methodists and mentally excommunicated their writings from serious consideration.

As discussed earlier, the Wesleyan hymns served as worship and as means of education for the (mostly) ill-educated converts. The Eucharistic hymns tackled the difficult and controversial area of sacramental theology. Here the Wesleys had to tread gently yet firmly. The Anglican *via media* allowed a wide variety of Eucharistic theology, from near Roman Catholic to almost Zwinglian. At the same time sacramental worship was at a low ebb among Anglican churches, with communion offered only quarterly in most churches. This was in part a result of the fact that the Deists had reduced the sacraments to poetic but graceless events. Such a viewpoint was unacceptable to the Wesley brothers. Note how in the following hymn theological ambiguity and mystery mingle with pastoral devotion (as in the Eastern church fathers):

> O the depth of love Divine,
> Th' unfathomable grace!
> Who shall say how bread and wine
> God into Man conveys!
> *How* the bread his flesh imparts,
> *How* the wine transmits the blood,
> Fills the faithful people's hearts
> With all the life of God!
>
> Let the wisest mortal show
> How we the grace receive,
> Feeble elements bestow
> A power not theirs to give.
> Who explains the wondrous way,
> How through these the virtue came?
> These the virtue did convey,
> Yet still remain the same. . . .

Sure and real is the grace,
    The manner be unknown;
Only meet us in thy ways,
    And perfect us in one.
Let us taste the heavenly powers;
    Lord, we ask for Nothing more:
Thine to bless, 'tis only ours
    To wonder and adore.[8]

This does not mean that the Wesleys had no specific theology on the Lord's Supper. John in particular had sifted carefully the evidence from biblical sources, the writings of the church fathers, and the Reformers to come to his own synthesis. It was a Eucharistic theology close to the original position of John Calvin.[9] It affirmed a real spiritual presence while denying the Catholic doctrine of real physical presence (transubstantiation). The Wesleyan position was not altogether original, as other Anglican divines had worked out similar positions.

In fact, for the introduction to the *Hymns of the Lord's Supper*, John imported as its introduction a work written by a great Anglican scholar of a generation earlier, Daniel Brevint (d. 1695), entitled *The Christian Sacrament and Sacrifice* (1673). John was not one reluctant to write out new materials when necessary, but he found Brevint's work so satisfactory that he merely edited it down, as he had done with his *Christian Classics* series.[10] Brevint argued that the Lord's table is not just a commemoration, but a *re-presentation* of the original and *once-only* sacrifice of the cross. The Wesleys' adoption of this understanding of the Eucharist, which viewed it as *sacrifice*, brought them too close to the Catholic theology for the comfort of his more orthodox critics. Partly for this, the Wesleys were labeled as "papists" by some of their opponents.[11]

The Wesleys also understood the Lord's table to be a sacrament of the forgiveness of sins, a doctrine from the early church and definitely *not* Roman Catholic. In his early sermon "The Duty of Constant Communion" John wrote:

> The grace of God given herein [in Communion] confirms to us the pardon of our sins, by enabling us to leave them. As our bodies are strengthened by bread and wine, so are our souls by these

tokens of the body and the blood of Christ. This is food for our souls; This gives strength to perform our duty, and leads us on to perfection.[12]

As we noted in their struggle at Fetter Lane, the Wesleys discovered that the Lord's Supper could also serve as a converting sacrament, capable of moving a person from nominal faith to living, experienced faith and assurance. During the height of this struggle with the stillness faction at Fetter Lane, John Wesley preached several sermons on the Lord's table. He has fortunately recorded their outline in his *Journal*:

> In the ancient Church, every one who was baptized communicated daily. So in the Acts we read, they "all continued daily in the breaking of bread, and in prayer."
> But in latter times many have affirmed that the Lord's Supper is not a converting, but a confirming ordinance.
> And among us it has been diligently taught that none but those who are converted, who have received the Holy Ghost, who are believers in the full sense, ought to communicate.
> But experience shows the gross falsehood of that assertion that the Lord's Supper is not a converting ordinance. Ye are the witness. For many now present know, the very beginning of your conversion (perhaps, in some, the first deep conviction) was wrought at the Lord's Supper.... Our Lord commanded those very men [the Apostles] who were even unconverted, who had not yet received the Holy Ghost, who (in the full sense of the word) were not believers, to do this "in remembrance of" Him.[13]

Though similar to the theology of Solomon Stoddard (ch. 4), there is no evidence of direct influence by the elder Puritan on the Wesleys. However, it is almost certain that Wesley was aware of the earlier Puritan and Anglican writers such as William Prynne and John Humfrey, who had written about the converting power of the Lord's Supper.

The Aldersgate experience, which many evangelical historians have seen as the demarcation point between the "Catholic Wesley" and the "evangelical Wesley," was in reality no such demarcation. Aldersgate gave Wesley the experience of assurance and enriched his faith, but it also enriched his appreciation of the sacrament and motivated him to more frequent reception of the Holy Communion.[14] By the 1750s John Wesley received communion on the average of three times a week, an incredibly high figure for the times. Charles was equally devoted to the sacrament, and when he celebrated it, he was often moved to tears.[15]

Although it was the Wesley brothers who educated the Methodists to appreciate sacramental worship, it was the Methodist public who responded with, dare we say, "enthusiasm" to the sacraments. The people tasted and found the Lord good (Ps. 34:8). It was the people who walked for miles to the sacramental services and then were often vilified by the local Anglican clergy even as they received the sacramental elements.[16]

HOLY ORDERS

John Wesley began his ministry with a high-church understanding of the role of bishops and the need for apostolic succession, but he adopted a more evangelical position as time went on. He went to Georgia believing that only a priest in the apostolic succession had the right to minister the sacraments. But there he saw the power of God fill the Moravian community and their sacramental occasions. This was reinforced as he witnessed a devout Lutheran community in Georgia. All this undermined his confidence in the traditional doctrine of apostolic succession.

In 1746 John Wesley read a book by the aristocratic scholar Sir Peter Kings, *An Inquiry into the Constitution, Discipline, Unity, and Worship of the Primitive Church*. Kings argued *against* the doctrine of apostolic succession (i.e., the teaching that the powers of the priesthood are passed down by an unbroken succession of valid ordinations). He also presented the argument that there was really only one order of ordained ministry and that a bishop was really just a priest who supervised other priests. As a consequence, priests could legitimately ordain others to the priesthood.[17]

This was a radical theory for an Anglican, and Wesley held it "in reserve" until the last years of his ministry, when he was forced to ordain ministers for the newly independent American states. A similar shift from high-church sacerdotalism occurred in his theology of sacramental confession of sins. At Epworth with his father and in Georgia, he believed that a priestly absolution was necessary for forgiveness of sins, but as he observed the Moravians and saw the good that mutual confession was doing in the Methodist bands, he came to recognize the lay role in ministering the forgiveness of sins.

SACRAMENTAL INNOVATIONS: THE LOVE FEAST[18]

The Wesley brothers not only brought new depth of worship to the Lord's Supper; they also made use of several sacramental forms to enrich the spiritual lives of their societies. These included the watchnight service (a monthly prayer service lasting from about 8:00 P.M. until midnight), a covenant service of rededication, and the love feast. We have already noted that the love feast was originally part of the Lord's Supper, so that here we have a recovery rather than an innovation.[19] These informal "lesser sacraments," or more properly "less recognized" sacraments, were often combined with the Lord's Supper and sometimes united one to another. Hester Rogers, wife of one of John Wesley's preachers, described the Christmas season of the Dublin Methodists in 1788:

> The Christmas festival was a most blessed season. On Christmas morning, at four o'clock, the preaching-house was well filled, and God was truly present to bless; many were awakened, and some converted. Four were justified at the watchnight on new year's eve. Several also found pardon at the love-feast, and many witnessed a good confession; but the time of renewing of covenant exceeded all; fourteen souls were that day born of God; some at their classes, and the rest at the sweet, solemn season of the covenant.[20]

Recall here how the Wesley brothers led the Moravian love feasts at the Fetter Lane Society. From the beginning of Methodism they took this obviously anointed rite and incorporated it into their scheme of worship. The love feasts quickly became an emblem of Methodists, particularly in the United Kingdom. They also served as a graduation ceremony or confirmation rite for new members into the Methodist societies. Attendance at a love feast was carefully limited by Wesley or his circuit preachers to members in good standing only. Admittance was by tickets, initialed by the Wesleys or other circuit preachers. In this the tickets functioned as tokens to the Scottish communions.

The Moravian form of the love feast was retained. Biscuits and water were shared, and then members testified to their born-again experience, their reception of the "second blessing," or other works of God in their life. The love feast was held quarterly in each circuit and limited to about one and a half hours. They were intensely emotional and grace-filled, with revival "exercises" being common. As news leaked out about the love feasts, the enemies of Methodism used the restricted rite to broadcast their suspicions of the radical "enthusiasm" of all Methodists, or in some cases invent salacious gossip. One ditty of the times ran:

> There saints, new born, lascivious orgies hold,
> Meek lambs by day, at night no wolves so bold . . .
> Together wanton pairs promiscuous run,
> Brothers with sisters, mothers with a son:
> Fathers, perhaps with yielding daughters meet,
> And converts find their pastor's doctrines sweet. . . .[21]

What is especially significant for our study is that the Wesley brothers accepted the love feast in spite of there being no Anglican precedent for it. As always, they claimed they were doing nothing other than restoring an ancient rite, not introducing a modern innovation. In fact, the biblical warrant for the love feast is clear (see ch. 9), although its *form* of celebration is not. The love feast is mentioned in some of the earliest church documents, such as the *Didache*.[22] Of course, what could not be proven was that the Moravian-Wesleyan use of it as a witnessing event was biblical.[23] But the Wesley brothers were practical in their spirituality, and the love feast simply proved itself an effective means of grace. Several local Methodist revivals were triggered by particularly devout love feasts. The decades-long Methodist revival in Yorkshire began and was fueled by successive love feasts and is long remembered in Methodist history.[24]

SACRAMENTAL INNOVATIONS:
THE COVENANT SERVICE[25]

Another effective sacramental form implemented by the Wesleys was the covenant service. Unlike the love feast, the Wesleys never saw one before it was introduced into a Methodist service. Again, the covenant service was not a Wesleyan invention, rather a development of a previous form. In this case, the covenant service was taken from Puritan experiments originating a century earlier.

As we noted in chapter 3, Puritan theologians had great regard for the covenant relationship between God and humankind. They saw the Old Testament descriptions of covenant renewal (see ch. 13) as pertinent to Christian life. Certain Puritan writers and pastors urged Christians to write out their obligations to God in the form of legal contracts. These contracts, often phrased in elegant legal language, promised faithful conduct, attentiveness to Bible reading, suppression of personal sins, and so on. These contracts were personal; that is, every Christian, depending on his or her spiritual state, promised specific standards of action for the coming year.

This practice continued in Wesley's time among some Anglicans and Dissenters. "Mad" Grimshaw of Haworth (ch. 8) was known for writing particularly detailed covenants and suffered much anguish at his inability to keep them perfectly.[26] Puritan pastors had attempted on occasions to have their entire congregations involved in such covenants. Jonathan Edwards had attempted this in 1741 with disastrous results (see ch. 4).

John Wesley was aware and appreciative of this Puritan tradition. The classic work of this genre, edited by Richard Alleine (1611–1681), was incorporated into Wesley's *Library of Christian Classics*.[27] In 1747 John preached a sermon series (now lost) on covenants with God. They were based on examining Old Testament covenant renewals described in Deuteronomy 29, 2 Kings 23, and 2 Chronicles 15. From Wesley's *Explanatory Notes upon the Old Testament* we have an idea of the core message:

> [The covenant] would help to increase their [the people's] sense of obligation, and arm them against temptation. And by joining all together in this, they strengthened the hands of each other.[28]

In these sermons John Wesley urged as the "application" that the people give themselves entirely to God; perhaps he even urged them to write out personal covenants as the Puritans had. However, after preaching this series (1747), no further sermons on the topic were given until the summer of 1755, when he brought the issue to the attention of the London Methodists. John Wesley had recently read of how a revival was sparked in Massachusetts in 1680 by a fervent covenant service. He wanted the same renewed fervor and revival for his societies. Wesley planned and held the first Methodist covenant service in mid-August of 1755. He acquired the use of the church at Spitalfields, which was much larger than the chapel at the Methodist Foundry. The service followed a Puritan tradition, but it involved the Methodists as a *congregation* rather than encouraging individual covenants. It began with hymns and prayers.

> After I had recited the tenor of the covenant proposed, in the words of the blessed man, Richard Alleine, all the people stood up, in testimony of assent, to the number of about eighteen hundred persons. Such a night I scarce ever saw before. Surely the fruit of it shall remain for ever.[29]

Note here how a single covenant was read, and everyone affirmed it by *standing up*. This was the sacramental action, resembling the altar call as it first developed in the following century. In another innovation, Wesley ended and solemnized the covenant service with a celebration of the Lord's Supper.

Naturally Charles Wesley composed an appropriate hymn, the last part of which went:

> . . . the bond of sure and promised peace;
> Nor can I doubt its power divine,
> Since sealed with Jesus' blood it is:
> The blood I trust, that blood alone,
> And make the covenant peace mine own.
>
> But, that my faith no more may know
>   Or change, or interval, or end,
> Help me in all thy paths to go,
>   And now, as e'er, my voice attend,
> And gladden me with answers mild,
> And commune, Father, with thy child![30]

The first covenant service set the pattern for similar services throughout the United Kingdom in the following decades. The Methodist congregations were first educated on the covenant service through sermons. This was followed with a day of prayer and fasting immediately prior to the service (like the Scottish holy fairs). In spite of its initial popularity and effectiveness, the covenant service never acquired a formal liturgy or status. Apparently, the Alleine model was considered satisfactory.

In the last decades of John Wesley's life it became customary for him to celebrate the covenant service with his London Methodists in the afternoon of January 1. This was preceded by a watchnight service. After 1782 the date was changed to the first Sunday of the new year. This tradition passed into English Methodism as the sacramental form of welcoming the new year. Unfortunately the service did not become established in the United States, principally because the rite was not included in John Wesley's modification of the *Book of Common Prayer* (see below), nor was it included in his *Book of Office*. Even in England the service declined in popularity and was mostly discontinued by 1900.[31]

In developing the covenant service the Wesleys may have been onto something more important that is generally recognized. Certainly they did not claim that the covenant service was necessary for salvation[32] and perhaps never saw it as anything more than another useful means of grace. But if the entire Bible is seen as relevant to Christian life, then the covenant renewals found in the Old Testament are valid models for similar sacramental acts of the church. The Puritans understood this partially, and the Wesley brothers made this into a living, corporate sacramental form.

That such a service did not pass on to the other denominations in Christendom reflects the limitations of the consensus theology of the times, which generally devalued Old Testament practices as irrelevant for the Christian.[33] The Wesley brothers, by contrast, were sufficiently open to the Spirit to discern the eternal biblical warrant and pastoral effectiveness of this sacramental form.

PARADOX OF WESLEY SACRAMENTAL PRACTICE

The Wesleyan revival was the most sacramental revival in church history, but paradoxically it was *not a liturgical revival*. That is, unlike the Anglican Tractarians of the Victorian period, the Wesley brothers had relatively little concern for precise liturgical forms. Whereas the Tractarians had great interest in investigating the history of medieval liturgies, vestments and their symbolic meaning, and so on, none of these things seemed important to the Wesley brothers. In fact, the Wesleyan revival was one of increasing sacramental expression and decreasing liturgical concerns.

Part of the reason for their liturgical disinterest was that the brothers knew how deceitful liturgy and sacraments without faith could be. That is, much of their Deist opposition came from churchmen who were "liturgically correct" but not born again, nor even Christian in a historic sense. Rather, they enjoyed the beauty, poetry, and decency of a good Anglican service. Similarly, many Anglicans who went to church for the social benefits and liturgical beauty were scandalized when the Wesleys demonstrated that faith in Christ was a necessary *basis* of real Christianity. Wesley identified this sub-Christian form of sacramental and church practice as "formalism" and saw it as a serious danger and counterfeit to the church.[34]

> We allow, though it is a melancholy truth, that a large proportion of those who are called Christians, do to this day abuse the means of grace to the destruction of their souls. This is doubtless the case with all those who rest content in the form of godliness, without the power. Either they fondly presume they are Christians already, because they do thus and thus, — although Christ was never yet revealed in their hearts, nor the love of God shed abroad therein: — Or else they suppose they shall infallibly be so barely because they use the means.[35]

What mattered to the Wesleys in regard to the Lord's Supper was faith, even if weak or exploratory, and a desire to receive a blessing, not the particular liturgical expression of the sacrament. Note how the Methodist societies accepted the Eucharist from local Anglican churches, high or low. Also, John Wesley discerned that the Scottish

Presbyterian communion service, tokens, white linens, and so on were a valid form of communion regardless of how different it was from Anglican practice. He allowed the Scottish Methodists to commune in that tradition.

Significantly, when John Wesley was finally forced to ordain Methodist ministers for America (1784) after the Anglican bishops refused to do so, he ordained them with a simple rite of prayer and laying on of hands, not the full rite of the *Book of Common Prayer*. John Wesley also knew that the frontier situation of the American Methodists demanded simplicity in liturgy. He prepared for the American Methodists an edited and reduced version of the *Book of Common Prayer*, in which everything was simplified. Even the Sunday service was cut down to allow more time for preaching and extemporaneous prayers.[36] The Wesleys understood that liturgy was necessary to corporate worship, but its refinement did not become a major concern.[37]

In the end, the Wesley brothers wound up being *sacramental revolutionaries*. Like Luther and the Reformers, they insisted that they did nothing but reestablish "primitive Christianity," and that indeed was their goal. By being open to the leading of the Spirit and observing the good fruit of renewed worship, they resurrected and re-created two sacramental forms, the love feast and the covenant service, which had been little noticed in the historic denominations.

THE WESLEYAN REVIVAL AS *VIA MEDIA*[38]

Although not noticed at the time, the Wesley brothers presented the Anglican Church with a grand opportunity to reestablish and refresh its central ideal, the *via media*.[39] In the vision of Richard Hooker and the other founders of Anglicanism, the *via media* was the special grace of the Church of England. It was to take the best insights of Reformation theology, especially its evangelical stress on salvation by grace alone, and combine them with the spiritual disciplines and sacramental worship of the traditional church.

The Wesley brothers did exactly that, and more. They brought passion to both the evangelical and Catholic sides of the balance.

They were better evangelicals than most Protestants and, *at the same time*, better at the disciplines of the spiritual life and more loyal to sacramental worship than most Catholics.

But the Anglican clergy did not notice. Instead, they were irritated by the unusual means that this new *via media* was using. They disliked field preaching, which threatened clerical authority. They felt extemporaneous prayers a presumption and an insult to the *Book of Common Prayer*. Hymn singing was vulgar, and most of all, the Methodists were "enthusiasts." One can understand in historical terms why they took these attitudes. Yet it is the responsibility of the clergy to practice discernment of spiritual matters beyond the immediate moment. By not embracing Methodism, the Anglican Church failed in discernment at a great moment of grace and opportunity. In the Middle Ages, the Catholic Church was confronted with a similar challenge with the ministry of St. Francis and his brothers, and to its credit it managed to welcome them into the structure of the church.

The final separation of Methodism and Anglicanism after 1784 meant that both camps would fail to sustain the *via media* that the Wesley brothers offered and indeed actualized in such parishes as St. Michael's at Haworth (Grimshaw) and John Fletcher's church at Madaley. The Anglican Church did reform in the nineteenth century, partly through the influence of the Methodists and other evangelicals and partly through the Tractarian movement. But the Tractarian movement stressed renovation through the traditions and liturgy of the pre-Reformation church and ultimately lost the evangelical passion for preaching salvation by grace. It was not by accident that its most notable advocate, John Henry Newman, abandoned the *via media* altogether and passed over into Roman Catholicism.

On the other side, the Methodists, away from the Anglican Church, eventually lost the Catholic component of the *via media*. This is not to say that Methodism was in any way a failure, for the nineteenth century would see its spectacular triumph in America (see ch. 12) as well as its substantial growth and influence in the United Kingdom. But the Methodists at the end of the nineteenth century were far from what the Wesley brothers had planned or imagined. Most significant was a serious decline in sacramental worship as the Methodists began looking more and more like other Protestant groups.

This is clearly demonstrated in the history of the Primitive Methodist Church in England. This was a split-off from Methodism, one of many in the nineteenth century, and was led by pious and uneducated laypersons. It was a Methodism of the exhorters without the Wesley brothers. The Primitive Methodists developed a worship life that included love feasts, prayer meetings, and class meetings, but the Lord's Supper was celebrated only once a quarter, like other good evangelicals! They were a fine denomination that continued to minister among the poor the way the Wesleys had a century before, but their separation from Anglicanism meant there was no one in the denomination educated to the high standards of the Wesley brothers who would teach the richness of the church's sacramental understanding.[40] Although the love feast served for a while to sustain the covenant graces of the Lord's Supper, it could not carry the entire load. We will note similar tendencies in American Methodism.

NOTES

1. *JWJ*, April 1, 1781.
2. Cited in L. Tyerman, *Wesley's Designated Successor* (New York: Phillip & Hunt, 1883), 25.
3. John C. Bowmer, *The Sacrament of the Lord's Supper in Early Methodism* (London: Dacre Press, 1951), ch. 7, "The Communion Service in Early Methodism."
4. Ibid., 195.
5. Evelyn Underhill, *Worship* (New York: Harper & Brothers, 1937). For discussion of Underhill's influential sacramental theology, see Todd E. Johnson, "Pneumatological Oblation: Evelyn Underhill's Theology of the Eucharist," *Worship* 68 (July 1994): 313–32.
6. Steven T. Hoskins, "Eucharist and Eschatology in the Writings of the Wesleys," *Wesleyan Theological Journal* 29 (Spring/Fall 1994): 71. This article is magnificent for its interpretation and depth of research. Unfortunately, evangelical writers have tended to minimize the role of the

sacraments in early Methodism; on this see Bowmer, *The Sacrament of the Lord's Supper*, ix.

7. #42, *Hymns on the Lord's Supper*.

8. #57, *Hymns on the Lord's Supper*.

9. Paul S. Sanders, "Wesley's Eucharistic Faith and Practice," *Anglican Theological Review* 48 (April 1966): 165.

10. Henry Robert McAdoo, "A Theology of Eucharist: Brevint and the Wesleys," *Theology* 97 (July/August 1994): 245–56.

11. See Augustus Toplady, *Arminianism: The Road to Rome!* (1754). Available at: www.swrb.com/newslett/actualnls/RHNarmin.htm.

12. "Duty of Constant Communion," 1.3.

13. *JWJ*, Nov. 1, 1739.

14. Sanders, "Wesley's Eucharistic Faith," 159.

15. Robert A. Leaver, "Charles Wesley and Anglicanism," in *Charles Wesley: Poet and Theologian*, ed. S. T. Kimbrough Jr. (Nashville: Kingswood, 1992), 151–75.

16. On this point see Hoskins, "Eucharist and Eschatology," 70.

17. Linda M. Durbin, "The Nature of Ordination in Wesley's View of the Ministry," *Methodist History* 9 (April 1971): 3–20.

18. An excellent general article is William Parkes, "Watchnight, Covenant Service, and the Love Feast in Early British Methodism," *Wesleyan Theological Journal* 32 (Fall 1997): 35–58. The standard source on the Methodist love feasts is Frank Baker, *Methodism and the Love-Feast* (London: Epworth, 1957). A useful summary article on the origins and celebration of the love feast throughout the ages is found in Paul Miller, "Let Us Break Bread Together," *Touchstone* 8 (September 1990): 29–33.

19. See ch. 9, note 22.

20. Hester Ann Rogers, *The Experience and Spiritual Letters of Mrs. Hester Ann Rogers* (Halifax: William Milner, 1855), 141–42, cited in Parkes, "Watchnight," 35.

21. Cited in Parkes, "Watchnight," 39.

22. Now available at several websites; for example: www.ocf.org/OrthodoxPage /reading/St.Pachomius/Liturgical/didache.html. In some form the love feast continued in use in the Western church until the eighth century.

23. Dom Gregory Dix, in an influential study of the early liturgy, *The Shape of the Liturgy*, argues that the Lord's Supper and the love feast were one original Jewish-Christian sacrament, formed in imitation of the Jewish fellowship meal (*chaburah*). The *Didache*, rediscovered in the 1880s,

pictures a love feast of the second century in which people remain *silent* and *listen* to a lector reading the Scriptures while eating a full meal.

24. Parkes, "Watchnight," 43 n. 19.

25. This section is based on the following articles: Rupert E. Davies, "The History and Theology of the Methodist Covenant Service," *Theology* 64 (February 1961): 62–68, and especially Frank Baker, "The Beginnings of the Methodist Covenant Service," *The London Quarterly and Holbourn Review* 25 (1955): 214–20.

26. Frank Baker, "'Mad Grimshaw' and His Covenants with God," *The London Quarterly and Holbourn Review* 28 (1958): 211–12.

27. Richard Alleine, *Vindicie Pietatis: or, A Vindication of Godliness . . .* (London: n.p., 1664), the actual "example" covenant of this work was written by his son-in-law, Joseph Alleine.

28. Cited in Baker, "The Beginnings," 215.

29. JWJ, Aug. 11, 1755.

30. Hymn #909, *A Collection of Hymns for Use of the People Called Methodists*.

31. The new year covenant service was reintroduced by the English Methodists in the 1930s, and the rite is reprinted as an appendix in the anthology *John and Charles Wesley*.

32. Davies, "History and Theology," 62–68.

33. See our discussion of this issue in ch. 13.

34. On this see the superb work by Henry H. Knight III, *The Presence of God in the Christian Life: John Wesley and the Means of Grace* (Metuchen: Scarecrow, 1992). Fr. Mark Pearson, the theologian and chaplain of the House of Bishops of the CEC (see ch. 15), has pointed out a modern parallel. He has noted that many charismatic Episcopalians distrust sacramental worship because they see liberal, gay, "high church" bishops lead flawless liturgies while holding the Scriptures and church tradition as disposable.

35. John Wesley, "The Means of Grace," Sermon #16, 2:5.

36. Frank Baker, in his *John Wesley and the Church of England* (Nashville: Abingdon, 1970), 251, calls the Wesley's edited *Book of Common Prayer*, "low church."

37. Ibid., chs. 14–16.

38. There is surprisingly little modern literature on the *via media*. I have found two articles helpful: John K. Yost, "Hugh Latimer's Reform Program, 1529–1536, and the Intellectual Origins of the *Via Media*," *Anglican Theological Review* 53 (April 1971): 103–13; and John E.

Booty, "Hooker and Anglicanism," in *Studies in Richard Hooker: Essays Preliminary to an Edition of His Works,* ed. W. Speed Hill (Cleveland: Case Western Reserve Univ. Press, 1972), 207–40.

39. On this point see Baker, *John Wesley and the Church of England,* "Introduction," ii–viii.

40. Herbert A. Marsh, "The Cultivation of the Spiritual Life in Early Primitive Methodism," *The London Quarterly and Holbourn Review* 22 (July 1952): 180–84.

FROM CAMP MEETING

TO ALTAR CALL

12

In a visit to a typical contemporary United Methodist Church in the United States, one can easily mistake its Sunday service for a Presbyterian or Church of Christ service. The worship centers on singing and the preached Word. Holy Communion is held perhaps once a month or even less, and the love feast not at all — being little more than a story told in Sunday school history class. Professor Paul Sanders of Amherst College, a noted Methodist historian, rhetorically asks: "How does it happen, considering its Wesleyan roots, that American Methodism places so little value upon the sacraments?"[1] How and why the American branch of Methodism lost its sacramental focus and became just like other Protestant mainline denominations is a story full of unfortunate circumstances and lost opportunities.

MOMENT OF GLORY: THE ANGLICAN/METHODIST REVIVAL IN VIRGINIA

Indeed, the desacramentalization of American Methodism could have been avoided. For several years during the colonial era Wesley's ideal of Anglican clergy cooperating with Methodist preachers and circuit riders became a reality and worked to bring revival to large sections of Virginia. It was a pattern reminiscent of what had occurred at "Mad" Grimshaw's parish in England (see ch. 8).

The hero of this colonial Anglican/Methodist revival was Devereux Jarratt (1733–1796). Jarratt was born into a working-class family that attended Anglican services dutifully but manifested little faith. As a youth he cultivated a love of horse racing and gambling common to the young men in colonial Virginia. He did, however, have an unusually accurate memory and excelled in school.

After finding and devouring a used arithmetic book, he landed a job as a math tutor at a local plantation. There the mistress of the plantation read evangelical sermons to the family. Jarratt was in earshot and came under conviction. He read further from the plantation library, including several Puritan authors, and developed a passion for spiritual writings. He taught himself Latin and Greek in order to read the Christian classics.

At this point Jarratt met "New Side" (revival) Presbyterians and under their influence taught himself classic Reformed theology. By 1760 he was preparing for Presbyterian orders, but when he examined the *Book of Common Prayer* he discovered to his surprise that it was a richly evangelical work! He returned to the Anglican fold and sailed to England for ordination into the Anglican priesthood. There he took the opportunity to listen to the revival preaching of both Wesley and Whitefield.

Back in Virginia and now a priest (1763), Jarratt took over the charge of Bath parish in Dinwiddie County (now the city of Richmond). The people expected a new round of moralistic preaching ("Masters, be kind to your slaves; slaves be obedient, etc."). Instead, this new priest proclaimed the gospel of sin, repentance, and salvation. For this he was maligned and shunned by fellow Anglican clergy as an "enthusiast" and even a "secret Methodist."

Jarratt soon gave further credence to those accusations. He developed a circuit throughout the area, preaching in homes and barns to clusters of interested believers. In 1772, Robert William, Methodist evangelist, came to Virginia and made contact with Jarratt. A warm friendship developed between the two. Jarratt determined to work the Wesleyan ideal of cooperation between Methodist preachers/ exhorters with himself as Anglican pastor. William forged the first Methodist circuit in Virginia to take advantage of Jarratt's offer. Other Methodists found the Jarratt household both a refuge and a place of friendship. An especially close relationship developed between Francis Asbury (first general superintendent of the American Methodists) and the Jarratt household.

During the 1770s Jarratt observed and participated in Methodist class meetings throughout the state. He wrote to Asbury:

> Such a work I never saw with my eyes. Sometimes twelve, some-times fifteen find the Lord at one class meeting. I am just returned from meeting two classes. Much of the power of God was in each.... Blessed be the Lord, that ever he sent you and your brethren into this part of his vineyard.[2]

By 1776 the William-Jarratt connection helped Methodist membership in Virginia reach over 1,600, a large number in view of the total population.[3] Jarratt soon was answering requests for ministry at Methodist meetings all over Virginia and South Carolina. At these meetings he celebrated the Lord's Supper, performed baptism, and even officiated at love feasts — a most un-Anglican activity! He welcomed Methodist exhorters and allowed them to preach from his pulpit (much to the offense of the other Anglican clergy). On several occasions Jarratt preached and Asbury exhorted.[4]

His own parish flowered into a sacramental/evangelical revival that paralleled Grimshaw's success.

> The sacrament of the supper had been so little regarded, in Virginia, by what were called *Church people*, that generally speaking, none went to the *table*, except a few of the more aged, perhaps seven or eight at a church.... But as soon as the people got their eyes opened to see their own wants and the necessity of a Saviour, and the nature and the design of the ordinance was shewn, and the obligation ... the number of communicants increased from time to time, so that in the year 1773, including those who constantly attended from other parishes, the number was at least nine hundred or one thousand.[5]

After the War of Independence, when the American Methodists officially separated from the Anglican Church (1784), Methodist leaders were no longer interested in cooperating with Jarratt. They could celebrate the sacraments in good conscience without his help. Jarratt was even attacked by his former allies as too "Calvinist." Also, the Methodist leaders, following John Wesley, preached against the institution of slavery and demanded that Methodists commit to the eventual manumission of their slaves. Although Jarratt was a great evangelist of the African slaves in his district, he did not believe that the Bible demanded general emancipation.

The Methodists in Virginia simply went their own way, and Jarratt ceased to be invited to Methodist functions. This turn of events broke his heart, for he had envisioned a renewed revival after the Revolution that was both sacramentally anchored with the Anglican Church and evangelically energized with Methodist exhorters.

METHODISM IN COLONIAL AMERICA: THE ACCIDENTAL DENOMINATION

Methodism itself was destined to become the predominant Protestant denomination of nineteenth-century America. Ironically, Methodism in America was not consciously cultivated by the Wesley brothers. Rather, Methodist laypeople, who sailed to the colonies out of economic motives but who loved the Methodist societies and system, established the movement. By the 1770s American converts to Methodism were serving as exhorters and preachers, but unlike England, many had never stepped into an Anglican church. For them, the Methodist midweek order of service — the dramatically preached Word and heartfelt hymns — was the only form of church service they knew.[6]

The assumption of the Wesleys that Methodists would be involved in the local Anglican church to receive sacramental ministry proved fallacious in America, where in some colonies the Anglican Church was practically nonexistent. Even in Virginia, where the Anglican Church was fully established and funded, there were no Anglican churches on the vast frontier. Where would the frontier Methodists go to receive the Lord's Supper or have their children baptized?

Some Methodist circuit riders and preachers broke church order, ordained each other, and began performing sacramental ministry without authorization. It took much of the energy of the Methodist leadership in America to keep its preachers loyal to the greater Methodist movement and suppress such irregular sacramental services. In England, the Wesley brothers lobbied hard to get an Anglican bishop to ordain their preachers for sacramental service in the colonies, but not a single one would agree. Finally, in 1784 John Wesley himself reluctantly ordained men to the American ministry.

THE LOVE FEAST AS METHODIST SACRAMENT

Thus for over two decades Methodism in America had developed into a church without the regular ministry of the dominical sacraments. This did not leave Methodists spiritually crippled, for they used other "means of grace." Preaching the evangelical gospel and joyous hymn singing became the hallmarks of their services everywhere in the new world. The love feast filled in for many of the occasions where other denominations would celebrate the Lord's Supper. The love feast was the distinguishing covenant sign for the Methodists and could be presided over by an unordained preacher without offending anyone. As the Wesley brothers had learned at Fetter Lane in London, the Lord's grace was often powerfully poured out on these love feasts. Jesse Lee, pioneer Methodist itinerant, wrote about an early Methodist meeting in Virginia that took place in 1776. This love feast, atypically, was open to non-Methodists:

> No meeting house in Virginia could hold the people. We had a large arbour in the yard, which would shade from the sun, two or three thousand people. The first day was a blessed season: but the second day was a day never to be forgotten. We held the love-feast under the arbour in the open air; the members took their seats, and other people stood all around them by hundreds. The place was truly awful, by reason of the presence of the Lord. Many of the members spake; and while some declared how the Lord had justi-

fied them freely, others declared how and when the blood of Jesus had cleansed them from all sin. So clear, so full, and so strong was their testimony, that while some were speaking their experience, hundreds were in tears, and others vehemently crying to God, for pardon and holiness.[7]

After 1784 Methodists were free to minister the dominical sacraments, but only those ordained as "elders" could do so. Not every preacher or circuit rider was an elder; thus, the earlier situation, where love feasts were easier to celebrate, often remained. Methodist Sunday services continued to be revival meetings structured around hymn singing and preaching, not a complete worship service.

In spite of the obstacles, the celebration of Lord's Supper, when offered, remained popular among the American Methodists. Up to the 1800s the sacrament was still understood as a converting ordinance. That is, Methodist "mourners" — those who had not received assurance of salvation — were welcomed to receive communion in the hope that they would receive that grace at the table. A pioneer Methodist bishop reported that in one case just such a mourner was "powerfully converted with the bread in her mouth."[8]

But circumstances were slowly robbing the Lord's Supper of this important function. The Supper was often celebrated in conjunction with the love feast. As in England, the latter was normally restricted to Methodists with signed tickets. Thus in America the Lord's Supper and love feast became associated with the "private" worship of the Methodists — those things that only full Methodists did. The Sunday service of singing and preaching was open to all. This became institutionalized, and by the 1830s communion was formally "fenced" for church members in full (converted) standing only, as in other Protestant denominations.[9]

Significantly, the Wesley brothers' *Hymns on the Lord's Supper* was never printed in America. Thus a major educational and theological source on the Lord's Supper was never as influential in America as it should have been. John Wesley prepared a specially reduced and simplified version of the *Book of Common Prayer* for the American societies, called *The Sunday Service*. Unfortunately, it was not popular with the itinerants; by steps it was reduced even further, and its remnants were incorporated into the Methodist *Book of Discipline*.[10]

Another factor in the decline of the Lord's Supper among American Methodists was the force and personality of Francis Asbury (1745–1816), the first general superintendent (bishop) of American Methodists. Asbury joined the Methodist Church in England as a boy. By the time he was eighteen, he was accepted as a local preacher. He was not university-educated and lacked grounding in the early church, which had so influenced the sacramental theology of the Wesley brothers. In 1771 he volunteered for duty in the colonies and began a tireless itinerancy that resembled that of John Wesley's. Asbury's less-than-Wesleyan understanding of the sacraments can be discerned from a letter he wrote to John Wesley in 1783, explaining the special circumstances of the Methodist societies in the colonies:

> I reverence the ordinances of God; and attend them when I have opportunity; but I clearly see they have been made the tools of division and separation for these three last centuries [Reformation period]. We have joined with us at this time those that have been Presbyterian, Dutch, and English, Lutherans, Mennonists, low Dutch, and Baptists. If we preach up the ordinances to these people . . . we shall drive them back to their old churches that have disowned them; and who will do all they can to separate them from us.[11]

Asbury's point was well taken, in that the American situation was not like that of the United Kingdom. Methodist inquirers and members could not be sent off to the Lord's Supper at a local Anglican church. Yet had Asbury had the same passion for the Lord's Supper as the Wesley brothers, some way would have been found to bring more frequent communion to the Methodists.

CAMP MEETING AND METHODIST REVIVALS

In fact, by the time Asbury wrote Wesley about the ordinances, the center of Methodist corporate worship in America had shifted away from the Lord's Supper and toward the camp meeting cycle. As we saw in Jesse Lee's account, Methodists were holding revival meetings in wooded areas and away from towns well before the Cane Ridge revival (1801).[12]

What the Cane Ridge revival did for the Methodists was to forge their love for outdoor meetings into a permanent institution. Bishop Asbury witnessed several frontier Presbyterian communion camp meetings. He ordered similar meetings for the Methodists, who had no reluctance to carry out his command. In a letter to the Baltimore Methodists, the most urban and sophisticated congregation in the United States, he explained:

> The campmeetings have been blessed in North and South Carolina, and Georgia. Hundreds have fallen and have felt the power of God. I wish most sincerely that we could have a camp-meeting at Duck Creek out in the plain south of town, and let the people come with their tents, wagons, provisions and so on. Let them keep at it night and day, during the conference, that ought to sit in the meeting.[13]

With these instructions Asbury combined the quarterly meetings that discussed policy, discipline, and administration with a revival camp meeting for the public. On the first day the leadership attended to church business while laypersons set up camp in regimented streets and avenues as well as areas for sanitation, cooking, watering the animals, and so on. The second day began with a morning love feast at 9:00 A.M. This was followed by a communion service before noon. Lunch was a long affair, which we would recognize as a "covered dish" social, lasting several hours. The afternoon was for the general public and given over to preaching, with occasional weddings and baptisms in between the preaching. In all of this we can detect the direct influence of the Scottish Presbyterian communion cycles. We should also note that the Methodist love feast spread to other denominations, especially those churches of the Restoration Movement that came out of the Cane Ridge revival.[14]

Perhaps the greatest characteristic of the camp meetings of this era was the consistency with which they produced revival.[15] They were open to unbelievers and inquirers who would come mostly for the food and "show," but more often than not they were converted by the fiery and anointed evangelistic preaching. The camp meetings helped keep revival fires burning within Methodist congregations long after it had passed elsewhere. While most historians date the end of the Second Great Awakening at about 1830, the Methodist camp meetings continued to generate local revivals for most of the nineteenth century. This was also due in part to the fact that Methodists had enthusiastically adopted a new sacramental form that arose during that era, the *altar call*, and incorporated it into their camp meetings.

THE ALTAR CALL AS THE SACRAMENT OF ARMINIAN EVANGELICALISM[16]

Exactly how and when the altar call developed is mired in historical fog, with various denominations claiming credit for it. An early form of the altar call was developed by the Methodist evangelist and elder William Penn Candler. He rode several circuits in the East Coast from the 1790s and developed a strong revivalist technique that anticipated the later ministry of Charles Finney. For instance, he organized Methodist prayer intercessors to pray for revival at coming camp meetings. By 1799 Candler was combining fiery sermons with an invitation to those who were moved with conviction "to come to the front and kneel," and there he and others could "pray for their salvation."[17] Similarly, several Baptist preachers on the frontier were urging those who attended their meeting to make an immediate commitment to the Lord.[18]

All of this was a radical change from the pattern of conversion so esteemed in the Puritan-Reformed tradition. As you may recall, the Puritans (and other Calvinists) believed that salvation was entirely dependent on God's eternal election. Thus the individual could do little more than *discern* election in his or her life. As we saw in chapter 3, this caused many difficulties in identifying who was really a Christian and thus part of the voting/communing local church.

Calvinist revivalists such as George Whitefield and the others of the Great Awakening believed that the duty of the revivalist was solely to present the gospel and allow the hearer to come to conviction.

After that each seeker must discern his or her call to be a Christian. Often revivalists of the era, particularly in America, would use a phrase for this such as, "Go to the woods!" This meant that the "mourner" now had to be alone in prayer and meditation to see if indeed God had called him or her to be among the elect. (In America there was always a grove of woods nearby, even in the larger towns.) Such a theology of election left little room for human action or prayer: If God had elected you, you would discern it; if not, prayers would not change his eternal decrees.

John Wesley, as an Arminian, believed that the mourner could be brought into the kingdom and into assurance through the means of grace that included prayer, attendance at Methodist band meetings, and reception of the Lord's Supper, and that the process from mourner to assurance would normally take time to complete. By contrast, the altar call was a more radical expression of Arminian theology. It assumed that human beings could activate a God-mandated *covenant* to receive the promise of salvation universally offered. As the altar call developed, the requirement for a sense of assurance of one's election was eliminated.

That the altar call did not just evolve from Methodist-Arminian evangelists such as William Candler but arose simultaneously from several sources, including Baptists, is one of the most important developments to come out of the Second Great Awakening. It indicates that the Holy Spirit was inspiring various groups and individuals at the same time for this purpose.

We noted earlier how the Scottish communion cycles were discredited in part because of the accusations of sexual immorality leveled by the critics (ch. 5). The Presbyterian leadership of the Kentucky communion-cycle revivals were aware of this criticism and were determined not to allow scandal to feed the critics of revival. With such large crowds attending, the traditional method of directing mourners "to the woods" would not work. Critics would claim that what went on in the woods was not just prayer!

At Cane Ridge, as a temporary expedient, the ministers designated a public area *within the camp area* where persons under conviction could go for prayer. Ministers and intercessors would pray with them there to receive the grace of assurance. Everything was above board and not hidden "in the woods." This area was called the "mourners' pen" by the revival leadership. The critics called it the "pig pen," in part because many who went there were slain in the Spirit, and their clothing was covered with mud. After Cane Ridge many camp meetings, especially those organized by Methodists, had a similar-type area, variously called "mourners' area," "mourners' pen," and later, referring to prepared benches, "mourners' benches."

CHARLES FINNEY AND THE NEW MEASURES FOR REVIVAL[19]

All of this was disturbing to the more traditional of the orthodox Calvinist clergy, who came to theological loggerheads with the ministry of Charles G. Finney (1792–1875). Finney was raised in a non-Christian family and, as a young man, joined the Masons partially to express his contempt for Christianity. He read to become a lawyer and bought his first Bible to check the constant references to the Bible in the law books of the era. He also joined a local church to satisfy his desire for good music (he was an excellent cellist) and, still an unbeliever, became its choir director.

As he listened to his pastor's sermons, he began an independent Bible search to verify the minister's Calvinist theology. His study of the biblical text led him to radical opposition to the Calvinist understanding of predestination. As he searched for the truth, he underwent a powerful conversion experience — yes, "in the woods," near his office. A few days later he had a visionary experience of Jesus. So powerful was his anointing in the first days of his conversion that several persons in his village fell into profound conviction after Finney said a few words to them. An elder of his church, long-converted and known for his devotion and "somber" disposition, fell into uncontrollable holy laughter when he dropped by to speak to Finney at his law office.[20]

Finney held his first revival meeting in 1825. His theology, like Wesley's, was anti-Calvinist, but he did not have an appreciation of the role of the sacraments in maturing a Christian's spiritual life. He taught a doctrine of Christian perfectionism that stressed the role of the Holy Spirit to empower the life of the Christian. As a revivalist, Finney consolidated many of the lessons of the Second Great Awakening. He organized systematic prayer meetings for revival before he began any preaching or revival meetings. He depended on "praying women" to be the heart of these intercessory prerevival meetings. From 1830 on he utilized the "anxious bench" to call mourners forward, and there at the front benches of the church he would kneel and pray with those who came forward. So strong was his anointing at these meetings that people would often feel release and assurance in a brief period.

Finney's ministry in New York State attracted much attention, including strong opposition by the more traditional clergy. They were upset at Finney's "new measures," specifically the "promiscuous" prayer meetings where men and women *prayed together* in public and, of course, the anxious bench, which was considered a heretical Arminian innovation.[21] By 1827 his critics had mounted a substantial pamphlet war against Finney's revival ministry, but, following the biblical pattern, a meeting was arranged between Finney and his chief critics in the small town of New Lebanon. The meetings lasted several days but produced no change of minds.

But in the long range the New Lebanon meeting produced a dramatic change in American evangelicalism. Finney, who never attended a day at seminary, held his own against his more educated and prestigious critics. More importantly, his revival meetings were manifestly more effective in bringing new converts into the kingdom than his orthodox opponents. The new measures of intercessory prayer and coming forward for salvation to the front of the church, along with the assumption that every hearer could choose to accept the invitation to salvation, became the standard for the next generation of evangelists. Lost was the sacrament of the Lord's Supper, including its lesser manifestation, the love feast. Finney's own revivals included no sacramental worship. For him, the sacraments were the concern of the local church and had nothing to do with the process of conversion or revival.

FROM THE MOURNERS' BENCH TO THE ALTAR CALL

Evangelist Dwight Moody (1837–1899) took the last step in disassociating the experience of assurance from the call to conversion. In a revival in London in the 1860s the press of the crowds was too intense to call mourners forward. As an improvisation he asked those who wished to receive salvation to "stand up." Many in the audience responded to this, and he used that gesture in many other revivals.[22] This evangelistic "invitation" had all the characteristics of a sacrament. It was a sign and action expressing God's covenant promise and transforming grace. Unlike the Puritan process of conversion, its center was not on a person's spiritual/emotional responses as a sign of God's election, but rather on God's faithfulness to do what the Scriptures promise.

Later evangelists modified the altar call in various ways. Billy Sunday, the ex-baseball player turned evangelist, asked seekers to come and shake his hand as a sign of receiving the gospel offer of salvation. By 1950 coming forward and repeating a prayer of repentance and acceptance of Jesus had become standard. Contemporary evangelists such as Billy Graham proclaim explicitly toward the end of the invitation that no "emotional" response is needed for God to accept the seeker — the opposite of the Puritan's quest of assurance.

It is also the post-Moody evangelists who separated the altar call from the Finney/Wesley understanding that the goal of every Christian life was radical holiness. Thus, by the first decades of the twentieth century the altar call changed from a *beginning* of Christian life to "fire insurance" that promised a heavenly afterlife. The altar call became the basis of the huge evangelistic campaigns of the twentieth century that electronic technology made possible, but also unintentionally it increased the blight of antinomianism, for through the altar call many Christians never proceeded to discipleship.

METHODISM IN THE TWENTIETH CENTURY

Just like English Methodists, American Methodists fell for the temptation of respectability. The love feast became tamer or less emotional in order to avoid gossip about enthusiasm, sexual innuendo, or disorder at their meetings. Eventually they turned into social occasions with fine tea and pudding cake. Gone was the Spirit-empowered sacrament. Similarly, the class meetings with their frank confession of sins became an embarrassment and turned into Bible studies, which discussed issues such as the emancipation of slaves and the temperance movement.[23]

The Wesleyan mix of evangelical preaching, small-group discipleship, sacramental worship, and personal ministry to the poor unraveled. The Wesleyan *via media* disappeared, and with it the ability to produce a people of extraordinary holiness.[24]

NOTES

1. Paul S. Sanders, "The Sacraments in Early American Methodism," *Church History* 26 (December 1957): 355. Professor Sanders's article is the single best source on the decline of American Methodist sacramental spirituality.
2. Letter from J. Wesley to D. Jarratt, June 24, 1777, printed in Francis Asbury, *The Journal and Letters of Francis Asbury*, ed. Elmer T. Clark (3 vols.; London: Epworth, 1958), 1:220.
3. Wesley M. Gewehr, *The Great Awakening in Virginia, 1740–1790* (Durham, N.C.; Duke Univ. Press, 1930), 150–55.
4. Asbury, *Journal and Letters*, April 17, 1783, 440.
5. Devereux Jarratt, *The Life of the Reverend Devereux Jarratt*, ed. John Coleman (Baltimore: Warner & Hanna, 1806), 102.
6. Sanders, "The Sacraments," 360.
7. Russell E. Richey, "From Quarterly to Camp Meeting: A Reconsideration of Early American Methodism," *Methodist History* 23 (July 1985): 203.
8. Lester Ruth, "A Little Heaven Below: The Love Feast and Lord's Supper in Early American Methodism," *Wesleyan Theological Journal* 32 (Fall 1997): 69.
9. Ibid., 65–70.
10. On the process see Sanders, "The Sacraments," 366–69.
11. Letter, Francis Asbury to John Wesley, printed in *Arminian Magazine* 14 (July 1791): 386.
12. Kenneth O. Brown, *Holy Ground: A Study of the American Camp Meeting* (New York: Garland, 1992), 5ff.

13. Richey, "From Quarterly," 202.

14. See the description of an 1841 love feast led by Walter Scott, frontier evangelist, at: www.mun.ca/rels/restmov/texts/wscott/scott1.html.

15. Richey, "From Quarterly," 208.

16. A book-length history of the altar call is much needed. For an outline of the process, I have depended on Bill J. Leonard, "Getting Saved in America: Conversion Event in a Pluralistic Culture," *Review and Expositer* 82 (Winter 1985): 111–27; William Oscar Thompson Jr., "The Public Invitation as a Method of Evangelism: Its Origins and Development" (Dissertation; Fort Worth: Southwestern Baptist Theological Seminary, 1979).

17. Kirk Mariner, "William Penn Candler and Revivalism in the East, 1797–1811," *Methodist History* 25 (April 1987): 138.

18. On the Baptist claims to the invention of the altar call, see Thompson, "Public Invitation," ch. 3.

19. Lewis A. Drummond has produced a masterful biography of Finney, *The Life and Ministry of Charles G. Finney* (Minneapolis: Bethany, 1985). Finney's autobiography has been a Christian classic since its publication. However, the reader should consult the most recent edition: Charles G. Finney, *The Memoirs of Charles G. Finney: The Complete and Restored Text* (Grand Rapids: Zondervan, 1989). Previous editions were edited and expunged controversial and dramatic spiritual experiences to please Victorian Christian sensibilities. The restored text is more "Pentecostal" than the earlier editions.

20. Finney, *Memoirs* (1989 ed.), 24.

21. The critics' view of Finney's ministry is expressed in one of the classics of Christian pharisaism: Lyman Beecher, *Letters of the Rev. Dr. Beecher and the Rev. Mr. Nettleton, on the "New Measures" in Conducting Revivals of Religion* (New York: Carrill, 1828).

22. David W. Bebbington, "How Moody Changed Revivalism," *Christian History* 9/1 (1990): 23–25.

23. On the decline of Methodism to a "respectable" denomination, see John H. Wigger, *Taking Heaven by Storm: Methodism and the Rise of Popular Christianity in America* (New York: Oxford Univ. Press, 1998), 87, 175ff.

24. Sanders, "The Sacraments," 369.

PART 4

BIBLICAL PATTERNS
AND CONTEMPORARY
OPPORTUNITIES

REFLECTIONS

ON THE BIBLICAL PATTERN

OF REVIVAL

13

REVIVALS WITHOUT THE LORD'S SUPPER

As we have seen, by the time Charles Finney began his revival ministry in the 1820s, the model of the Word *and* the Lord's Supper as a vehicle for revival began to diminish. With the revival ministry of Dwight Moody (1837–1899), Finney's innovation of revivals without the traditional sacraments was solidified as the evangelical pattern. Since then no major evangelist has incorporated the Lord's Supper as part of the revival cycle—although a few have urged immediate baptism after the conversion experience.

Was the elimination of the Lord's Supper and its replacement with the altar call a Spirit-inspired development, or was it an unfortunate mistake? The noted Christian historian Iain Murray has recently said a loud Yes to the second question in a thoughtful and provocative book, *Revival and Revivalism: The Making and Marring of American Evangelicalism.*[1] Murray argues that evangelicals should return to the revival methods that stressed prayer and personal repentance rather than the emotionalism of an altar call. We have pointed out how the *abuse* of the altar call, especially when combined with the doctrine of eternal assurance, has contributed to the blight of American antinomianism (ch. 2).

Nevertheless, it is also true that the era since the 1830s has been the most revival-rich in church history. The revivals of the current age include the great Finney and Moody campaigns, and their tradition has continued through such figures as Billy Sunday and Billy Graham. The Pentecostal revivals, which include the Azuza Street revival and the Pentecostal movement, the charismatic renewal, and the current wave of revival (Toronto/Pensacola), follow the pattern of avoiding the Lord's Supper as a revival event.

In truth, contemporary evangelists such as Billy Graham and Rinehard Bonnke have, in sheer numbers of conversions, outpaced all of the traditional sacramental revivals of history. It is hard to see how, for instance, the current Bonnke revivals in Africa could accommodate any sort of communion service. In a recent revival campaign in Benin, West Africa, the Rev. Bonnke and his ministry team attracted 640,000 persons during their six-day campaign and received 200,000 responses for salvation. The ministry team was overwhelmed by that response, as they had brought only 120,000 copies of their discipleship booklet, *Now That You Are Saved.* Thankfully they coordinated with the area Christian churches to assure that those who made a decision for Christ were channeled into active fellowships.[2]

To criticize that many of the persons who make the altar call at such events eventually backslide is to miss the point that many others do in fact become mature Christians. The current rapid expansion of Christianity in the Third World would not have been possible without the new sacramental form of the altar call. Further, most mature evangelists, such as Graham or Bonnke, go to great lengths to cooperate with local churches to assure that the convert's discipling follows the altar call.

All of this raises an important question: Is the association of revival and the Lord's Supper now obsolete? Should the great Scottish revivals and the Wesleyan revival be seen as charming chapters of church history that have little relevance for the modern church? Is the fact that God now seems to be pouring out his grace of revival mostly through evangelists who do not use the Lord's

Supper during revival or even teach about it as necessary for the new believer make this sacrament obsolete as a revival tool?

If Christianity were ruled by statistical analysis, we might indeed conclude that such is the case and indeed declare the altar call the new sacrament of evangelization — end of argument. However, Christians must always look back to the biblical evidence as a "reality check" and affirmation of current practice. In fact, both the Old and New Testament revivals have a strong sacramental component that is too often overlooked by modern readers, who look at the biblical data through contemporary, nonsacramental categories. Looking carefully at the biblical witness will help locate the divine plan for the role of the Lord's Supper in revivals.

THE "CHRONICLER" AS OLD TESTAMENT THEOLOGIAN OF REVIVAL[3]

Several related Old Testament books deal centrally with the cycle of sin and revival: 1 and 2 Chronicles (originally one work) and the books of Ezra and Nehemiah (also probably one work). The writer (or editor) of these works, called the "Chronicler" by scholars, wrote perhaps as early as the late sixth century B.C.[4] This was a time when the Second Temple was functioning as the center of Jewish worship, but Israel was no longer politically independent. The Chronicler was probably a Levitical scribe and singer or musician — his works have a lot of detail about the music ministry of the temple.

It has also been noted that the Chronicler's writings downplay the role of the classical prophets such as Isaiah or Hosea. Along this line, note the incident in the book of Nehemiah in which local prophets accept bribes to give false utterances against rebuilding the wall of Jerusalem (Neh. 6:10–14). This is not something that reflects well on the office of the prophet. Instead, the Chronicler takes an almost Pentecostal view that the Spirit of God and prophetic utterances are universally spread.[5] For the Chronicler, the classic prophets such as Isaiah and Hosea are *part* of the voice of God to Israel and Judah, but they are not the entire voice. There are also lesser "seers," momentary speakers of God's word, such as a pagan pharaoh

(2 Chron. 35:20–22) and a soldier, a "chief of the Thirty," who had the Spirit of God come on him to give a valid prophecy (1 Chron. 12:18). These are messengers of God who did not have the formal prophetic office. Presumably the Chronicler would not have been surprised by the visionary and prophetic experiences of the Scottish revivals or the Cane Ridge revival, where even children prophesied.

The Chronicler used many sources, most notably 1 and 2 Kings, but also the prophetic books of the Bible, memoirs, and other sources we no longer have. These he forged into a theological interpretation of the history of the rise, fall, and restoration of the Israelite nation from the time of David and Solomon to the beginning of the Second Temple period. He focused on the southern kingdom of Judah, which included Jerusalem and its beloved temple.

The Chronicler's longest work, 1 and 2 Chronicles, is not the favorite Old Testament reading for most Christians. The work begins with lengthy genealogies and includes details of temple worship that bore many of us. It is also history, and therefore one may be tempted to downgrade it as less useful than Old Testament books such as Proverbs or Psalms.[6] But principally, because it is an Old Testament book, some of the Chronicler's assumptions are alien to modern readers. For starters, the Chronicler understands that God manifests his character through *both* mercy and retribution. If one disobeys the precepts of the law of God, and especially if one falls into idolatry, retribution will be severe and certain — on this earth, and not necessarily in the afterlife.[7] Many contemporary Christians have been raised with the idea that God has so much "unconditional love" that his retribution is merely a rhetorical threat.

The Chronicler also assumes that the full, true worship of God is *corporate* worship, which takes place within the context of the temple cult, with its divinely established covenant rites of the Mosaic law. This is not to say that the author is an Old Testament legalist, for throughout the work is a deeply embedded understanding that proper worship must include sincere and wholehearted devotion to the one God of Israel. This is dramatically highlighted when the Chronicler cites King David's charge to his son Solomon with his duties as king:

> And you, my son Solomon, acknowledge the God of your father,
> and serve him with wholehearted devotion and with a willing
> mind, for the LORD searches every heart and understands every
> motive behind the thoughts. If you seek him, he will be found
> by you; but if you forsake him, he will reject you forever.
> (1 Chron. 28:9)

This stark choice is repeated throughout the work and becomes the
judgment peg of the kings of Judah and Israel.

Finally, the last section of Chronicles shows the kingdom of
Judah overrun by the Babylonians. Jerusalem is sacked, the people
are killed or exiled, and the temple itself is destroyed. Although there
is also a hint of the coming restoration of the temple, this is not a
Hollywood ending. The contemporary reader may receive the
impression that Chronicles is mostly a book of divine retribution —
and like Lamentations, a record of spiritual tragedy.

That is an unbalanced view. Although 1 and 2 Chronicles record
the history of the destruction of the kingdoms of Israel and Judah,
embedded in that tragic narrative is the pattern for restitution and
revival — a hopeful theme. It is the good news of God's promise that
no matter how apostate his people become, revival is possible.
Without exaggeration it can be said that the Chronicler is the Old
Testament *theologian of revival*, and his writings present for us a
focused pattern for revival and restoration. Although the details of
the revivals in Chronicles, Ezra, and Nehemiah are different, the
general pattern is the same. A sinful and apostate nation must repent,
reject idolatry, seek God, and obey his laws and commands.
Obedience and loyalty to the Lord is manifest especially in the corporate worship and covenant ordinances of the Mosaic law.

The Chronicler divided his first work, the books of Chronicles,
into two major historical sections. The first describes the establishment of the divine pattern for temple worship under David and
Solomon (1 Chron. 11–2 Chron. 9). The second section, the rest of
the work (2 Chron. 10–36), details the waves of apostasy, idolatry,
and disloyalty to the Lord — but with glorious examples of revival.

The Chronicler's description of David's reign focuses on the
restoration of the ark of the covenant to its proper place as center of

Israel's worship. The ark is brought to the newly conquered capital, Jerusalem, by its proper Levitical and priestly escort. David then sets in place all that is necessary for the priests to perform the daily sacrifices of the Mosaic law. As a result, David's kingdom is strengthened and expanded (1 Chron. 18). The high point of this first section is the dedication of the temple under Solomon. During the praise songs by the singers and musicians God sets his seal of approval on the temple with his special presence as a cloud of glory that occasioned the original "fallings"—that is, the priests faint away under the power of God as the temple ceremony proceeds (see 1 Kings 8:11).

> The trumpeters and singers joined in unison, as with one voice, to give praise and thanks to the LORD. Accompanied by trumpets, cymbals and other instruments, they raised their voices in praise to the LORD and sang:
>
> "He is good;
>   his love endures forever."
>
> Then the temple of the LORD was filled with a cloud, and the priests could not perform their service because of the cloud, for the glory of the LORD filled the temple of God. (2 Chron. 5:13–14)[8]

This was followed by Solomon's dedicatory prayer, which includes a lengthy supplication asking God to forgive any future sins of the people and pleas for *future* restoration and revival:

> When they sin against you—for there is no one who does not sin—and you become angry with them and give them over to the enemy, who takes them captive to a land far away or near; and if they have a change of heart in the land where they are held captive, and repent and plead with you in the land of their captivity and say, "We have sinned, we have done wrong and acted wickedly"; and if they turn back to you with all their heart and soul in the land of their captivity where they were taken, and pray toward the land you gave their fathers, toward the city you have chosen . . . then from heaven, your dwelling place, hear their prayer and their pleas, and uphold their cause. And forgive your people, who have sinned against you. (2 Chron. 6:36–39)

Sometime during the week of dedication the Lord appeared to Solomon in a dream and reaffirmed Solomon's request in words that have been often quoted in recent decades:

If my people, who are called by my name, will humble themselves and pray and seek my face and turn from their wicked ways, then will I hear from heaven and will forgive their sin and will heal their land. (2 Chron. 7:14)

THE THREE REVIVALS OF THE FIRST TEMPLE

After Solomon's reign came the kingship of Rehoboam. He "did evil because he had not set his heart on seeking the LORD" (2 Chron. 12:14). In his greed for power he foolishly forced the northern tribes into rebellion and divided the kingdom into the northern part, Israel, and the southern, Judah (including the city of Jerusalem). The national decline actually began under the latter part of King Solomon's reign, when he allowed the allure of foreign wives to dampen his fervor for the Lord (1 Kings 11). This is *not* mentioned by the Chronicler, who wishes to present the reign of Solomon as perfect.

After the reign of Rehoboam's son, Abijah, Asa inherited the throne of Judah and immediately began warring against the creeping idolatry that had settled on the land: "He removed the foreign altars and the high places, smashed the sacred stones and cut down the Asherah poles" (2 Chron. 14:3). Then, after a decade of peace and prosperity, the Ethiopians attempted to invade Judah. Asa called on the Lord and routed the invaders with a much smaller army. The Judean army sacked the enemy camp and took many cattle (the mobile commissary of ancient armies). As King Asa made his triumphal return, he was met by Azariah, a man on whom the "Spirit of God came," who gave Asa words of prophetic encouragement: "But as for you, be strong and do not give up, for your work will be rewarded" (15:7).

The messenger's words encouraged Asa to initiate another wave of reform and idol cleansing. Many from the northern kingdom flocked to Judah "when they saw that the LORD his God was with him" (2 Chron. 15:9). Asa then proclaimed a Passover-like feast, and the captured Ethiopian cattle were sacrificed before the Lord — and served as the entrée. During this feast Asa led the people into a renewal of their covenant with God:

> They took an oath to the LORD with loud acclamation, with shouting and with trumpets and horns. All Judah rejoiced about the oath because they had sworn it wholeheartedly. They sought God eagerly, and he was found by them. So the LORD gave them rest on every side. (2 Chron. 15:14–15)

The period of prosperity and religious faithfulness continued under Asa's successor Jehoshaphat. Unfortunately, the kings following Jehoshaphat were less faithful to the Lord. The decline became precipitous under the reign of Ahaz, who not only cast idols to worship but also sacrificed his sons as burnt offerings to those very idols — the deepest level of apostasy (2 Chron. 28:2–3). The Chronicler details the defeats and disasters suffered by the kingdom of Judah as a result of Ahaz's apostasy. These events set the stage for the greatest of the First Temple revivals, under Ahaz's son Hezekiah.

When the youthful King Hezekiah ascended to the throne in Judah, the temple was boarded up, and worship of the Lord had been discontinued. He immediately called in the priests and Levites to open and cleanse the temple — a process that took several weeks. The first service of the reopened temple was a sin offering for the sins of the previous generation. The king then called for a thank offering from the people, and the response was overwhelming — a sign that the revival had come: "Hezekiah and all the people rejoiced at what God had brought about for his people, because it [revival of worship at the temple] was done so quickly" (2 Chron. 29:36).

At this point "the king and his officials and the whole assembly in Jerusalem decided to celebrate the Passover in the second month" (2 Chron. 30:2). It was a month later than its mandated time because the priests had not been properly consecrated. Hezekiah converted the Passover into a "revivalistic" event for all God's people by inviting the tribes of the northern kingdom, Israel, to share the Passover.

This was in spite of the fact that Judah and Israel had recently fought a series of bitter wars.

For the most part the northern tribes ridiculed Hezekiah's invitation — they were content with their own gods. Some from the north did come, but these and the other Jews from outside Judah had not properly consecrated themselves according to the Mosaic law (Ex. 12:43–49; Num. 9:10). They should have been disqualified from participating in the Passover. Hezekiah prayed that the Lord would overlook this requirement:

> "May the LORD, who is good, pardon everyone who sets his heart on seeking God — the LORD, the God of his fathers — even if he is not clean according to the rules of the sanctuary." And the LORD heard Hezekiah and healed the people. (2 Chron. 30:18–20)

The "healing" in this passage refers to healing from ritual impurity. The whole assembly then "celebrated the Feast of Unleavened Bread for seven days with great rejoicing, while the Levites and priests sang to the LORD every day, accompanied by the LORD's instruments of praise" (2 Chron. 30:21). All this was so good that everyone agreed to extend the feast and celebrate *another* seven days. This calls to mind the revival at Cambuslang in 1742, with its unprecedented second communion.

This revival, strengthened by the observance of the Passover and Feast of Unleavened Bread, spilled out into further reforms and revival. The people returned to their cities and destroyed the idols and local worship centers. Hezekiah reorganized the daily temple service so that it would be regular, and the priests, supported by the tithes of the people, dedicated themselves to the study of the law. Soon the tithe donated for temple worship was so abundant that new storehouses had to be built to contain the produce.

The Chronicler describes Hezekiah as a new David. True temple worship was restored and idolatry suppressed, and the law of Moses became normative in the kingdom of Judah. Positive earthly consequences resulted: Judah prospered, and with God's miraculous intervention, an assault from the huge Assyrian army was rebuffed (2 Chron. 32).

① Moses changes ⊙ mind — Ex. 32:9-14

② Hezekiah — ⅠⅠⅠⅠ — 2 Kings 20:1-7

Unfortunately the two kings who followed Hezekiah again "did evil in the sight of the LORD" and reestablished witchcraft, child sacrifice, and idolatry in Judah. This sets the scene for the last revival in Chronicles, the one led by King Josiah. This was a last hurrah of true temple worship before the dispersion and exile of Judah and them destruction of the temple.

③ Josiah inherited the throne as a boy of eight. By the time he was sixteen he began a cleansing of Judah from the idolatry of the two previous regimes. In the process of cleansing and repair the high priest discovered the scroll of "the Law of the LORD that had been given through Moses" (2 Chron. 34:14). This was probably the book of Deuteronomy. When the book of the law was read to King Josiah, he realized how far his people had departed from God's command. The king tore his clothes as a sign of repentance and sent his advisors to seek a prophetic word on the matter. The prophetess Huldah gave the word of God: The sins and apostasy of Judah were beyond remedy, and Judah was doomed. However, because Josiah had sought the Lord and repented, "I [the LORD] will gather you to your fathers and you will be buried in peace. Your eyes will not see all the disaster I am going to bring on this place and on those who live here" (34:28).

Josiah immediately busied himself in bringing Judah into more rigorous conformity with the law of Moses. Perhaps he was mindful of the ancient Jewish understanding of "changing God's mind" through prayer and repentance. That understanding went as far back as Moses' plea to God not to destroy the Jewish people for worshiping the golden calf (Ex. 32:9–14). King David had gone on a fast to try to save his newborn child in spite of the word of God from the prophet Nathan (2 Sam. 12:7–23). Josiah was presumably also aware of the prayer of King Hezekiah, which had added fifteen years to his life in spite of the initial word from God through Isaiah that he would die immediately (2 Kings 20:1–7).[9]

In any case, Josiah organized a covenant-renewal service. This took the form of an assembly of the men of Judah in which the law was read, and Josiah vowed to obey the requirements of the law: "Then he had everyone in Jerusalem and Benjamin pledge themselves to it; the people of Jerusalem did this in accordance with the covenant of God, the God of their fathers" (2 Chron. 34:32). Josiah also encouraged the Levites to become teachers of the law. As the other righteous kings of Judah, he reinstated the observance of the Passover and its accompanying Feast of Unleavened Bread.

> The Israelites who were present celebrated the Passover at that time and observed the Feast of Unleavened Bread for seven days. The Passover had not been observed like this in Israel since the days of the prophet Samuel; and none of the kings of Israel had ever celebrated such a Passover as did Josiah, with the priests, the Levites and all Judah and Israel who were there with the people of Jerusalem. (2 Chron. 35:17–18)

The only serious error of Josiah as king was one connected with a military decision. He did not discern that Neco, the pharaoh of Egypt, was on a mission from God to fight the Babylonians (2 Chron. 35:22). Josiah refused to give the Egyptian army safe passage through Judah but instead went out and gave battle. He lost both the battle and his life, and he was buried to the public chants and laments of the prophet Jeremiah.

In spite of Josiah's splendid spiritual accomplishments, the Lord did not change his mind about destroying Jerusalem and punishing the people, and Huldah's (and Jeremiah's) prophecy came to pass. Within less than twenty-five years after Josiah's death, Jerusalem was captured, its people killed or exiled, and the temple destroyed. The consequences of the apostasy and evil done by the kings and people of Judah had brought God's severe judgment. This, however, did not cancel the promise of further revival and restoration — the theme that the Chronicler hints at in the last paragraph of 2 Chronicles and elaborates in the books of Ezra and Nehemiah.

REVIVAL AFTER THE BABYLONIAN EXILE: EZRA AND NEHEMIAH

The book of Ezra records how after the years of "Sabbath rest" in exile, a contingent of Jews returned to the ruins of Jerusalem to rebuild the temple and reestablish the worship of the Lord their God. The Chronicler's main concern in this work is to show how the returning exiles, under first Zerubbabel, a prince, and later Ezra, a priest and scribe, cleansed themselves in order to become the restored people of God.

When the exiles returned, they found Jerusalem in ruins. They trusted the Lord for protection and built a temporary altar to begin the daily sacrifices mandated by the law. They also celebrated the Feast of Booths (Ezra 3:4). The temple foundation was laid, but the work was stopped because of local opposition.

Under the prophetic encouragement of Haggai and Zechariah, work on the temple started up again and was eventually finished. The Jews then gathered to dedicate the temple: "For seven days they celebrated with joy the Feast of Unleavened Bread, because the LORD had filled them with joy" (Ezra 6:22). Only then, when the community was strengthened with proper worship, did the central drama of the book of Ezra unfold: dismissal of foreign wives and children.

The story of the purified Jewish community is continued in the book of Nehemiah. This work completed the Chronicler's cycle by showing the remnant Jewish community safe behind newly built walls and spiritually protected by a reinstated Mosaic law. This occurred through a great revival led by Nehemiah the governor and Ezra, who earlier had led the community to dismiss foreign wives and children.

The book of Nehemiah opens at the court of the Persian king Artaxerxes I (465–424 B.C.). Nehemiah, personal cupbearer to the king, prays to God for the restoration of the Jews and the rebuilding of Jerusalem's walls with promises found in Deuteronomy 30:2–4. God answers that prayer, and Nehemiah is given a royal commission to rebuild the walls of his beloved city.

Soon after Nehemiah arrived in Jerusalem, he oversaw the rebuilding of the walls. He shamed the ruling class Jews into forgoing all usury and to free enslaved Jews. The work on the walls was completed in spite of opposition from local chieftains and an attack of false prophecy by prophets bought by the opposition (Neh. 6:10–14). Nehemiah then called a convocation of the returned exiles to dedicate the walls and reestablish the holy covenant of the Jews with God. Ezra the priest began the convocation with praise and worship and proceeded to read the Mosaic law. He read from morning to night, and priests assisted him in explaining the law to the people.

> Then Nehemiah the governor, Ezra the priest and scribe, and the Levites who were instructing the people said to them all, "This day is sacred to the LORD your God. Do not mourn or weep." For all the people had been weeping as they listened to the words of the Law. (Neh. 8:9)

As Jonathan Edwards might have said, the crowd had been "exercised" by a spirit of conviction, which surprised the leadership.

> Nehemiah said, "Go and enjoy choice food and sweet drinks, and send some to those who have nothing prepared. This day is sacred to our Lord. Do not grieve, for the joy of the LORD is your strength."
> The Levites calmed all the people, saying, "Be still, for this is a sacred day. Do not grieve."
> Then all the people went away to eat and drink, to send portions of food and to celebrate with great joy, because they now understood the words that had been made known to them. (Neh. 8:10–12)

The next day the people gathered for further instruction in the law of Moses. They found in the law the command to celebrate the Feast of Booths.

> So the people went out and brought back branches and built themselves booths on their own roofs, in their courtyards, in the courts of the house of God and in the square by the Water Gate and the one by the Gate of Ephraim. The whole company that had returned from exile built booths and lived in them. From the days of Joshua son of Nun until that day, the Israelites had not celebrated it like this. And their joy was very great.
> Day after day, from the first day to the last, Ezra read from the Book of the Law of God. They celebrated the feast for seven days, and on the eighth day, in accordance with the regulation, there was an assembly. (Neh. 8:16–18)

That assembly on the eighth day was the opposite of the one they had just celebrated. The people fasted and wore sackcloth, and they repented of their sins and the sins of their fathers in rejecting the law of God. Finally, the assembled Jews recommitted themselves to God and to obedience of the law through a renewed covenant. In this case a covenant that outlined the obligations of the law was signed by the leadership of the renewed community.

THE CHRONICLER AS SACRAMENTALIST

It is obvious that besides being a revivalist, the Chronicler was also a sacramentalist.[1] He positioned the liturgy of the Israelite feasts and the covenant rites of temple worship in the midst of, and *causally connected with*, revival. Other factors were also important in his presentation of revival. Repentance was a major factor, of course, as in renouncing, with great tears and weeping, the idolatry and syncretism that continually infiltrated Israel and Judah.

Also critical for the Chronicler's understanding of revival and restoration was the role of royal leadership. The spiritual orientation of the king set the course of loyalty to the Lord and his temple worship on the one hand, or apostasy and idolatry on the other. This makes sense in an age of absolute kings. The Chronicler would have been surprised by the course of events in America and the United Kingdom, where revivals have occurred under ungodly kings or presidents. Cane Ridge and the Second Great Awakening, for example, began under the presidency of Thomas Jefferson, a Deist and possibly the least religious president of the United States in the nineteenth century (see ch. 7).

But after all is said and done, it is the covenant acts — the feasts (especially Passover and the Feast of Booths), the covenant renewals, and the daily temple sacrifices mandated by the law — that are for the Chronicler the "means of grace" to strengthen the Jewish community and clear the channel to heaven for God's blessings. Nevertheless, it is fair to admit that nowhere does the Chronicler use the word "sacrament" (a word that does not appear anywhere in Scripture) or "means of grace" or other such phrases. In fact, the understanding of the Old

Testament rites and ordinances as true sacraments — covenant signs that mediate grace — goes against centuries of Christian theology, an issue we need now to deal with more closely.

WERE THE OLD TESTAMENT COVENANT RITES TRUE SACRAMENTS?[11]

Although the word "sacrament" does not occur, in regard to its mandated feasts, the Old Testament does use the word "ordinance" (which in church history has become a synonym for "sacrament"):

> The LORD said to Moses, "Say to the Israelites: 'On the fifteenth day of the seventh month the LORD's Feast of Tabernacles begins, and it lasts for seven days. . . . Celebrate this as a festival to the LORD for seven days each year. This is to be a lasting ordinance for the generations to come; celebrate it in the seventh month.'" (Lev. 23:33, 41)

A similar passage is found in Exodus in reference to Passover:

> You shall observe this rite [Passover] as an ordinance for you and for your sons for ever. And when you come to the land which the LORD will give you, as he has promised, you shall keep this service. (Ex. 12:24–25 RSV)

The problem for many contemporary Christians in accepting the Passover, the Feast of Booths, or the other Israelite feasts as true sacraments lies in theological instruction and assumptions derived from early Christian theology. The issue goes back to the anti-Judaic prejudices of certain patristic writers, especially St. Augustine (354–430). Although Christianity began as a Jewish sect, relations between synagogue and church soon took an acrimonious turn. By the end of the second century it was no longer possible to be both a Jew and a Christian.[12] The rabbis excommunicated all Christians from the synagogue, and Christians retaliated by using harsh terms to describe the Jews' rejection of the gospel.[13]

St. Augustine, bishop of Hippo in North Africa, laid the foundations of Western Christianity's sacramental theology with his prolific writings. Unfortunately he also accepted the anti-Judaic beliefs of the early church.[14] Moreover, he spent part of his adulthood among the Manicheans, a religious sect that believed the Old Testament was written by an evil god of vengeance and only the New Testament was inspired by the Holy Spirit. When Augustine became a Christian, he discarded that extreme view but continued to have problems in appreciating the Old Testament. Thus, in Augustine's view the Old Testament sacramental feasts, temple service, and rites were "types," foreshadowings of the Christian sacraments, but were not valid, grace-giving actions in themselves.[15] Thus illogically, the rites and festivals gave no blessings to those who obeyed and performed them in the Old Testament times, but they were "instructional" for New Testament Christians (who had not yet been born!). For Augustine the only valid sacraments are those directly instituted by Christ and performed through the church.

Augustine's debasement of the Old Testament sacraments was hotly disputed by theologians in the Middle Ages.[16] For example, St. Bonaventure totally disagreed and saw the Old Testament festivals (especially Passover) as sacraments and truly grace-giving. In his view, "the sacraments were instituted [by God] from the beginning to cure the sickness of sin, and they will endure until the end of time."[17] Although Bonaventure understood the primacy that Jesus played in establishing the church's sacramental ministry, he also understood that the sacraments had their origins in the Father's love and nature. For instance, Bonaventure believed that God established the sacrament of matrimony at the Garden of Eden, that it continued after the Fall among all peoples, and that it continues as a valid sacrament even among the heathen. Similarly, God established the sacrament of repentance (penance) as a spiritual universal. This can be seen as active in the ministries of the Old Testament prophets, who called the people of Israel to repentance and reconciliation with the Lord.

Unfortunately, St. Thomas Aquinas, who developed what became the official Roman Catholic theology of the sacraments, sided with Augustine. True sacraments were restricted to those sacred actions found in the New Testament and to those that could be linked to Jesus. For instance, St. Thomas claimed that baptism was instituted by Jesus when he received John's baptism.[18] The opinion that Jesus directly instituted sacraments of the church became the orthodox opinion of Roman Catholicism and later influenced Protestant theology as well.

Significantly, several of the Reformers battled this theological opinion and credited the Old Testament feasts (notably, the rite of circumcision and especially the Passover) as valid sacramental acts — in effect following the tradition of St. Bonaventure. John Calvin especially held to a high view of the Old Testament covenant rites, including circumcision, as valid sacraments.[19] Puritan writers, including Solomon Stoddard (ch. 4), shared this more generous view of the Old Testament. However, as evangelical Protestantism drifted into the Zwinglian view of the sacraments as merely memorial, the high view of Old Testament covenant rites as true sacramental acts became irrelevant. Thus, most Protestant theologians aligned themselves with St. Augustine's opinion that the Old Testament rites were merely "types" or shadows of New Testament sacraments and disregarded Calvin's opinion.

A reading of Luke 7:28–30 indicates that St. Bonaventure and John Calvin were correct and that St. Augustine and St. Thomas were wrong. In these verses Jesus is talking about the ministry of John the Baptist, and Luke adds a significant comment.

> "I tell you, among those born of women there is no one greater than John; yet the one who is least in the kingdom of God is greater than he."
>
> (All the people, even the tax collectors, when they heard Jesus' words, acknowledged that God's way was right, because they had been baptized by John. But the Pharisees and experts in the law rejected God's purpose for themselves, because they had not been baptized by John.)

In these verses, Jesus locates John the Baptist as an old-covenant prophet, and yet (as the comment by Luke demonstrates) his baptism contained an *effective grace*. It opened the ears of its participants to the gospel of Jesus.[20] When a person accepted baptism and entered into this God-inspired rite, that person received a specific grace. Those persons who refused baptism did not get it. In other words,

Old Testament covenant acts are sacraments and do have a grace-mediating capacity, just as the New Testament sacraments.

THE SCOTTISH COMMUNION CYCLE
AS THE FEAST OF BOOTHS

Retrospectively, we may conclude that what happened in the Scottish communion cycles, including Cane Ridge, and in the camp meetings that followed, was a *recovery of the sacrament of the Feast of Booths*. It is not difficult to detect the hand of the Holy Spirit in shaping this recovery during the century and a half that it took to form the communion cycles. All the essential elements of the Feast of Booths were reactivated: a dramatic decrease in social pretensions and separations by removing the individual from his or her home (a major emblem of social standing), the charity and joy (and grace) of food sharing, and fellowship regardless of class or economic standing. These were combined with preaching the Word, repentance, and rededication. Certainly in the communion cycles there was the added and greater grace of the Lord's Supper. Thus grace was heaped upon grace, perhaps the secret of their success in the face of such persistent opposition within and without the church. This may also explain why the camp-meeting tradition has been such a successful and enduring part of American Christianity.

The connection to the Feast of Booths was not understood, or at least publicly discussed, by even the staunchest defenders of the Scottish communion cycles. The anti-Semitic heritage of orthodox theology had closed their eyes to the possibility that imitating any of the ancient feasts could be an occasion of grace. Ultimately this theological gap exposed the communion cycle to ridicule and disintegration, so that without the comparison to the Feast of Booths the communion cycles were indeed regarded as unscriptural.

PAUL'S CAUTION

Recent decades have seen an unprecedented upsurge of interest in, and appreciation of, the Jewish heritage of Christianity. Many Christian churches have experimented with celebrating a Christian Passover on Good Friday night instead of the usual somber vigil. My suggestion that there is a grace gained from celebrating the Feast of Booths (consciously or unconsciously) places this work within that ongoing movement.

However, we should also be aware that the "return-to-Jewish-roots" movement has a danger. We must begin with Paul's warning to his churches not to be in bondage to Jewish traditions:

> Therefore do not let anyone judge you by what you eat or drink, or with regard to a religious festival, a New Moon celebration or a Sabbath day. These are a shadow of the things that were to come; the reality, however, is found in Christ. (Col. 2:16–17)

In this perspective, Augustine's argument against the validity of Old Testament sacraments is an exaggeration of Paul's warnings. The apostle's revelation was that a dependence on the Jewish calendar and festival cycle for salvation or righteousness debases the effectiveness of the cross and is a legalistic bondage. But his words do not rule out the possibility that a person can freely receive a blessing of grace from the celebration of Old Testament feasts. After all, Paul himself kept a number of Jewish rites and rituals in his own personal life (cf. Acts 21:20–26; 1 Cor. 9:20).

In sum, our enthusiasm for the grace possibilities from the Christian celebration of Passover or the Feast of Booths must be tempered by Paul's warning. The Old Testament sacraments may very well be eternally valid, but they are not critical for salvation or for the development of the mature Christian life. Rather, they must be seen as additional blessings available to believers of every era.

NEW TESTAMENT REVIVAL IN JERUSALEM[21]

Turning to the New Testament, the book of Acts presents the great and seminal revival that began at Pentecost and that birthed the Christian church. The revival sequence of Acts 2 can be easily discerned to be sacramental. The disciples were waiting and praying in the upper room for the reception of the Holy Spirit in response to Jesus' last command (1:4–5, 8). The Holy Spirit then descended in dramatic form, with wind and tongues of fire as outward evidence. All those in the upper room received the gift of tongues and presumably other gifts of the Spirit. Peter then stepped out to an assembling crowd and preached an anointed sermon, calling for repentance and proclaiming the lordship of Jesus.

As a result, the crowd was "exercised," as Jonathan Edwards would say (Acts 2:37, "cut to the heart"), and they asked, "Brothers, what shall we do?"

Peter replied, "Repent and be baptized, every one of you, in the name of Jesus Christ for the forgiveness of your sins. And you will receive the gift of the Holy Spirit" (Acts 2:38). After further urging three thousand were immediately *baptized* (2:41). Luke then describes the life of the revival community in Jerusalem:

> They devoted themselves to the apostles' teaching and to the fellowship, to the breaking of bread and to prayer. Everyone was filled with awe, and many wonders and miraculous signs were done by the apostles. All the believers were together and had everything in common. Selling their possessions and goods, they gave to anyone as he had need. Every day they continued to meet together in the temple courts. They broke bread in their homes and ate together with glad and sincere hearts, praising God and enjoying the favor of all the people. And the Lord added to their number daily those who were being saved. (Acts 2:42–47)

We should note certain characteristics of this prototype revival. The new Jewish-Christian community devoted themselves to learning God's Word through the apostles. They continued public worship at the temple and had an unusually strong communal life, which expressed itself in the sharing of material goods and property. The divine *presence* was strong in their midst and manifested in every individual, feeling a special sense of awe and fear of the Lord, and in the constant working of miracles through the apostles.

In the midst of all of this was a constant sacramental observance similar to that of the Old Testament revivals, except now the covenant signs were the ones mandated by their Lord. That they practiced immediate baptism is clear. Here there is no lengthy catechuminate as in the later centuries of the church.[22] However the

[handwritten notes in top margin: "@ Pentecost Gifts / ① Ev. / ② Tongues / Holy Spirit / ③ Healing / ④ preaching/..."]

form or formula of baptism is not described and may have been, in its beginning at least, only in the name of Jesus, as is hinted at in the revival in Samaria (Acts 8:16).

Similarly, the meaning of the "breaking of bread" is unclear. Biblical commentators are practically unanimous in declaring this to be a form of the Lord's Supper. This was certainly an Agape meal, a love feast in which the new believers experienced and celebrated the Lord's presence. For the Jewish Christians the words of institution may not have been as important as giving thanks to God for the elements — a pattern derived from the Passover and continued in Jewish fellowship meals of the times.[23] The phrase "ate together with glad and sincere hearts" may also indicate that the love-feast element was predominant in the Jerusalem community over the more somber "memorial" of Christ's death motif described in the Gospels.[24] In any case, some form of the Lord's Supper and baptism stood at the center of the Jerusalem revival.

The Wesleyan Revival as Acts 2

We can now understand that the Wesleyan revival was close in character and grace to the revival described in Acts 2. This is not surprising, for the Wesley brothers strove consciously to recreate "primitive Christianity" among their societies. Like the first Christians in Acts 2, the early Methodists experienced a deep presence of the Holy Spirit. The Wesley brothers preached an "apostolic" (evangelical) gospel, stressed small group fellowship, and practiced sacramental worship to the point of seeking to recover the fullness of the original love feast/Lord's Supper. In addition, the Wesleyan revival incorporated the Old Testament sacrament of the periodic covenant renewal. About the only element of the Jerusalem church that the early Methodists did not practice was the community of goods. It must be noted, however, that their concern and charity to the poor followed the original apostolic *intent*. We will discuss further the fullness of the Wesleyan revival below (ch. 16).

With this biblical perspective we can also see that the Scottish communion cycles and the Wesleyan revivals presented the church not just with charming chapters of church history but with *the high point of a revival mode*. These older revivals re-created with deeper fidelity than modern revivals the *biblical pattern* for renewing the people of God.

NOTES

1. Iain H. Murray, *Revival and Revivalism: The Making and Marring of American Evangelicalism, 1750–1858* (Carlisle: Banner of Truth Trust, 1994), ch. 11, "The Illusion of a New Era." This is not meant to imply, however, that Murray endorses a return to the Lord's Supper as having a role in revival.

2. The Rinehard Bonnke website is www.cfan.org, where one can follow the news of this amazing ministry.

3. This section is based on the seminal article by Donald F. Murray, "Retribution and Revival: Theological Theory, Religious Praxis, and the Future in Chronicles," *Journal for the Study of the Old Testament* 88 (June 2000): 77–99.

4. The majority academic opinion of the past century has held that one author or editor was responsible for the books of Chronicles, Ezra, and Nehemiah. Some recent scholars have questioned this opinion and posited that the similarities in style and theological outlook are due to a disciples' "school" or fellowship. The ultimate answer may be irresolvable this side of eternity. For the single-author opinion, which I have chosen because it in our case simplifies matters (and if wrong does no harm), I have depended on the work of the noted Old Testament scholar Peter R. Ackroyd, especially his recent work *The Chronicler in His Age* (Sheffield: Sheffield Academic Press, 1991).

5. William M. Schiniedewind, "Prophets and Prophecy in the Books of Chronicles," in *The Chronicler as Historian*, ed. David J. A. Clines and Philip R. Davies (Sheffield: Sheffield Academic Press, 1997), 204–24.

6. Fortunately, the books of Chronicles has received recent favorable attention from Bruce Wilkinson's best-selling work on prayer based on the two-sentence "prayer of Jabez" embedded within one of the Chronicler's lengthy genealogies (1 Chron. 4:9–10). See *The Prayer of Jabez: Breaking Through to the Blessed Life* (Sisters, Ore.: Multnomah, 2000). This book has been ridiculed as materialistic and simplistic by liberal critics, but it is really an excellent work that demonstrates the simplic-

ity and power of prayer. See Philip Zaleski, "In Defense of Jabez," *First Things* 106 (October 2001): 10–12.

7. For a study of the Old Testament description of the relationship between a person's moral acts and the consequences in personal and national history, see Gerhard von Rad, "The Essentials of Coping with Reality" in *Wisdom in Israel* (Nashville: Abingdon, 1972), esp. 124–37.

8. See also 2 Chron. 7:1–3.

9. The whole idea of changing God's mind seems to be heretical within classical Christian theology, based as it is on second- and third-century Hellenistic philosophy, but it has received much attention in the current controversy over "Openness Theology." For an introduction to this topic, see the cover story of the May 21, 2001 issue of *Christianity Today*, "Does God Know Your Next Move?"

10. Many Old Testament scholars would agree with this; for example, see the work by William Johnstone, *2 Chronicles 10–36: Guilt and Atonement* (Sheffield: Sheffield Academic Press, 1997).

11. The following section was informed by the seminal article by A. H. C. Van Eijk, "The Difference Between the Old and the New Testament Sacraments as an Ecumenical Issue," *Bijdragen* 52 (1991): 2–36.

12. One group, the Ebionites, attempted to be both Christian and Jewish, but they were considered heretical by both Jewish and Christian leaders. The Ebionites saw Jesus as Messiah, though not the divine Son of God, and rejected the writings of Paul. See Eusebius, *Ecclesiastical History*, 3.27.

13. In contrast, Paul's writings reveal the rejection of Christ by the Jews as *providentially necessary* for the salvation of the Gentiles, and eventually "all Israel will be saved" (Rom. 11). The anti-Semitism of the early church must be considered yet another unfortunate byproduct of the *delay* in accepting Paul's letters as Scripture. We noted earlier (ch. 1) that without Paul's writings the early church created a theology of the Holy Spirit that was lacking a full understanding of the gifts of the Spirit.

14. Clark M. Williamson. "The *Adversus Judaeus* Tradition in Christian Theology," *Encounter* 39 (Summer 1978): 273–96; also Craig A. Evans and Donald A. Hagner, eds., *Anti-Semitism and Early Christianity* (Minneapolis: Fortress, 1993). Anti-Semitism may date to the writing of the Gospel of John, when relations between the synagogue and church were already testy. Note the manner in which the term "Jews" in John's Gospel is employed rather consistently in a negative way.

15. Marcel Dubois, "Jews, Judaism and Israel in the Theology of Saint Augustine," *Immanuel* 22/23 (1989): 162–70.

16. A summary of this issue is found in Van Eijk's, "The Difference Between the Old and the New Testament Sacraments."

17. Cited from John Francis Quinn, "Saint Bonaventure and the Sacrament of Matrimony," *Franciscan Studies* 12 (1974): 101.

18. *Summa Theologica* 3.66.2. The entire *Summa* is available from the web at www.newadvent.org/summa.

19. John Calvin, *Institutes of the Christian Religion*, 4.21–23.

20. It would be accurate but undignified to call John's baptism the sacrament of "the big ear"; it is far better to give it a Latin name: the sacrament of the *auris magna*.

21. The literature on the book of Acts and on the Acts 2 revival is extensive. Of the many excellent biblical commentaries I found particularly helpful the volume in the Anchor Bible commentary by Joseph A. Fitzmyer, *The Acts of the Apostles* (New York: Doubleday, 1998).

22. In defense of the catechuminate (i.e., the lengthy preparation, including exorcisms, and instruction of the believer before baptism), the Jews in Jerusalem knew the moral law of God through the Jewish Bible, whereas the converts of the Roman Empire did not, and thus they rightly had to be morally instructed before baptism.

23. Werner Elert, *Eucharist and Church Fellowship in the First Four Centuries*, trans. N. E. Nagel (St. Louis: Concordia, 1966), and the classic work by Dom Gregory Dix, *The Shape of the Liturgy* (Westminster: Dacre Press, 1945), ch. 4, "Eucharist and the Lord's Supper."

24. For an excellent review of modern biblical research on the New Testament church's practice of the Lord's Supper, see John L. Boyle, "Practice of the Eucharist in the New Testament," *Worship* 44 (May 1970): 289–91, and Myles M. Bourke, "New Testament and the State of the Liturgy," *Worship* 44 (March 1970): 130–42.

WHEN REVIVAL CAME

TO ST. MICHAEL'S

14

The Sunday service at St. Michael's Episcopal Church in Gainesville, Florida, began traditionally enough with a hymn from the Episcopal hymnbook and a vested procession. Soon, however, the service showed the signs of revival. The "Gloria," the traditional prayer of praise sung or recited by the congregation at the opening prayers, was replaced by lively contemporary praise songs, led by a talented, female African American worship leader. Toward the end of the praise songs the service took another unexpected turn. The Rev. Joan Mattia, the copastor, took the hand of an acolyte and began marching around the altar. The acolyte grabbed the hand of another acolyte, who in turned took hold of one of the lay readers. Pastor Joan headed for the center aisle, and soon half the congregation was in a "Jericho march" around the outside aisles of the church.

I first visited St. Michael's in April 1996 along with my wife, Carolyn. After meeting the copastors, a husband and wife team, at the national charismatic conference in Orlando in 1995, I had been invited to observe their services and preach. Lou and Joan Mattia had both gone to Virginia Episcopal Seminary (noted then for its evangelical persuasion), and both had been ordained to the priesthood in the Episcopal Church. They had participated in the charismatic renewal since the 1970s. When they accepted the call to be copastors to St. Michael's, they already had a reputation as unabashed charismatics. However, no one anticipated the whirlwind of revival that would sweep that church in their tenure.

After I gave a brief sermon that Sunday in April, Joan and Lou conferred briefly and felt led by the Spirit to cancel the standard "prayers of the people." In its place she gave an altar call for those who wished to receive a touch of God for healing or other needs. About a quarter of the congregation responded. Lou and Joan laid hands on the line of people who came forward, and a majority of them fell backward into the ready hands of "catchers" (a liturgical position not yet included in the *Book of Common Prayer*).

The service went on to the offertory and then to the Eucharistic prayer, where the words of consecration were spoken. Ever since revival had swept St. Michael's, both Lou and Joan had felt special energies flow through them at the words of consecration. At times the presence of God was so heavy at the altar that it was difficult for them to continue the service. This Sunday the distribution of the communion elements took place in an atmosphere of joy that could be seen in the faces of the people. At the left altar rail a woman slumped on the rail after she received the cup. She slowly sprawled over the kneeling cushion and floor, where she stayed until after the service was over. On the right a young man slumped down even before he had received the elements. He began to twitch and growl. Fr. Lou quickly discerned this as a demonic manifestation and with discrete hand motions summoned a deliverance team from the worshiping congregation. Three men and a woman helped the young man to the vesting room, directly behind the altar area.

Carolyn and I followed to observe. Although we were experienced in deliverance ministry, we were visitors and chose to observe and pray silently. It was obvious that the deliverance team was experienced. In fact, it included an evangelical missionary who had a worldwide ministry and an African American couple experienced in healing and deliverance. The deliverance was completed in minutes.

The ministry team took the man to the altar, where together they received communion.

This exciting service, which integrated the preaching of the Word, liturgy, sacrament, and the Holy Spirit's manifest presence, was normal to St. Michael's time of revival. It surprised no one present. How the copastors and congregation came to this stage of spiritual power and maturity is a fascinating story that includes an object lesson in both the cost and fruit of revival. Without conscious imitation of the early Methodists, St. Michael's was functioning in the Weselyan pattern of Reformed Anglicanism. The evangelical gospel was preached regularly, the congregation was subdivided into small home fellowships (which meet weekly for prayer and encouragement), and the church sponsored many outreaches, including assistance to the less fortunate in the area. Penetrating this all was a rich sacramental worship guided by the *Book of Common Prayer*, which centered on the weekly Eucharistic Sunday service, and a welcoming stance to the divine intrusion of the Holy Spirit.

A Brief History of St. Michael's

St. Michael's was founded in 1958 at the far edge of the then small university town of Gainesville, Florida. It took ten years of slow but steady growth for the church to become a self-sustaining congregation. The congregation was socially and theologically conservative, typical of the Gainesville area, which has more in common with south Georgia than Florida. In the 1970s the Cursillo movement made an important impact on parish life, and many of its members were made aware of the necessity of being "born again" through this ministry and its reunion groups.

In 1984 Fr. Stephen Jecko was called as rector. He had embraced the charismatic renewal and slowly introduced renewal concepts to the church. However, an element of anticharismatic members (and vestry persons) was present in the church. Fr. Jecko's first years were contentious as he sought to please both pro- and anticharismatic factions. The church settled into a pattern common to many mainline churches: traditional services on Sundays for all and special charismatic "healing" services on Wednesday nights. It was a polite understanding. The traditionalists were content with the Sunday service while the charismatics could exercise the gifts of the Spirit on Wednesdays and in the home fellowship groups.[1] Fr. Jecko left St. Michael's in 1990 to become canon at the cathedral in Jacksonville, and he subsequently became the bishop of Florida (St. Michael's diocese).

After much earnest prayer the congregation called Lou and Joan Mattia to be their "co-rectors." When the Mattias came to St. Michael's, Joan was the first female rector in the North Florida district, and there was considerable opposition to having a woman priest among the congregation. For the first six months everything went relatively smoothly, with the "Liturgical-Sunday-and-Pentecostal-Wednesday" pattern holding. Suddenly strong opposition to Joan's ministry surfaced. It seemed as if the traditionalists in the congregation would barely accept a woman priest, but they had expected a demure Southern lady. Joan was an assertive woman with a prophetic edge that was sometimes interpreted as tactlessness.[2] The traditionalists organized a campaign against Joan and requested that the bishop remove the Mattias.

Warring Against the Principalities

While this controversy stormed, prayer intercessors at St. Michael's prayed for God's protection for Lou and Joan. They understood that the fervent opposition signified a battle against spiritual "principalities and powers" and not their traditionalist brothers and sisters. The vestry backed Lou and Joan and spent hours of their time in supportive prayer. About this time it was learned that St. Michael's might have been built on former slave quarters of a plantation.[3] In addition, St. Michael's had been repeatedly defaced with occult rituals and symbols. Cultic symbols had been carved on the church's doors and the walls spray-painted with occult markings. A cat had been hung at the entrance of the church.

Lou and Joan led a procession of about sixty parishioners around the property, asking the Lord to cleanse the property of the grief and sorrow of past sins. Praise songs broke out, and the perimeter was sprinkled with holy water. At the open spot on the church property, known as a place where some local teens indulged in sex and drugs, the group stopped, and Lou and Joan celebrated a brief Eucharist.[4] From that time worship seemed to flow more freely. Opposition to Joan's ministry spent itself. The church was ready for the next move of the Spirit.

BUD WILLIAMS BRINGS THE "TORONTO BLESSING" TO ST. MICHAEL'S

In early 1994 St. Michael's vestry met to pray and plan for the coming year. They discerned that God was calling St. Michael's to a deeper dimension of life in the Spirit. News of the dramatic ministry of Fr. Bud Williams had circulated. Fr. Williams was an Episcopal priest from Lakeland, Florida, who had attended the seminal Rodney Howard-Brown revival in Lakeland at the Carpenter's Home Church (1993) and had subsequently been anointed as an evangelist of what is now known as the "Toronto Blessing." That particular wave of revival is most often associated with the phenomenon of laughing in the Spirit. That is, a person, or a group, or the whole church might begin to laugh during church service for no obvious, conscious reason. This often brings joy and peace in the individual's life. This has been a constant if infrequent phenomenon in Christian revivals and spiritual life.[5]

Lou and Joan had met Bud years before and traveled with him during June 1993 in England, where they witnessed the operation and growth of the "laughing revival." The revival was particularly influencing and refreshing Anglican churches throughout the United Kingdom. Tapes of Bud's revival sessions had circulated among the vestry, so that everyone in position of authority at St. Michael's knew what the stakes were when they called him to come and hold revival at St. Michael's.

The Bud Williams revival was held April 11–15 (Monday through Friday), 1994, at St. Michael's sanctuary. The First Assembly of God canceled its own services for the week so that the whole congregation could attend. The church was packed, with extra chairs in the aisles and narthex. The attending public represented at least forty-five churches from the Gainesville and North Florida area.

Many who attended spent "carpet time" (resting in the Spirit) as they came forward to receive blessings at the hand of Fr. Williams. People were healed of emotional and physical ailments, including the instant healing of a serious heart condition and the disappearance of a cyst that was about to be operated.[6] Joan was healed of the grief and bitterness she felt from the first years of struggle at St. Michael's.

The gifts of the Spirit manifested mightily every night in healing, word gifts, and deliverance. One evening a man with a demonic spirit was literally elevated from the floor several times and thrown back down as the power of God expelled the evil spirit. In a later service Lou experienced anxiety about the possible reaction of some members of his congregation to the revival, and the Lord gave him a vision of Lot and his wife leaving Sodom. He felt the Lord tell him, "Don't turn round or go back; do not return to the place of fear of men!"[7]

St. Michael's after the Williams' Revival

When Fr. Williams and his team left, St. Michael's and several other congregations in the Gainesville area were recharged and freshly anointed for ministry. The people at St. Michael's noticed immediately a bold new spirit of witnessing and much increased joy. The first Sunday after the revival was telling as to what had happened to St. Michael's congregation. At the 10:30 service the formal "Gloria" was replaced by praise songs, followed by tongues and prophecies. Joyous laughter broke out during the sermon and offertory. Joan delivered a brief sermon entitled "Don't Put God in a Box" and then encouraged several from the congregation to witness to what the Lord had done for them during the revival. Mrs. Anita Doyle, the senior warden and a cradle Episcopalian, had always been somewhat skeptical about biblical revelation. The Lord dealt with her during "carpet time" in the revival, and she stood, waved her Bible, and proclaimed that she "truly believed what the Bible had to say."[8]

As Lou said the words of consecration in the Lord's Supper, he felt a jolt of energy empower every word. Joan, standing to his side, fell under the power at the same moment, as did several acolytes and several members of the congregation (cf. 2 Chron. 5:14). Joan recovered in time to distribute the consecrated elements. After the communion there was an altar call for those wishing to receive a touch of God, and again many were felled by the power of God. The following Sundays the powerful presence of God continued to manifest itself. For example, the very next Sunday much laughter broke out, and several communicants found themselves "stuck" to the altar rail as they experienced a special presence of the Lord.

AN EXTRAORDINARY HEALING

The Lord's special presence at St. Michael's is demonstrated in the healing of "L. M.," a woman in her forties who fled from Canada to avoid an abusive husband. While in Canada she suffered from the London flu (spring of 1973), a severe form of the Asiatic flu. This eventually led to the development of fibromyalgia — a rare wasting disease that causes severe muscle and joint pain, skin problems, and digestive disorders. L. M. was diagnosed with the disease by Canada's leading physician of fibromyalgia in 1989.[9] She was placed on a heavy medication schedule and for a while experienced some remission. However, her ultimate prognosis was not good, and she was not expected to survive past six years.

When she came to Florida, L. M. was suffering severely, with increasing weakness. On September 3, 1995, she attended the Sunday service at St. Michael's and was slain in the Spirit in front of the altar along with several others. She crawled up to the alter rail to receive communion and was slain again as she received the wine. When she came to, she was healed from fibromyalgia. The next time she went to her doctor, she was able to go through the standard blood pressure test with only nominal discomfort. Previously it had caused such severe pain as to leave her immobilized for half a day. She has been symptom free of her disease since her healing.

L. M. experienced another extraordinary healing at the altar rail at the beginning of 1996. When she was a girl, she had hurt her back, and periodically since had attacks of sciatica (nerve pain in the leg and thigh) from the injury. L. M. had been in pain for three weeks when she went to receive communion:

> Joan Mattia, priest, served me the wafer and found herself unable to remove her hand from mine. Neither could I remove my hand. It was like an electric circuit was completed when she touched me, and the power of God flowed to and from Joan and me. After a time (30 seconds, 2 minutes?) Joan was able to remove her hand and proceed on down the rail, but we were both very drunk in the Spirit as a result. When I received the wine, I fell back as though pushed backwards and lay under the power for a long time.
>
> When I rose up my spine cracked several times. I could feel the bones move. I was healed![10]

L. M., who is an intelligent and articulate woman, reflected on the healing ministry at St. Michael's:

> The atmosphere at St. Michael's is not one of a hyped expectation of physical healing, rather an atmosphere in which one is constantly aware that God is present and active. This gives one the support necessary, the faith necessary to stay in the healing process until the full results are in place. The emphasis is not so much on healing as it is on God, His Presence, and daily evidence of His power at work among us. Every Sunday one goes to church knowing that everyone to whom they speak will report wonders and helps from God that have changing results. We have the privilege of watching each other overcome, grow, change, and become new. The metamorphic process is visible in all the people in our church. It is quite glorious on an ongoing basis.[11]

L. M. continues in good health, regularly attending St. Michael's and serving in many capacities, including volunteer work at the office and thrift store.

THE COST OF REVIVAL

The grace of revival was freely given, but it has been costly to St. Michael's. As much as one-half of the congregation left. Aside from those who left from a sense of conviction, many also left out of a sense that the revival had "gone too far." Several of the "patriarchs" of the church (and major financial supporters) had barely accepted the charismatic elements then in place and were deeply offended by the revival under Bud Williams. A lunch that had been scheduled months earlier took place the Sunday afternoon after revival. When Lou and Joan showed up, they were obviously shunned by their hosts and other older families.

Financial contributions fell dramatically during May and June of 1994. One of the traditionalists explained to Lou that a large contribution would be in jeopardy "if they didn't go back to the old way of celebrating the liturgy." The exodus occurred even among several charismatic families who had stuck with Lou and Joan through all of the earlier battles of their ministry at St. Michael's. It seemed that the holy laughter and the "disorderliness" within the orderly Episcopal liturgy was too much for them as well.

The summer after revival was a difficult one for the St. Michael's congregation in spite of its many blessings. The sudden exodus of so many families was especially burdensome as old friendships were severed. This was tempered by new people coming in who were hungry and thirsty for God's refreshment. Parish income dropped by over 20 percent, and suddenly there were bills that could not be met. Cuts were made in the budget, including cuts in the Mattias' salary, but still there were some outstanding bills. At the August vestry meeting clergy and vestry persons placed the unpaid bills on the floor, and they all stood on the bills, praising the Lord and claiming his provision. Not accidentally tithing increased dramatically from those families that remained, and by the end of 1995 all the bills were paid with total income returning to prerevival figures.[12]

It took several years for the number of persons attending Sunday services to recover to their prerevival statistics. Certainly revival at St. Michael's did not bring a stampede of new members as it did at Pensacola, Florida, or Holy Trinity Church in Brompton, England. Revival was costly to St. Michael's, but every person we asked affirmed that the blessings, graces, and mercies that St. Michael's had received from the Spirit's moving in revival were more valuable than the heartbreak and trouble that followed.

Perhaps more important to the universal church is the glimpse that St. Michael's gives as to the face of revival in the future. The clergy and members of St. Michael's have accepted not only the gifts of the Spirit, as was learned in the charismatic renewal, but they have also embraced the *presence of the Spirit* and accepted his *divine intrusion* into their activities and liturgy to a degree not often seen in churches from any tradition, let alone liturgical churches. The Wesleyan pattern had come to a new fullness.

A visitor to today's St. Michael's would not likely find the dramatic revival manifestations just described. Certainly the healing ministry remains strong, and the gifts of the Spirit continue to operate in this charismatic congregation. The new pastor has been part of the charismatic renewal movement for decades, but he does not directly encourage revival manifestations. Lou and Joan were called to become missionary teachers to the Anglican diocese of Mpwapwa in Tanzania. They are currently teaching at the Provincial Anglican Seminary, St. Philip's, educating African pastors seeking advanced degrees.

St. Michael's, like so many Wesleyan congregations of the eighteenth century, was strongly touched by God's reviving hand, but it lives as a congregation in the *ordinary presence* of his covenanted gifts and sacraments, but with the special memory of how revival can manifest itself in the life of a liturgical church. We will now turn our attention to another congregation in Florida where revival did not come on as quickly, but where the balance between the preached Word, the sacraments, and divine presence has been especially powerful.

NOTES

1. This is a common pattern among many mainline churches, but it rarely is completely successful. If the charismatics expand, the traditionalists flee; if the traditionalists prevail, the charismatics wither and are marginalized.
2. Changes in pastors are normally difficult; many adults see a new minister as "chaplain," one who holds the institution together, rather than as "pastor," one who spiritually leads. It normally takes three years for a minister to be fully accepted as pastor.

3. This has not been documented, but there is an old African American cemetery adjacent to the church property.

4. Account described in letter to author by the Mattias, May 29, 1996.

5. See Guy Chevreau, *Catch the Fire: The Toronto Blessing* (London: Marshall Pickering, 1994), and more critically, James A. Beverley, *Holy Laughter and the Toronto Blessing*, (Grand Rapids: Zondervan, 1995). On holy laughter early in the ministry of Charles Finney, see the comments in ch. 12.

6. Letter from Lou and Joan Mattia to The Rev. Canon Steve Jecko, April 29, 1994. Copy in author's file. Knowing of the predilection for charismatics to be careless and exaggerating about healing claims, the leadership of St. Michael's has attempted to document instances of miraculous and medically inexplicable miracles that occurred during the week of revival.

7. Interview with author, April 22, 1996.

8. Letter, Mattia to Jecko, April 29, 1994.

9. Copy of diagnostic letter about L. M. from Dr. Liam Martin, medical faculty member, University of Calgary, is on file both at St. Michael's and author's office.

10. Letter from L. M. to author, August 12, 1996.

11. Ibid.

12. Annual Report, St. Michael's Episcopal Church, 1995.

Word, Sacrament, and Presence at Christ the Redeemer Church

15

The Saturday evening youth service at Christ the Redeemer Church in Ponte Vedra Beach, Florida, was already under way.[1] I had missed a turn before I found the parking lot of the modern concrete and glass building that was the home of a new and unusual church. The audience for this Saturday evening service, mostly late teens and young couples, were already deeply into worship singing. The lyrics were projected on two large wall screens on both sides of the central stage. The worship was led by a handsome young man wielding a guitar, accompanied by a small band and a half-dozen singers. Spotlights bathed the stage in shifting colors, and a hidden smoke generator created an artificial fog bank that made it seem as if the band and choir were in a cloud.

After twenty minutes of praise music a young woman came forward and began a skit as a woman who was imprisoned and lonely, and a young man at the other end described his plight as a homeless person. Then two others came forward and told why they did not really have enough time in their busy schedule of work, family, and church to minister to others. An unseen narrator read the words of Matthew 25:34–40:

"Then the King will say to those at his right hand, 'Come, O blessed of my Father, inherit the kingdom prepared for you from the foundation of the world; for I was hungry and you gave me food, I was thirsty and you gave me drink, I was a stranger and you welcomed me, I was naked and you clothed me, I was sick and you visited me, I was in prison and you came to me.' Then the righteous will answer him, 'Lord, when did we see thee hungry and feed thee, or thirsty and give thee drink? And when did we see thee a stranger and welcome thee, or naked and clothe thee? And when did we see thee sick or in prison and visit thee?' And the King will answer them, 'Truly, I say to you, as you did it to one of the least of these my brethren, you did it to me.'" (RSV)

The brief skit (lasting about six minutes) made the biblical point better than most sermons I have heard.

All this is much like many a Vineyard church, which are noted for their successful attempts to reach the unchurched with the gospel by all means conventional and unconventional. Yet there is one important distinction: A large and obviously permanent altar is fixed in the center of the stage. It was already set with the communion elements.

The service proceeded with another traditional element, the reading of the Scriptures taken from the standard lectionary of the Episcopal Church. Three laypersons came to read the selections, but unlike most liturgical churches, a layperson read the Gospel portion. After the readings Dan Williams, bishop and pastor of Christ the Redeemer Church, stepped forward to give the homily. He was dressed in a denim shirt and Dockers. My visit took place the week after the 2000 presidential election, while the certification and recount controversies were in progress. Williams, a staunch Republican in private life, talked about the need for Christians to model a more civil tone than secular politicians during the current time of political controversy.

After his homily Bp. Williams returned to his seat in the front row, and the priest celebrant, a young man in his early thirties, came to the altar to speak the words of consecration. He too was dressed in slacks and a shirt without tie. It was a brief rite, using the words of

Jesus from 1 Corinthians 11:23–25, with a few additions from the *Book of Common Prayer*. The communion elements (strips of pita bread for dipping and wine) were distributed by both the priest and an elderly couple, who obviously delighted in their task and managed it with unusual grace. The closing benediction was a song entitled "I Believe," which served as a modern-day creed. Its Pentecostal elements are evident:

> I believe that God came to see us
> I believe He was an ordinary man
> I believe He left us with His Spirit
> I believe He wants to fill every man
> I believe there is mercy every morning
> I believe He's the Ancient of Days . . .
> I believe in the unity of brothers
> I believe that we're different yet the same
> I believe where two or more are gathered
> He's in the midst and He's taking away the shame
> I believe if I say unto this mountain
> "Be rooted up and cast into the sea . . ."
> I believe if I pray without doubting
> The lame will walk and the blind are going to see.[2]

So enthused was the audience's rendition that it was repeated several times before the service finally came to a close.

The service took almost two hours, but I saw no one leave before the end. Several persons lingered after the service for conversation and prayer in the sanctuary. Others filed into the youth room converted into a café, where coffee and punch were served. There a group of "twenty somethings" and late teens socialized and played board hockey or checkers. The café finally closed at 2:00 A.M.

SUNDAY SERVICES

The early Sunday service (9:00 A.M.) at Christ the Redeemer Church was more traditional but still lively enough to attract a wide range of participants, young and old. The praise music that opened the service was every bit as charismatic as the Saturday evening service.

However, in this service the altar had been carefully laid out with fine embroidered linen, and the celebrants wore matching stoles — the only form of vestments ordinarily used at Christ the Redeemer. Bp. Williams repeated his Saturday-evening sermon dressed in a suit and tie, but no stole. The Eucharistic service was again brief but complete.

Later that day Bp. Williams explained to Carolyn and me that he plans to make the 9:00 A.M. service the most traditional of his services. He is aiming this early service to be attractive to the more liturgically inclined persons in the area, many of whom come from Roman Catholic and Episcopal backgrounds. It will increasingly resemble a Rite II service of the *Book of Common Prayer.*

It is the 10:30 service that is the most manifestly Spirit-filled of the services. During the opening worship period of praise songs on the Sunday we were there, people steadily drifted to the altar rail for intense prayer. A few sobbed in repentance and petition, with others kneeling alongside praying and ministering to their spiritual needs. Such ministry at the altar has become normal at the 10:30 service. That Sunday Bp. Williams discerned a special anointing at the altar and encouraged the congregation to continue in prayer and encouraged others to come to the rail for ministry.

After a few moments a woman came to him and whispered a message. Bp. Williams then announced that he had received a "word from the Lord," namely, that the Lord was visiting the congregation with healing. He asked those who had been healed by the Lord in previous services to come forward and begin praying for others. A half-dozen in the audience came forward to minister, and others came to receive healing prayer. The altar-rail area became crowded with people seeking healing, and others, laypersons and clergy alike, ministered with the laying on of hands and intercessory prayer.

A lay elder approached one of the worship leaders and prayed over a young man. He then smacked the young man in the mouth and apologetically explained that the Lord instructed him to do that. The young man graciously accepted the incident.[3] Later in the evening the young man explained that the "healing smack" had indeed produced a miraculous result. It instantly freed him of a longstanding stuttering condition, one in which years of therapy and effort had been expended to no avail.

The healing interlude at the altar lasted about a quarter of an hour. Then Bp. Williams moved to continue the service. To get back to schedule he directed the lectionary readings to be bypassed and went directly to the sermon. The communion service followed, and as at the earlier services the elements were distributed by two married couples, who added a special charm and grace to the communion distribution. The final benediction was the same song, "I Believe," sung at the earlier service. There was no formal processional, although Bp. Williams made it a point to slip out during the final chorus and post himself at the door to greet the public as they filed out.

The unusual mix of modern and traditional found at Christ the Redeemer is called *convergence*. This new movement has arisen within the last thirty years among churches and church groups all over the world. These churches seek to combine an evangelical zeal and understanding of the gospel with a Pentecostal appreciation and use of the gifts of the Spirit, all of which are expressed in liturgical/sacramental worship.[4]

Most convergence congregations are "high church." That is, they normally use a full traditional liturgy, and their clergy are vested in classic vestments (albs, chasubles, stoles, etc.). A majority of convergence churches in America follow the liturgy of the Episcopal *Book of Common Prayer*. One example is the Church of the Messiah in Jacksonville, Florida, a short drive north of Bp. Williams's church.[5]

But the services at Christ the Redeemer Church point to a form of convergence that is "low church." The liturgy and the lectionary are taken as suggestions, not commandments. Full vestments are worn only on high holidays, such as Easter or Pentecost Sunday (a high holiday at Christ the Redeemer!), or at weddings, where the vestments add a sense of tradition and photogenic color. The Nicene Creed is said monthly at all services as a reminder of the doctrinal unity of the church. On the other Sundays the "I Believe" functions as the creed, or a sung and modernized version of the Apostles' Creed is used.

This low-church convergence has been highly successful for Bp. Williams and his congregation. The church was begun in the Williamses' living room in 1992; it now averages about nine hundred persons attending weekend services, and it continues to grow. This makes it one of the largest contemporary convergence congregations in America. This low-church convergence is not accidental but a carefully thought-out strategy by Bp. Williams and his staff to meet the spiritual needs of the people in his area. Its purpose is to create a church that is both contemporary yet connected with the heritage and sacramental structure of the church catholic.

DAN WILLIAMS'S JOURNEY INTO CONVERGENCE[6]

Bp. Dan Williams began life in a devout Christian household. His family moved from an Independent Baptist to a Southern Baptist affiliation in his childhood years. At age five, during a local tent revival, young Dan gave his life to Christ. From then on, Bible memorization, Sunday school, and Christian youth camps made up a large part of his childhood. As a teen he experienced a brief period of rebellion, but by the time he was seventeen he had returned to the church fold. At eighteen he married his stunningly beautiful bride, Sharon, and was licensed to preach by his Southern Baptist congregation. They had discerned a strong calling on his life.

At this time Dan and Sharon were fully "orthodox" in the Baptist faith, believing that, for instance, Catholics were all unsaved and sub-Christians and that Pentecostals were deluded in their claims of Spirit-filled gifts. At a home prayer meeting, however, they discovered the youth minister of their church praying in tongues and healing the sick by the laying on of hands — the very Pentecostal delusions they had been warned about! Though suspicious, both knew they wanted the exuberance and joy that the youth pastor had. Shortly after Dan went off to a scheduled Baptist youth conference, and while at solitary prayer, he received the gift of tongues. Sharon followed shortly in the Pentecostal experience, but their Baptist church could not tolerate such doctrinal nonconformity and disfellowshiped them.

Thus released, Dan and Sharon went off to become missionaries in Latin America, where they served in Costa Rica and Ecuador under several different denominations. During this period Dan was recognized as a gifted pastor and ordained through a Pentecostal denomination. However, the Williamses noticed that many of the independent Pentecostal and charismatic churches in their area fell into contention and doctrinal errors. They learned to appreciate the Episcopal form of church government to the more traditional denominations as better suited to avoid dissension and maintain biblical oversight.

The Williamses returned to the United States where Dan broadened his church experiences by serving in a Methodist church and then as youth pastor at St. Peter's Episcopal Church in Jacksonville (one of the great charismatic churches of the Episcopal Church). There he learned about the depth and beauty of sacramental worship and experienced convergence with an Episcopal flavor. He was invited by the bishop of the diocese, Frank Cervany, to receive ordination as an Episcopal priest, but Dan prayerfully discerned this was not God's will for him.

Through these different church postings, God was filling Dan and Sharon's hearts with a great love for *all* of the church, regardless of the denominational specifics. This included a love for the Catholic Church, in spite of its less-than-Christlike opposition to the evangelical movement in Latin America. In 1981, with the role of missions still at the center of their hearts, Dan and Sharon put their energies into founding a missionary service agency called Calvary International.[7] As its leader Dan helped plant and staff over a thousand churches in the former Soviet Union and has also been active in Central and South America. Additionally, Calvary International has established over thirty Bible schools all over the globe, several in the dangerous "10/40" window of non-Christian countries.

The Founding of Christ the Redeemer Church

By 1989 Dan and Sharon felt a special call to found a church where the evangelical, Pentecostal, and sacramental could be blended —

convergence. They worked for three years to disengage from Calvary International and hand leadership over to competent hands. By January 1992 they were able to move ahead and establish a church in their home with four couples; they called it Christ Chapel. By May of that year, growth had forced them to move to a conference room of a local Marriott Hotel. In March 1993 the congregation moved to an elementary school, and after that a storefront at a strip mall. Later that year they passed the significant figure of 250 persons in regular attendance. This is a major milestone for any church — lesser numbers makes auxiliary services such as nursery, youth ministry, and Sunday schools difficult.

The church renamed itself Christ the Redeemer Church, and in June 1996 they purchased a twelve-acre plot of land in Ponte Vedra Beach, just south of Jacksonville. Because of the congregation's willingness to tithe and even go beyond tithing, Pastor Williams and his flock were able to move into a new, custom-built church building in July 1999.

Part of what made this expansion possible was the strong leadership and specific vision that the Williamses had for their congregation. It was based on much prayer, on their broad experience in church planting, and on interactions with churches in many parts of the world. This is articulated in the church's mission statement, which the Williamses call the "four distinctives."[8]

The first distinctive is "an unflinching resolve to recognize and promote the priesthood of all believers." This is a reaffirmation of the Reformation insight that every believer is a priest before the Lord (1 Peter 2:9–10). In spite of the fact that Christ the Redeemer has ordained clergy and values its "apostolic succession," the laity are given wide authority in ministry. Bp. Williams makes it clear that the ordained clergy "is not a group which exclusively holds and retains the power to minister, but rather, they are coaches and teachers with the distinct purpose of involving all of God's servants in effective ministry."[9] Each quarter the church runs a four-hour course for newcomers that includes a "spiritual gifts" inventory to guide every person to an appropriate ministry. The newcomers are encouraged to join one of nineteen care groups — home fellowships, where they learn the skills of intercessory prayer for one another's needs and actively practice the gifts of the Spirit. From there they are moved into one of the many church ministries.

The second distinctive is a "vigorous devotion to train a generation of young people to fulfill their God-given destiny." Indeed, one of the noticeable things about Christ the Redeemer Church is the large numbers of children and youth present. Children are given Bible instruction in the nursery, not just entertained. For example, recently the kindergartners were taught about the story of Jonah and the big fish. To dramatize Jonah's experience the kids were all "tossed overboard" into the arms of another staff member, and then all were crowded into a darkened restroom (the fish's belly). Middle schoolers have a separate program from high schoolers. Three of the full-time staff members are youth or children's pastors.

The third distinctive is "an absolute dedication to the fulfillment of the Great Commission in this generation." This distinctive represents the Williamses' continued heart for missions. Christ the Redeemer maintains close relations with Calvary International and cosponsors many of its projects. Members of the church are involved in many short- and long-term mission projects. Its budget of missions and missions support is over $300,000 a year.

The last distinctive is that of convergence, namely, "a full expression of the historical and contemporary streams of the Church where the sacramental, Evangelical and charismatic converge." It is significant the way convergence is defined. In most of the convergence churches the "liturgical" element is given equal weight to that of the sacramental, as in defining a "sacramental/liturgical" component of convergence. Bp. Williams's view of convergence affirms the importance of the sacramental worship but does not give great weight to the liturgical and ritual aspects of convergence. It is his opinion that accenting the liturgical and ritualistic is not biblically mandated, whereas the life of sacramental worship is plainly seen in the New Testament church. Further, he believes that high-church liturgy is alien to many Americans, who place a premium on informality and relaxed dress. Note too that convergence is listed as the last of its distinctives. It is almost an instrument to achieve the other three goals.

RELATIONSHIP WITH THE CEEC

As Christ the Redeemer was being birthed, Dan Williams became aware of other churches and groups that were also on the convergence journey. He looked at the Charismatic Episcopal Church (CEC) and decided its policy on not ordaining women was not where the Lord was leading his church. He did, however, feel an attraction to the Communion of Evangelical Episcopal Churches (CEEC).[10] This communion of churches is similar to the CEC in its pursuit of the Anglican and Celtic tradition of spirituality, yet it ordains women to the clergy and is looser in organizational structure. Bp. Williams had extensive conversations with the CEEC leadership and formed a close friendship with them. The bishops of the CEEC recognized Williams's gifts and accomplishments and offered to ordain and receive him as a bishop within the CEEC. However, he discerned that it was not God's will for Christ the Redeemer Church to be part of the CEEC.

> The reticence I had to join them in full communion as one of their clergy is their resolve to express their faith with Anglicanism with a Celtic expression as their center ... while I love the Episcopal system of government and the Liturgical/Sacramental approach to worship, I do not have the same level of desire for much of the symbolism that comes along with traditional Anglicanism.[11]

Significantly, the bishops of the CEEC affirmed the validity of Pastor Williams's calling in working out a low-church form of convergence. Rather than ending their relationship, they offered to ordain Williams into apostolic succession as an independent bishop. He would have their blessing and commission to organize a new convergence communion. Thus understood, in February 1999 Williams was ordained and consecrated a bishop by Archbishop Boosahda and two other CEEC archbishops. They agreed to have formal intercommunion. That is, CEEC clergy can preach and celebrate the sacraments at Christ the Redeemer and vice versa. Further, Bp. Williams was invited to serve on the CEEC advisory board, a position he accepted.

Contemporary/Early Church

When I visited Christ the Redeemer I had already heard of their low-church convergence, and I expected to see a contemporary sort of worship and church life. I did, but I also had the sense that what I was seeing was remarkably close to the worship of the early church. The records of the early church reveal a pattern in which the bishop *presided* over the liturgy but stayed on the sidelines. It was a presbyter (priest), or sometimes even a layman, who said the Eucharist, and lay readers read the Scriptures.[12] This is what happens at Christ the Redeemer.

Even the reticence of the clergy to use traditional vestments echoes the practice of the early church. High-church convergence theologians claim that the Old Testament regulations for temple worship reveal that God's best plan for the gathered church is a vested priesthood. However, the history of the early church is different. The bishops and presbyters wore the contemporary garb of a Roman gentleman, an alb and chasuble. This was done because the early church was an underground church, subject to persecution, and specifically Christian vestments would have been an unnecessary danger. It was only after the legalization of Christianity in the fourth century that the Roman gentleman's garments became ritualized and elaborated into priestly garments. Thus in a sense, the dress of the clergy at Christ the Redeemer Church, like most Protestant churches, is the cultural equivalent of the dress of the early underground church.

Christ the Redeemer's low-church convergence gives Bp. Williams and his staff great freedom to experiment with the liturgy. One of the trends noticeable in many parts of the church is a reincorporation of Jewish traditions and feasts. For example, this year for the second time, Christ the Redeemer celebrated the feast of Hanukkah in conjunction with the local Jewish synagogue, Beth El (not a messianic Jewish community). That Bp. Williams could encourage such a festive holiday right at the beginning of the traditional Advent season, where the traditional accent is on a sober self-denial, is a sign of the freedom that a low-church convergence church can exercise.

We mentioned earlier that Christ the Redeemer had experienced impressive numerical growth. More important, if less numerically definable, is the obvious faith and love of the congregation. The Christians who attend this church are moving in the Spirit of God, growing in his gifts, and being empowered by the sacraments to be a powerful witness to their community. The children who attend church here are growing up in an envelope of protection from the evils of the secular world and a vibrant, powerful faith that will make them not only survivors, but also apostles to their generation.

As I experienced the worship at Christ the Redeemer and interviewed its members, I had the uncanny feeling that what was happening here was a fulfillment of the Wesley brothers' dream for a reformed church. As we saw earlier (ch. 11), John Wesley had a theology that was highly sacramental but lightly liturgical and ritualistic, and he was even willing to experiment with new worship or sacramental forms. John Wesley was gifted in motivating and empowering Methodist laypersons for evangelism and church service while maintaining an appreciation for the priesthood and church order. All of this is present at Christ the Redeemer in large measure. It is a place where God's Word is preached consistently, the sacraments are ministered regularly and devoutly, the presence of God is discerned spiritually and manifested with miraculous healings, and discipleship is carried out with utmost care.

NOTES

1. The website for Christ the Redeemer Church is www.christ-the-redeemer.com.
2. From the CD "In the Spirit," words by Don Potter, copyrighted by Eagle Star Productions, division of Morning Star Fellowship Church, Charlotte, North Carolina. Original CD can be ordered: 1-800-542-0278. Used by permission.
3. Such dramatic actions are not uncommon in old Pentecostal circles. Smith Wigglesworth, the famous English Pentecostal man of faith, was noted for occasionally punching his supplicants into miraculous healings.

4. There is little literature on the convergence movement. Among the few items are Wayne Boosahda and Randy Sly, "The Convergence Movement," which can be downloaded at www.theceec.org/11convergence. html, and Robert Webber, *Sign of Wonder: The Phenomenon of Convergence in Modern Liturgical and Charismatic Churches* (Nashville: Star Song, 1992). Two new denominations have arisen to carry out the vision of convergence: the Charismatic Episcopal Church (CEC) (www.iccec.org) and the Communion of Evangelical Episcopal Churches (CEEC) (www.theceec.org). Both have documents relating to convergence on their websites. The author was ordained a priest of the CEEC in March 2000.

5. The Church of the Messiah is one of the best high-church convergence congregations in America. The clergy vest for every service, and incense is used at its Sunday services. This church is also gifted with an unusually talented and effective liturgical dance ministry, a form of worship expression common to many convergence churches. This church was founded by an Episcopal priest, Fr. Dale Howard. He led his congregation out of the Episcopal Church because of its increasing heresy and antibiblical practices and into a convergence denomination called the Charismatic Episcopal Church. That denomination was founded in 1992 to carry out convergence that is doctrinally orthodox and liturgically traditional.

6. The following information on Bp. Williams is taken from an interview the author had with Bp. Williams and his wife on Nov. 19, 2000, and a printed handout (entitled "My Journey") by Bp. Williams, which is available on request from Christ the Redeemer Church, 190 S. Roscoe Blvd., Ponte Vedra Beach, FL 32082.

7. For information on this active and effective missionary agency, see their website: www.calvary-international.org.

8. The four distinctives are in the handout given to newcomers when they walk in the door.

9. Anonymous, "The International Communion of Christian Churches," Church of the Redeemer handout, 3.

10. See note 4 for more on these two denominations.

11. Williams, "My Journey," 4.

12. On the classic description of the early-church liturgy and on how it developed in its many varieties and was formalized in the Middle Ages, see Dom Gregory Dix, *The Shape of the Liturgy* (Westminster: Dacre Press, 1945).

Conclusions

16

God's Providential Activity

In this concluding chapter we must stress that we are not claiming that the Finney pattern of revivals, with the altar call but without either the Lord's Supper or baptism, is wrong. We earlier pointed out that this type of revival has been gloriously fruitful all through the twentieth century. It must be considered providential for the needs of the age. Perhaps what has happened is that the "best" — revival plus the Lord's Supper — has been hidden for a season for another purpose. This is not uncommon in God's plan of salvation. We see a biblical example in Paul's insight that the Jews providentially rejected Jesus as Messiah so that the Gentiles might be brought into the church. But the best situation of all will occur in the end of the age, when Jews will become part of the body of Christ (Rom. 11).

> Again I ask: Did they stumble so as to fall beyond recovery? Not at all! Rather, because of their transgression, salvation has come to the Gentiles to make Israel envious. But if their transgression means riches for the world, and their loss means riches for the Gentiles, how much greater riches will their fullness bring! (Rom. 11:11–12)

In other words the best in the kingdom of God happens when what was eliminated is restored and added to what substituted it. Paul says that the kingdom of God will reach its full glory and maturity when the temporary subtraction of the Jewish people is ended and they return to the kingdom, to add to the new, and unexpected, Gentile church.

Similarly, we can begin to understand that coming revivals will restore the fullness of Scripture. They will have the elements of modern revivals, including the altar call, but will restore the place of the dominical sacraments, especially the Lord's Supper, to the center of revival activity. We saw hints of this in the last two chapters.

A concurrent move is taking place in some evangelical and charismatic churches with the restoration of the Lord's Supper as a weekly event in Sunday worship. Such pastoral leaders as Richard Eslinger and Charles Rice are urging evangelical congregations to recover the Lord's Supper as the *response to the sermon.* Eslinger noted that the "invitation [altar call] took the place of the Eucharistic invitation to the Lord's Table and consequently served to set preaching and sacrament in opposition to each other."[1] This is especially relevant to the contemporary evangelical-charismatic scene when the altar call is employed far beyond its original use as a vehicle for entrance into the kingdom. I have witnessed in the last few years altar calls for rededication to serve others, for healing, for release from financial burden, and so on. All of these requests for Christian empowerment and freedom could have been *better* focused through the Lord's Supper.

PROVIDENTIAL AND DEMONIC?[2]

Having affirmed that the decline of both the Scottish communion cycles and the sacramental stage of the Wesleyan revival was under God's providential permission, we must not exclude the opposite: that the opposition to, and obscuring of, the Lord's Supper in revivals was *primarily a demonic action* to limit the effectiveness of revivals.

Let us explore how unseen spiritual powers can influence Christian thoughts and actions. Several years ago Frank Peretti published a wildly successful novel, *This Present Darkness*, in which the conflicts between Christian and New-Agers in a small university town were pictured as representing the actions and motivations of heavy and demonic powers.[3] As much as we should celebrate the success of the Peretti work for bringing the concept of spiritual warfare to the general Christian public, his view does not do justice to the subtlety of the biblical evidence. In Peretti's novel demons influenced the thoughts and actions of the New-Agers, to the point where they were practically automatons. Christians, or at least the heroes of *This Present Darkness*, were not subject to such negative influences. Rather, their intercessory prayers empowered the good angels to overwhelm the demons.

The biblical evidence is both more subtle and more shocking. Humans, both Christians and non-Christians, are subject to demonic and heavenly influences at all stages of their spiritual lives. According to the Chronicler, pagan kings such as Cyrus could be influenced by the Spirit of God to do great works for the people of God.[4] The book of Ezra opens with these words:

> In the first year of Cyrus king of Persia, that the word of the LORD by the mouth of Jeremiah might be accomplished, the LORD stirred up the spirit of Cyrus king of Persia so that he made a proclamation throughout all his kingdom and also put it in writing: (Ezra 1:1 RSV)

Conversely, Christians — even Spirit-filled believers who studied at the feet of the apostles — could be influenced by the demonic. Note the incident of the lying couple, Ananias and Sapphira, recorded in Acts 5:3–4, whose heart "Satan . . . filled."

But biblical revelation is even more complex than this. A person may be strongly influenced by the Spirit of God one moment and by unholy spirits the next. In Matthew 16:13–23 Peter gives his famous confession of Jesus as the Christ, the Son of God. Jesus discerns that Peter said so by direct revelation of the Father. "Jesus replied, 'Blessed are you, Simon son of Jonah, for this was not revealed to you by man, but by my Father in heaven'" (16:17). A short time later, Jesus began to instruct his disciples about his coming sufferings and crucifixion. Peter rebuked the Lord, believing that the Messiah would never meet such a fate. "Jesus turned and said to Peter, 'Out of my sight, Satan! You are a stumbling block to me; you do not have in mind the things of God, but the things of men'" (16:23).

All of this is further complicated by the issue of the "flesh." In Paul's use of the word, which gives us its main biblical definition, flesh does not simply mean our bodily appetites. Rather Paul, following rabbinic sages of his day on the understanding of sin, understood the word to include all unsanctified desires, fears, and structures of the mind, such as the desire for prestige or search for security based on wealth.[5] Thus, the demonic can manipulate a person's specific "flesh" structures to entice one into sin and away from holiness and an effective ministry in the kingdom of God.

Let us go back to the example of the revival communions at St. Patrick that we described in the introduction to this book. None of the people involved in the decision to shut down the revival communions (Fr. Gray, Fr. Belt, or anyone else) was "possessed." Yet as imperfect Christians they had unsanctified structures in their minds that served as a base for the demonic to manipulate away from understanding and affirming the special grace that had been given. Perhaps Fr. Gray feared losing some of the more traditional members of the church. Perhaps Fr. Belt had an attachment to traditional theology of communion as a "private" occurrence between Jesus and the individual communicant.

On more certain grounds I can relate my own motives during the demise of that mini-revival. I was at the time director (convener) of St. Patrick's healing group, the OSL. When Fr. Gray informed me that he was going to restrict lay altar intercessors to those in the OSL, I had two thoughts. I saw the move as a step in the wrong direction and felt teaching from the pulpit could correct any developing problems. Nevertheless, I liked the idea of being responsible and in control of the altar intercessors. Instead of sharing my doubts about his decision and perhaps having Fr. Gray consider some alternative, I said nothing. My "flesh" desire for spiritual authority kept me silent. In other words, we were all influenced to shut down the mini-revival by a mix of demonic manipulations of our fears, vanities, and all the "flesh" structures of our minds.

MORE IMPORTANT CONSIDERATIONS

Christian historians have no right to come to conclusions about the extent of demonic influences in persons of history. They cannot pretend to have the unfaltering discernment of the Holy Spirit; any such attempt is pure pretension.[6] To reduce historical narrative to judgments on demonic and angelic influence is to reduce history to fiction, as in a Peretti novel.

Scripture is the model for this discernment reticence. The Bible's historical books present narrative that is comprehensible with normal human emotions, ambitions, sins, virtues, and frailties. Very sparingly does an author delve into the deeper spiritual entities behind human thought and action. The exceptions are a mere handful: King Saul being afflicted by a demon and attempting to murder David (1 Sam. 19:9), Satan entering Judas and betraying Jesus (Luke 22:3), Daniel describing the spiritual warfare in the heavenlies (Dan. 10:13). *+ Demon Posesim in min. of*

Thus, at most, we can suspect but cannot assert that, for instance, *Jesus* Jonathan Edwards's stand against the converting power of the Lord's Supper had more to do with his "flesh" perfectionism and its manipulation by the demonic than solid biblical arguments.[7] Similarly, the anonymous minister who penned *A Letter from a Blacksmith* may well have been an excellent pastor trying to protect his congregation from heresy, but probably the unsanctified areas of his mind allowed his reasoning to be manipulated for great spiritual destructiveness in opposing the Scottish communion cycles.

What went right in Wesleyan revival and why it was so effective may be partially attributed to the fact that both the Wesley brothers lived lives of superior sanctification. The demonic had less to manipulate in their mental structures than in most Christian leaders. A comparison with Martin Luther immediately comes to mind. Luther did a tremendous service to the church universal by reaffirming the doctrine of justification by faith.[8] Yet he was an imperfect Christian, possessing a vulgarity of language that often shocks modern Christians who read his informal writings. More seriously, Luther expressed a disdain and prejudice against the Jews that has echoed down German history with tragic results.

* Demons controling humans

This last comparison brings us again to the Wesley brothers and their revival.

WESLEY ON SUSTAINED REVIVAL

At the beginning of the twentieth century the famous French historian Elie Halevy noted how similar French and English society were during the eighteenth century and how differently they had developed in the nineteenth century.[9] In the eighteenth century both societies had large areas of civil and religious corruption and unbelief and grievous social inequalities. France went into revolution, dictatorship, and the terror of the Napoleonic Empire, and it was ultimately defeated. England experienced no violent revolution but slow, constant reform. Halevy believed that the difference was due to the impact the Methodists had on English society. The long Wesleyan revival (1739–1830)[10] had evangelized much of the underclass and peasantry of England. It had ministered to them with meaningful social service and was particularly effective in reducing alcoholism. As a result, the English lower class became patriotic, law-abiding citizens. The French underclass and peasantry remained subject to radicalization precisely because there was no equivalent to the Methodist movement in French Catholicism.[11]

Over a century earlier, in June 1755, John Wesley came to a similar reflective insight about his movement. His societies were now established and flourishing throughout the United Kingdom, and there was the beginnings of a noticeable reformation in the public morality of England. He wrote in his Journal:

> From a deep sense of the amazing work which God has of late years wrought in England, I preached in the evening on those words (Ps.cxlvii, 20), "He hath not dealt so with any nation"; not even with Scotland or New England. In both these God has indeed made bare His arm, yet not in so astonishing a manner as among us....
>
> God has wrought in Scotland and in New England, at several times, for some weeks or months together; but among us He has wrought for near eighteen years together, without any observable intermission. Above all, let it be remarked that a considerable

number of the regular clergy were engaged in that great work in Scotland; and in New England above a hundred, perhaps as eminent as any in the whole province, not only for piety, but also for abilities, both natural and acquired; whereas in England there were only two or three inconsiderable clergymen, with a few young, raw, unlettered men; and these opposed by well nigh all the clergy, as well as the laity, in the nation. He that remarks this must needs own, both that this is a work of God and that He hath not wrought so in any other nation. . . .

I was considering what could be the reason why the hand of the Lord (who does nothing without a cause) is almost entirely stayed in Scotland, and in great measure in New England. It does not become us to judge peremptorily, but perhaps some of them may be true: (1) many of them became "wise in their own eyes"; they seemed to think that they were the men, and there were none like them. And hence they refused God the liberty of sending by whom He would send, and required Him to work by men of learning or not at all. (2) Many of them were bigots, immoderately attached either to their own opinions or mode of worship. Mr. Edwards himself was not clear of this. But the Scotch bigots were beyond all others, placing Arminianism (so called) on level with Deism, and the Church of England with that of Rome. Hence they not only suffered in themselves and in their brethren a bitter zeal, but applauded themselves therein. . . . (3) With pride, bitterness and bigotry, self-indulgence was joined; self-denial was little taught and practiced. . . . No marvel, then, the Spirit of God was grieved.[12]

Allowing for some exaggeration as a result of his love of his Methodist societies, there is great insight in Wesley's analysis. The First Great Awakening in the American colonies and the Scottish revival at Cambuslang did actually have long-range fruit in increased church attendance and devotion among church members. George Whitefield passed through Scotland in 1748 and noted how refreshed and full of zeal many churches there were.[13] It is probable that Wesley was unaware that the Scottish Presbyterian revivals had been going on for a century.

Yet Wesley's core argument is essentially correct. The long-range fruit and continued growth of the Wesleyan revival *far outpaced* the more sensational revivals of the colonies and Scotland. Wesley lays the majority of the blame for the shortness of these other revivals on the established clergy, specifically their sectarianism. It is also true that Methodism received support from only a handful of educated ministers, and of these only John Fletcher could be considered distinguished in learning. Wesley was correct in pointing out that the highly educated clergy of both Scotland and New England could not sustain revival in their congregations past a year or even less. We saw earlier how Jonathan Edwards lamented and fulminated over his own Northampton congregation for not sustaining the powerful revivals that visited his town (ch. 4).

Beyond these factors Wesley had a glimpse of the deeper issue. The Methodist way of life — that is, the holistic package of Christian life and discipleship — was the differentiating factor in sustaining revival. The secret lay in its robust mix of factors that imitated the life of the first Christian community described in Acts 2. The Wesleyan mix is especially relevant for our day, which is also a period of revival. For clarity let us review those factors.

The Word in preaching. At the origin and core of every revival, whether biblical or during the church age, lies the clear preaching of God's Word, and especially one's need to understand one's own sin situation and accept God's gracious offer of forgiveness and salvation. This is the one indispensable element of revival. No revival can take place without this, though some revivals have taken place with *only* this.

One of the strangest revivals in history occurred in colonial Virginia in Hanover county during the 1740s (two decades before Jarratt's Anglican-Methodist revival). A devout layman, Samuel Morris, began reading Martin Luther's sermons to his family. Soon neighbors crowded into his home to hear his readings. Morris was invited to neighboring towns to read the sermons, and soon "reading houses" were built throughout the county — no hymns, no preaching, no sacramental worship, no public prayers, just the reading of anointed sermons. But the Spirit of God fell mightily, and many persons were converted.[14]

In regard to the Methodists, it was not just the Wesley brothers but the whole first generation of itinerants and circuit riders who also preached "fire from heaven" in their sermons and exhortations. Their gospel preaching included constant reminders to churchgoers that they must be born again and not merely be members of the established church in order to be saved. This was an offensive doctrine to many, but a necessary and effective one for the course of revival. On an individual level, Methodists were encouraged to exhort their neighbors, so that every Methodist was in effect an evangelist of sorts.

The sacraments. We have already given a chapter to this, so here it is only important to draw out some further implications of Wesleyan sacramental worship. Methodist sacramental piety brought to the worshiper God's faithfulness as reflected in his covenant nature. That the Lord's Supper could be validly given by a faithless, apostate clergy, which was often the case in eighteenth-century England, merely highlighted that fact that God's faithfulness was not dependent on human virtue. We should also note that the reintroduction of the love feast proved to be a major recovery and grace for the Methodists.

The intense sacramental life of the early Methodists gave an inherent protection from antinomianism. The Wesley brothers understood and taught the sacraments as part of the means of grace to achieve ever higher levels of the Christian life. This automatically checks the antinomian tendency to be satisfied with one's present spiritual state. In this they reflected the understanding of the Eastern Church and the medieval Western Church as well.[15]

The contrast between the Methodist sacramental practice and the Puritans and Scots is striking. The Wesley brothers believed that the Lord's Supper could be given to "inquirers"— those who believed in orthodox doctrine but had not yet received the grace of assurance (similar to the position of Solomon Stoddard). Thus, countless persons were incorporated into the Methodist system and brought firmly into revival by the grace of the Lord's Supper. In this sense the sacrament enlarged the population of those who personally experienced God's touch and remained steadfast Christians beyond the passing phenomena of public revivals such as the fallings or holy laughter.

This stands in contrast to the Scottish Presbyterian and New England revivals, where the Lord's Supper was severely restricted. One can only guess at how many persons in New England and Scotland were initially touched by the grace of revival and were positive toward it, but since they did not have the experience of assurance, they were shut off from the Lord's Supper and its continued graces and eventually slipped into nominalism or spiritual indifference.

(3) **Presence of the Spirit.** The Wesleyans were neither scandalized nor stopped by the manifest presence of the Spirit in their meetings. They institutionally absorbed what Jonathan Edwards had preached, that the activity of the Holy Spirit on the human soul and body sometimes produces disruptive phenomena, but that such phenomena should neither be encouraged *nor suppressed*. Here John Wesley's authoritative position as head of the Methodist societies was a blessing. Because Wesley had ruled that the "exercises" were acceptable when they did occur in a Methodist meeting, they were not controversial, and the leadership did not have to dispute the issue. In American Methodism the exercises and manifestations in fact were expected at camp meetings, and a preacher whose sermons produced the "fallings" was marked for promotion to bishop!

In contrast, Jonathan Edwards's teaching on the exercises was at best controversial during the First Great Awakening and subject to the derision of the antirevival clergy. In the sixty years following, to the beginning of the Second Great Awakening, his teaching had gained wide acceptance among Presbyterian ministers, but it was by no means the authoritative word as John Wesley's was among the Methodists.

Beyond the exercises issue, the Wesley brothers provided leadership that was open to the Spirit's direction even if it stretched conventional understanding of propriety and ministry, as in the expanded role of women in ministry. We have already noted how the brothers also stretched the sacramental ministry of their societies past the conventional to include the love feast and covenant service. The Wesleyan revival was not as much a traditionalist movement as it was a Spirit-led movement that maintained its grounding in biblical revelation and the early church.

(4) **Small-group fellowship and discipleship.**[16] Beyond these three factors of Word, sacrament, and presence, there were other distinctives that enabled the Methodist revival to last a century. As we saw

in the description of the Bristol revival (ch. 10), wherever Wesley preached, he immediately set up a small group for discipling. Confession of sin was integral to the life of the bands. The band and class leaders gave pastoral counsel and spiritual direction to every Methodist at the small-group level. This was unique to the Methodist (and Moravian) plan of small groups. It was found nowhere else in Christianity at the time. The prayer societies of the time common both to Scotland and New England were overly formal and included few of the pastoral functions of the band and class meetings.

The clergy of the era were blinded to the benefits of small groups by the weight of tradition. For centuries the church had been organized with the clergy dispensing and laypersons receiving spiritual instruction. In the Methodist bands and classes, however, lay leaders functioned as pastors. This was too revolutionary to be taken seriously. It was easier to mock the low educational level of the band leaders. It has only been in the current century that the usefulness of the small group has been rediscovered by the rest of the church.

The Methodist band and class meeting was much like the Holy Club at Oxford. It was focused on a methodical application of the means of grace such as prayer, fasting, the sacraments, biblical and devotional reading, and acts of mercy (such as visiting the imprisoned or the sick). Simplicity of life — as in dress (a major factor in the eighteenth century, when dress had important class and prestige implications) — moderation in food, and frugality in all things were also stressed.

A robust hymnology. Closely related with sacramental worship is the category of sacred song. Practically every major move of God is expressed by a fresh hymnology or sacred music. The American First Great Awakening is somewhat an exception to this as the conservative theology at the time restricted hymn lyrics to paraphrasing the Psalms. Here the Wesleyan revival excelled perhaps over all other revivals in history. The hymns of Charles Wesley continue to bless Christians on all continents, and hopefully the *Hymns on the Lord's Supper* will have a resurgence.[17]

Practical ministry for the poor. The Wesleyan revival was also distinguished by its consistent and conscious assistance to the poor.

Though most Methodists belonged to the lower classes of English society, they made heroic sacrifices to save and collect money for the poor.

(7)   **The goal of Christian perfection for all.** The controversial goal of Christian perfection, or "perfect love," ensured that every Methodist took the means of grace seriously and understood that deep holiness was his or her personal and achievable calling. This goal was yet another check against antinomianism. As the individual Methodist came into the "order of salvation" — appreciation for the free gift of salvation, then attention to the "means of grace" — his or her focus shifted to the demands of the Sermon on the Mount. This most famous of Christ's teachings was systematically preached by the Wesley brothers as a realistic program for every true Christian, although it demands an unusual degree of holiness.[18]

This element of the Wesleyan revival has special importance for the current revival. Critics of the charismatic renewal movement (1960–1985) have often pointed out that it lacked a theology of repentance and holiness. This was the failure that caused so much pain and embarrassment in the 1980s as one charismatic leader after another was exposed for immorality or corruption.

RECONSIDERING JONATHAN EDWARDS'S LAMENT

We can now better understand Jonathan Edwards's frustration and confusion with his own Northampton congregation. It had been visited by the Spirit of God in two powerful waves of revival. Yet the people quickly drifted away from the intense piety and devotion of the revival period. Edwards believed this drift to be a function of their spiritual carelessness and inherent sinfulness. Some of that may have been true.

However, when we compare the Puritan church with the Wesleyan societies, we can see that the main problem lay elsewhere. The Puritan churches, like the other churches at the time, were not set up to maintain high levels of lay piety. It had fewer support structures with which to buttress the initial move of revival. Small-group fellowship and discipling were not understood, and sacramental life was restricted, formal, and traditional. The other factors that the Methodists stressed, such as the spiritual disciplines and the attentiveness to the means of grace, were active in the Puritan church but were not cultivated "methodically."

All of this is of great relevance for the church of the twenty-first century. There is now a worldwide revival going on. In America it is being called the "Third Great Awakening." Revival is always a gracious visitation of the Spirit that cannot be absolutely quantified, nor can it be discerned how it will last. The Wesleyan revival has shown, however, that Christian churches need to adopt the biblical models described by the Chronicler in the Old Testament and Luke in Acts 2 of Word, sacrament, and presence for revival to be sustained and nation-transforming.

NOTES

1. Richard L. Eslinger, *Pitfalls in Preaching* (Grand Rapids: Eerdmans, 1996), 128. See also Charles L. Rice, *The Embodied Word: Preaching as Art and Liturgy* (Minneapolis: Fortress, 1991).

2. I am deeply indebted in this section and the following to the extraordinarily insightful work by James Kallas, *The Satanward View: A Study in Pauline Theology* (Philadelphia: Westminster, 1966).

3. Frank Peretti, *This Present Darkness* (Wheaton, Ill.: Crossway, 1986).

4. Cyrus's part in the restoration of the temple is described in Ezra 1.

5. W. D. Davies, *Paul and Rabbinic Judaism* (New York: Harper & Row, 1983).

6. See a fine discussion of this in Harry S. Stout, "Biography as Battleground," *Books and Culture* (July/August 1996), 5.

7. The reader may well ask how a Christian historian can air any suspicion under the guise of history. The answer is in the particular. This book has both a historical content and *a pastoral purpose*. It encourages a recovery of the sacramental component of revivals, and it warns readers to beware of judging revival and spiritual activities by their superficial aspects. Reflect on your own thought patterns and motives! Let us not repeat the errors of those who thought of the Cambuslang revival as mere "enthusiasm" or the Wesley brothers as sacramental fanatics.

8. As I was writing the draft to this chapter (November 1999), news came that Catholic and Lutheran theologians had signed a joint statement on the meaning of justification by faith that basically affirms the Lutheran view.

9. Elie Halevy, *A History of the English People in 1815*, intro. G. Wallas, trans. E. I. Watkin and D. A. Barker (New York: Harcourt Brace, 1924).

10. These dates represent only the most intense years of the Wesleyan revival. Methodism and its offshoots continued in various stages of revival and expansion all through the nineteenth century. For example, the Holiness movement, a form of "reformed" Methodism that stressed Wesley's concept of perfectionism, came into revival itself in the 1880s and led into the Pentecostal revival of the twentieth century. See Vinson Synan, *The Holiness-Pentecostal Movement in the United States* (Grand Rapids: Eerdmans, 1971).

11. This view was widely accepted until the past decades, but in most academic circles it would now be considered naive or even "reactionary." The problem lies not with Halevy's original insights or scholarship, but with the fashion of contemporary historians to disregard the influence of religion on society or to attribute positive social change only to "enlightened" (i.e., secular) economic and political forces. Thankfully, a newer generation of Christian historians has exposed the prejudices of this viewpoint and has reexamined and appreciated Halevy's scholarship. See Luke L. Keefer, "John Wesley, the Methodists, and Social Reform in England," *Wesleyan Theological Journal* 25 (Spring 1990): 7–20.

12. *JWJ*, July 22 and 23, 1755.

13. See Arthur Fawcett's work, *The Cambuslang Revival: The Scottish Evangelical Revival of the Eighteenth Century* (London: Banner of Truth Trust, 1971), 166.

14. On this strange revival see Wesley M. Gewehr, *The Great Awakening in Virginia, 1740–1790* (Durham, N.C.: Duke Univ. Press, 1930), ch. 3, "The Militant Presbyterians," pp. 47ff.

15. See the influential work by the medieval monk Pseudo-Dionysius, *Ladder of Perfection*, available in *Pseudo-Dionysius: The Complete Works*, trans. Colm Luibheid (New York: Paulist, 1987). It is only in the current period of high heresy and apostasy in the First World churches that sacramental life has been distorted into libertinism. Specifically, among liberal liturgical Anglicans and Episcopalians, receiving the Lord's Supper is taken as an affirmation that any biblically deviant lifestyle is acceptable and even a grace.

16. See the superb new work on this topic by D. Michael Henderson, *John Wesley's Class Meetings: A Model for Making Disciples* (Nappanee, Ind.: Evangel, 1997).
17. I pray that some Christian millionaire will endow special yearly awards, something like the Oscars, for the best paraphrase of a Wesley hymn or the best musical modernization of a Wesley hymn. Perhaps the awards would be called the "Chucks"!
18. Of John Wesley's forty-four "standard" sermons, which make up the heart of Wesleyan theology, thirteen are on the Sermon on the Mount. Available at: http://wesley.nnu.edu/sermons/standards.htm.

Index

without the Lord's Supper,
213–15
and the Word in preaching,
268–69
Rogers, Herbert, 31
Rogers, Hester, 184
Roman Catholicism
and apostolic succession,
183–84
and the Bollandists, 31
charismatic, 37, 44
and confession, 24–25
and confirmation, 25–26
and the decline in sacramental
spirituality, 34–35
decline in America, 33–34
elementary school education in,
23–27
ethnic, 38
factions within, 36–37
and gifts of the Spirit, 25–26, 39
and Hispanics, 23
and Holy Communion, 24–27
and the Jesuit order of priests,
28–29
and miracles, 27–28, 29
moderates in, 30
and moral discipline, 66–67
nominal, 15, 23, 33–34
nuns of, 21–22, 23–24, 36
orthodox, 29–33
prep school education in, 27–28
radicalism in, 30–32, 35, 36
response to Martin Luther, 62
and revivals, 14
in the 1950s, 23–27
in the 1960s, 28–33
and sacraments, 12, 25–27, 27,
61–63

and the Second Vatican
Council, 30, 36, 38
and secularization, 32–33, 38–39
theological liberalism in, 29–33
traditionalist, 36
and transubstantiation, 26, 61,
62–63, 181
and university education, 28–33
and the *via media*, 191–92
and views of Protestantism, 22
and wineless communion,
61–62
and worship, 26–27

sacraments. *See also* baptism;
Lord's Supper
and the Chronicler, 226–27
and communion tokens, 94–96
and covenant services, 186–88
definition of, 12–13, 61–62
and evangelical-charismatic
churches, 47, 52–53
evangelistic use of, 75–79
John Calvin on the, 64
John Wesley on the, 157–61
lesser, 12
Martin Luther on the, 62–63
and Methodists, 179–83,
189–90, 269–70
and the Mount Paran Church
of God, 47
and the Old Testament, 226–34
and Presbyterians, 130–31
and Puritans, 65–66
and Reformed theology, 12–13,
61–63
and revivals, 16–17
and Roman Catholicism, 12,
25–27, 27, 61–63

We want to hear from you. Please send your comments about this book to us in care of the address below. Thank you.

GRAND RAPIDS, MICHIGAN 49530 USA

WWW.ZONDERVAN.COM